## Thanks

To everyone at WayoftheBern, StillSandersforPresident, SandersforPresident and DNCleaks subreddits, to the Thompson Timeline Facebook page, and all the other Bernie and Green Facebook groups, to all the people who became the media and livestreamed Standing Rock and the convention, to everyone at Standing Rock, the the nurses union, to all the Bernie delegates and protesters in Philadelphia, above all to Renee Boehm for all her work editing and helping with this book, to everyone who volunteered, donated, went to rallies, and voted for the Bernie Sanders campaign, thanks.

A people that elect corrupt politicians... are not victims... **but accomplices**.

George Orwell

# Table of Contents

# The Democrats' Rap Sheet

# THE FADE OUT:

## THE OBAMA-CLINTON ELITE GAVE US WAR, OLIGARCHY, BIG BROTHER, PROPAGANDA AND TRUMP

### by Will Pflaum

thefadeoutbook@gmail.com

https://www.createspace.com/69956

facebook.com/TheFadeOutbyWillPflaum/

**YOUR COMMITTEE NEEDS A HAIRCUT.**

**T**HE FADE OUT: THE OBAMA-CLINTON ELITE GAVE US WAR, OLIGARCHY, BIG BROTHER, PROPAGANDA AND TRUMP by Will Pflaum demonstrates that the breakdown, failure and criminal activity of the Democratic party lead to the Trump presidency. The first half of the book offers blow by blow proof of how the Democratic party cheated in the 2016 primary, how Obama failed as president, how the DNC under the influence of the Clintons was little better than a mafia, and offers evidence that leaders of the Democratic party under Clinton and Obama are guilty of election law violations, theft and war crimes. The Pied Piper memo, the "Congrats" email, the Froman spreadsheet, the Podesta echo chamber memo of 2007, the Doug Band memo: the scandals reported in Wikileaks should be widely known and understood. The reason they are not better known is that the mainstream media is complicit in all of these scandals.

The second half of the book offers a vision of what America could be if we were able to break out of the confines of mainstream media propaganda, put an end to American imperialism, redistribute the wealth and confront global climate change. We would be on our way to this better future, if not for the cowardice of Obama and the feckless, corrupt Democratic party. Instead, Obama and the Democrats handed the imperial presidency to Trump. Instead of a start to better tomorrow under President Sanders, the Democrats chose to put their own interests ahead of the world and played chicken by propping up Trump as Hillary's useful bogeyman.

In 2016, Wikileaks offered us a once in a lifetime chance to get an up close look at how oligarchs corrupt the political process. Both parties obey the same masters, the media lies, all of our wars were against the interests of the American people, we could break free of fossil fuels if we wanted to and the rich run the government for themselves. You can use this handy volume to prove the fact that America is not a democracy. Share this work with your friends.

WILL PFLAUM, father of four, small business owner in upstate New York, is an anti-corruption activist at SunshineOnTheHudson.com, filing multiple Freedom of Information lawsuits against local government to reveal widespread corruption, podcaster at Phlogiston, blogger on Medium, author of books *Juba, Dog Stories, Under Two Maples, M.O.G.E.* and an upcoming biography of the Spanish artist Pazzis Sureda. BA from the University of Michigan, he has two master's degrees from Columbia University in anthropology and education.

If the Democratic Party made an ad for Coke

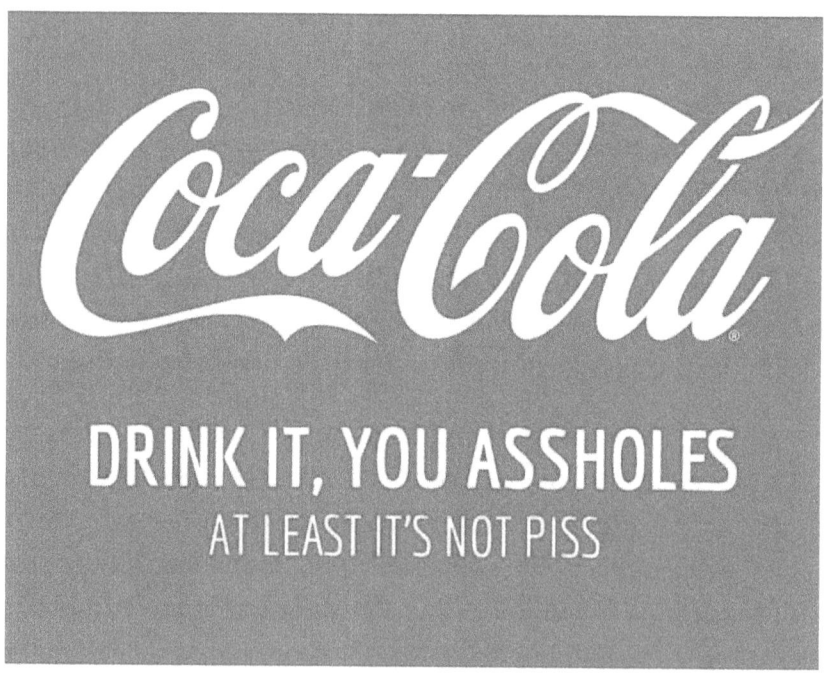

# On issues

**Naomi Klein** ✓
@NaomiAKlein

What do you call it when you do the same thing over and over again and expect different results? Oh yeah: the Democratic Party. #DNCChair

2/25/17, 10:22 AM

1000 DEMOCRATS LOST THEIR SEATS SINCE 2008

HEY, HEY, CAN WE HAVE A LITTLE CIVILITY HERE?

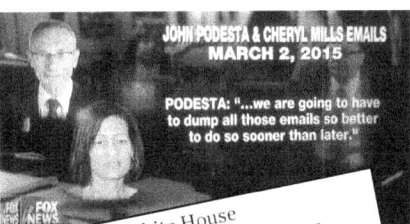

JOHN PODESTA & CHERYL MILLS EMAILS
MARCH 2, 2015

PODESTA: "...we are going to have to dump all those emails so better to do so sooner than later."

FOX NEWS

On Thursday, the White House acknowledged that an American hostage, Warren Weinstein, had been inadvertently killed in a U.S. operation earlier this year. Weinstein, along with an Italian hostage named Giovanni Lo Porto, died in what has been described as a drone strike against al-Qaeda militants along Pakistan's border with Afghanistan.

American hostages have died as a result of U.S. military action before – just last year, journalist Luke Somers was fatally shot while U.S. Navy SEALs tried to rescue him from al-Qaeda captivity in Yemen. But Weinstein appears to be the first hostage killed by the U.S. government's controversial drone operations.

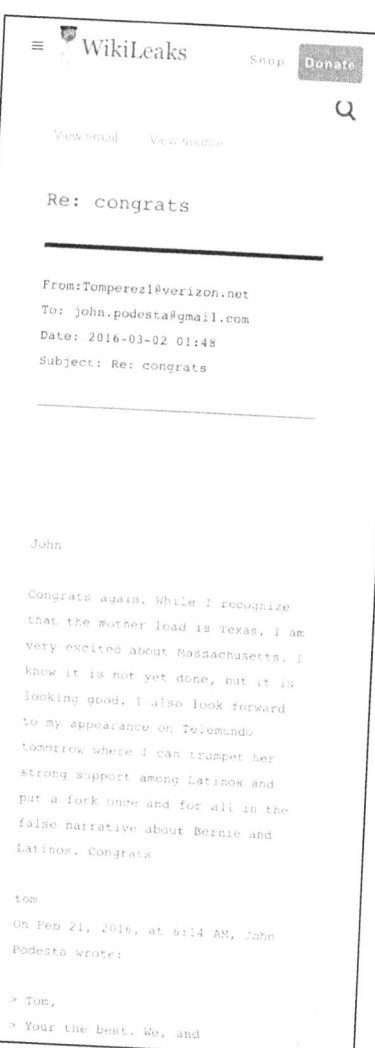

≡ 🔍 WikiLeaks     Shop  Donate

🔍

View email    View source

Re: congrats

From: Tomperez1@verizon.net
To: john.podesta@gmail.com
Date: 2016-03-02 01:48
Subject: Re: congrats

John

Congrats again. While I recognize that the mother load is Texas, I am very excited about Massachusetts. I know it is not yet done, but it is looking good. I also look forward to my appearance on Telemundo tomorrow where I can trumpet her strong support among Latinos and put a fork once and for all in the false narrative about Bernie and Latinos. Congrats

tom

On Feb 21, 2016, at 6:14 AM, John Podesta wrote:

> Tom,
> Your the best. We, and

# Introduction

**T**he phrase behind the title of this book—*"compliance is fading"*—comes from an email to John Podesta, head of Obama's transition and Hillary's campaign chair, released by Wikileaks in October 2016. Bill Ivey, a Democratic insider and occasional appointee, wrote to Podesta on March 13, 2016 (Podesta Wikileak ID 3599), "... compliance is obviously fading rapidly. This problem demands some serious, serious thinking - and not just poll driven, demographically-inspired messaging."

We all can tell something went wrong in 2016. Might be Russia, or maybe the FBI, or subborn lefties, or racists, or something... Here's my answer: the United States of America is not a democracry. This truth should comfort you. It's not that our people are hopelessly racist or militaristic. The people have been locked out. As a people, we can end the disconnect between the rhetoric and pretense of democracy by refusing to comply, offering the elites, all elites, all authorities, no assumption of deference. Be stingy with your respect and admiration.

Compliance: this goes right back to John Locke, the 18th

century political philosopher. If we have a social contract, if the people consent to be governed, the people must also be able to withdraw their consent. When you do not comply, you dissent.

Why dissent? Neither party is legitimate, Trump is dangerous, the Supreme Court is full of hacks, the media lies, the leaders only use the military to hurt the interests of the people, anti-American hatred abroad is largely justified, our spy agencies do evil, racism continues unabated, the rich rule, we're getting poorer, nothing works right, other countries are better governed than we are, the world is warming, the sea is going to rise and we're not doing anything to stop it. And now the good news: compliance is fading, as Ivy said.

If want to change the decline of America as outlined in the above paragraph, you cannot be a Democrat. On July 25, 2016 some of got this sinking feeling, "the Democrats are so terrible, Trump is going to win." We were right. Now, while the media is ginning up alarmism over Trump's continuation of the twenty or thirty year rule of the unconstitutional imperial presidency, a real crisis is unfolding again right under the talking heads clogged up noses: the Democratic National Committee (DNC) elected Tom Perez. No big deal? If Trump wins in a landslide in 2020 after wising up and passing Medicare for all or some legislation from Bernie's playbook, it'll be a big deal. That sinking feeling is back. Last time, I posted on Facebook. This time I'm writing a book. The Democratic Party is coming apart, dying, and there is nothing to stop Trump from doing whatever he wants.

DNC bylaws, Article V, section 4: "In the conduct and management of the affairs and procedures of the Democratic National Committee, particularly as they apply to the preparation and conduct of the Presidential nomination process, the

Chairperson shall exercise impartiality and evenhandedness as between the Presidential candidates and campaigns. The Chairperson shall be responsible for ensuring that the national officers and staff of the Democratic National Committee maintain impartiality and evenhandedness during the Democratic Party Presidential nominating process." No one on planet earth or any other planet thinks the Democratic Party remotely complied with this provision of their own bylaws in the 2016 primary.

The store, the only one in your town, offers you a choice between corn chips and potato chips. But you want something healthy at a reasonable price. If they offer you an empty box of orange covered, grabbing crackers (with connections to Russia), you still don't have a real choice. If you continue to dissent, and other customers accuse you of forcing them to eat disgusting crackers (with real hair!) and dream of the good old days of corn and potato chips, what do you do? Maybe write a book explaining what a delicious, balanced diet would taste like?

You can cite statistics and buy ads until the cows come home but I have had transmission trouble with more than one GM van. I will not buy another van made by GM, or for that matter any vehicle they make most likely for at least 20 years. You can't convince me to change my mind. It's too late: I won't be in the market for a car for a long time, and even if they cost a lot more, I will prefer Toyota and Honda.

Same deal with the Democratic party. I had a Democrat in office already for years and it didn't work well. You're not going to smooth talk me, find another charismatic Obama clone to trick me into voting for a Democrat again. Your brand is shot and you're going to continue to lose market share. In 2016, the Democrats did so much damage to their brand that even if they tried, they wouldn't shake it off for 20 years. But, and this is bad, they aren't even trying to shake it off. Fire the CEO. Your brand is tanking. Nope, not these geniuses.

In 1932 the people elected FDR 1.0 and liked what they got. They stayed loyal to the Democrats, with residual good feeling, right into the early 1990s, when the Democrats finally lost the House of Representatives for more than one consecutive cycle for the first time since 1932. In 2016 we had FDR 2.0 ready to go and the party did him wrong. Trump is a big, illiterate, bad-tempered baby who knows nothing but still thinks he is genetically superior and thought being president would be fun. He thinks rich people are obviously better in every way than non-rich people. Thanks for the Pied Piper strategy, Democrats. You put this monster in the White House.

Ivey in the "fade out" email was right. This book is meant to encourage the noncompliance he noted. I hope this book will be a shot of defiance to anyone confused by the oscillation between the alarmist Blue Dogs and the truly alarming actions of the Trump administration. And anyone who cares about the lives of working people, racial justice, constitutional principles, peace and the environment might want to abandon the Democratic party after reading this book. I hope so. The Blues have had their chance and they gave us nothing but war, decline, fake elections and Trump.

It's easy to be confused. Trump is truly dangerous, as he does not understand the principles of democratic government and thinks of people in dehumanizing, stereotypical ways. But the Democrats only enable and promote him. The Democrats created Trump. With real opposition, Trump would not be dangerous. The current Democratic party is nothing but a doormat, allowing more and more rightward drift and offering no resistance to Trump.

It's terrible that Trump is holding on to his business while being president. But here is what Hillary said when she was paid to speak at the Goldman Sachs Builders And Innovators Summit, October 29, 2013,

> *SECRETARY CLINTON: Yeah. Well, you know what Bob Rubin said about that. He said, you know, when he came to Washington, he had a fortune. And when he left Washington, he had a small fortune.*
>
> *MR. BLANKFEIN: That's how you have a small fortune, is you go to Washington.*
>
> *SECRETARY CLINTON: You go to Washington. Right. But, you know, part of the problem with the political situation, too, is that there is such a bias against people who have led successful and/or complicated lives. You know, the divestment of assets, the stripping of all kinds of positions, the sale of stocks. It just becomes very onerous and unnecessary.*

At this same meeting, Hillary seemed to call for someone like Donald Trump to run for president and defeat someone like her:

> *You know, I would like to see more successful business people run for office. I really would like to see that because I do think, you know, you don't have to have 30 billion, but you have a certain level of freedom. And there's that memorable phrase from a former member of the Senate: You can be maybe rented but never bought. And I think it's important to have people with those experiences. And especially now, because many of you in this room are on the cutting edge of technology or healthcare or some other segment of the economy, so you are people who look over*

*the horizon. And coming into public life and bringing that perspective as well as the success and the insulation that success gives you could really help in a lot of our political situations right now.*

Right. Why rent Clinton when you can be an oligarch in office yourself? Listening to Hillary speaking to bankers at her paid speeches, it's hard to figure out what her people see as wrong with Trump. Isn't this what she wanted? A businessman? Who doesn't have to sell his assets? The rich should rule directly, instead of through minions like Clinton. These pesky reporting requirements are the only problem preventing direct banker government. The "opposition" party to the billionaire rule, for "working families"? Right. Here is her paid speech for Morgan Stanley, April 18, 2013:

> *And I want to say to James and everyone at Morgan Stanley, thank you for lending me Tom Nides for the past two years. There was a bit of a culture shock at first. When I sent him to Baghdad and Kabul and other such places, he had to spend the night in containers that served as the housing for visiting diplomats, even deputy secretaries. You should have seen his face when he learned there were no stock options at the State Department. But he soon not only settled in very nicely, he became positively enthusiastic when I told him we did have our own plane. So Tom, once again, I'm in your most capable hands.*

So Tom got a job with her at the State Department, since being a rich banker is such good training for dealing with situations like Afghanistan and Iraq, or maybe because he was well connected and thought he'd like to play diplomat and feel yet more important. Nice to be a high government official: you get a plane! It's just like being a banker! No difference at all! And Hillary, as always, remains in your loving banker embrace either way.

This Hillary debacle was not a one-off slip. The whole party, everyone who endorsed her, has to pay the price. They all knew what she represented. The Democrats remain toxic: at best dangerously inept, self-interested and corrupt, often utterly deluded and complacent. Hillary seemed to be running clearance for Trump in her paid speeches. Absorbed in comfortable bubbles of convenient spin, party and media elites want to shift the blame to anyone, including the left, even if such a strategy of dishonesty might let Trump win again in 2020. They let Trump win in 2016. They'll cheat again. They put themselves over the country, the party, and humanity itself once. They have learned nothing. The greatest threat to America and the world is not Trump but the Democratic Party of the United States: world's most incompetent institution.

The voters did not comply with the media and two party elites in 2016. Unfortunately, while Ivey was counselling deep thought, Podesta was working on the Pied Piper strategy to trick his way out of rising discontent like a master Machiavellian. Clever strategy: who would really support Trump, right? Too clever, Podesta should have listened to Ivey. But Podesta knew the logical place to find "not just poll driven, demographically-inspired messaging" was with Bernie. Ivey could not have been more on point. But people have a hard time understanding something that they make money by not understanding. Podesta and company would not tolerate a turn to a genuine democratic message.

That's an important part of this book: how the Democrats blew it. They won't take the blame, resign and reform. It's not just an annoyance: the fate of the human race is in play but these guys want to keep their jobs, which they richly deserve to lose. Go get a job on the open market if you guys are so smart. Tragedy and farce, history is littered with little people who desperately crave a feeling of importance. Podesta, Pelosi, Schumer Hillary, Obama, Biden are all putting their pride above country even now. They had their chance to lead. They failed. They must step aside. Democrats are whistling past the graveyard.

"You are to blame for Trump because you didn't vote for Hillary and now I don't like you anymore!" Snub you, nose up in the air… We then quote Sarah Silverman at the Democratic Convention, "You're being ridiculous." Is there anything more ridiculous than Silverman calling for the military to overthrow Trump? Or a Hillbot blaming Trump on someone other than Clinton and Obama? The truth is here in this book if you want to know: the Democrats you love and admire are entirely responsible for Trump. Hillbots of America, wake up. These clowns are leading you to your destruction.

Our side, the ones who see both parties as fake one percenter frauds, has been sidelined, if not silenced. If you listen to NPR, CNN, Fox or mostly read the New York Times, there might be a truth and a path, a vision for America, evidence we can make this vision reality, but a set of ideas, aspirations and facts of which you are not aware due to systematic censorship. So, you see, this book is meant to counter years of propaganda and let you understand our anti-oligarch view of where we've been, where we should go and how to get there.

Here, I offer you another option than arguing with your liberal friends: give the Blue Dog Democrat in your life this book. Buy copies for all your liberal friends. Maybe they are so closed to new information they won't read it, but if they do actually read this book, if you, my Blue Dog friend, maybe you will reconsider some of your assumptions. Republicans: are you as closed minded as Democrats? This book is also for you.

Here's just a little tidbit to whet your appetite: Hillary Clinton decided on Tim Kaine as VP in July 2015 ("A little unseemly" ID 2986#efmABHAB3AB6ACN). Yet even after that was published, Tim Kaine cited with emotion his selection in his concession speech, as if we couldn't read the truth at Wikileaks. Denial. Or, to make the big drug companies happy, the Clinton Foundation, after refusing to donate anything to help famine victims in Africa, then worked to keep the price of AIDS drugs high in Africa (ID 36248). That's just in passing. One of many facts you might not know.

An entire book is necessary because of the volume of information necessary to categorically prove propositions such as, "Bernie would have won." Anyone who believes in science and empirical evidence and has been paying attention to the relevant data in 2016 will know that this statement is as true as "human activity is causing the planet to warm." Both "Bernie would have won" and "humans are warming the planet" require inferences based on evidence. The case that Bernie would have won is stronger.

All these arguments, with evidence, wrapped up nicely in one place, a book: no need to cut and paste a mess of links. The Democratic primary was rigged, etc. Here is all of the data, in one handy volume. That is one of the purposes of this book: a reference.

Here is an example of the disdain the party holds for us ninety-niners: "Bernie and his people have been bitching about super delegates… Throw Bernie a bone…[…]….his people will think they've "won" something from the Party Establishment. It doesn't make a difference. We don't lose" (ID 5423#efmAMyAPDAoKAqBAshAs8AzAA2x). We can never trust the Democrats again. Better to let the Republicans win. Or, it'll be meaningless bones forever. The people who said things like "throw Bernie people a bone" got promotions and jobs for their friends after losing.

Yes, the 2016 Democratic primary is in the past. Legal redlining through the 1970s is in the past, even as the practice is "still a thing" as reported in the Washington Post on May 28, 2015, but that history of redlining explains as much as any other factor why Black households were relatively late to home ownership. The Haymarket affair in Chicago is in the past but you cannot understand the international workers movement without knowing what happened on May 1 in Chicago. Urban Renewal in the 1970s is in the past, pretending to be liberal, helped to write residential segregation into the infrastructure in many US cities. The repression of workers movements during the Red Scare of 1919 is in the past but that history helps explains why the United States never developed a worker's party like every other industrialized nation in Europe and North America. The race riots and lynchings of the same year are in the past but you can see how racism has prevented full organization of workers then and in so doing, see how it is happening again now. The FBI COINTELPRO repression of radicals in the 1970s is in the past but that history helps explain why police brutality continues to be a problem in the United States, among other results.

The crime of 2016 is in the past, the Obama-Clinton coup against the will of the people, but it's not over or irrelevant by a longshot. This book is meant to help make sure that there is no whitewash of what happened and no narrative of 2016 that is false but well armed, backed by rich corporations, pushed into the sphere of public discourse dishonestly by those who do not want the American people to come together around a coherent program for improvement which opens any cracks in the seamless web of propaganda and the single party pretend politics to demand a redistribution of wealth, a new deal for the environment and an end to the war machine.

The next problem is with "democratic socialism." Somehow, our liberal friends think they are linked in some way to Goldman Sachs partners and other oligarchs, that their interests or worldview is similar to the way George Soros and his ilk see the world, or that they are better off siding with the rich over the working class. This is a mistake.

Our democratic socialist vision in no way means you cannot have nice vacations, or a country house, or that you should be embarrassed for buying expensive clothes or something. Well off people will be better off than they were before. Professionals will have more options for their children's education. Their children will grow up in a better world. There will be more people to go to movies and buy cars and wealth will increase. We're not out to get you. We have a compelling vision that will improve conditions for ninety-nine percent of the people, and the one-percenters will still be rich and will also live in a better, fairer, safer society. Our proposals for what to do are entirely reasonable and common sense ideas to clean up the planet and make sure people have decent lives. Don't get it twisted. Even the majority of the top one-percenters will live better and have a better future if we break out of the military industrial, crony financial services, polluting trap.

If you can use the book to pass off to Blue Dog friends, that would be great. If by some freak accident I, the author, actually make money off this self-published book, don't worry. I will, if I get any money, which I think highly unlikely, extremely, setup a page somewhere with a poll and ask readers to what cause the excess money should be donated, which candidates, organizations, etc. I'm a Bernie fan, so you probably suspect I'll keep my word.

The Hollywood Reporter broke the news on December 29, 2016 that the alt-right impresario Milo Yiannopoulos will publish a book with Threshold Editions, an imprint of Simon & Schuster. He will get hundreds of thousands of dollars to spout racist, right wing nonsense. The gatekeepers at Simon & Schuster are probably all Hillary supporters, based on people I know in similar positions. But business is business. They know there is an alt-right market, and Yiannopoulos has a cool haircut. Then, his comments on pedophilia broke and the deal fell through--not because the publisher suddenly had some kind of standards as to what they believe they'd like to contribute to the public dialogue, but due to scandal.

This is the kind of thing that could drive someone who wants real reform nuts. Here we are, taking all this flack for not falling in with the Democrats, here we are the only ones who state simple truths such as the Democratic party cheated Bernie's people, here we are the only ones with an actual program that could in fact make a positive difference to America and the world, stop the wars, redistribute the wealth, and we cannot get through the gatekeepers to the people and tell them: there is a better way. You can see some of it in Northern Europe. We can do even better than that. We don't have to decline. We don't have to go to war. Take this book, give it to them to eat, do this in remembrance of him. Break through the gatekeepers.

Democrats routinely roll over in the face of any right wing opposition and hand them contracts and approve their racist nominees. Then they say the ninety-niners are too strident or something.

To an extent, I am writing to cut out a piece of the historical record from the side of the ninety-niners about 2016. Any book with a different point of view has to refute the evidence presented here. There is evidence: Podesta sent the Pied Piper memo. Anyone presenting an alternative view of the 2016 crime scene election has to address what we can clearly read in Wikileaks. The Democrats continue to pretend the curtain was not pulled all the way back on their fake political show. We see the Wizard of Oz now, Democrats, and he is a con man. Only a naive mark falls for a con like the Democratic party. They are for the oligarchs and themselves. You are not super rich. They don't give a damn about you. If you still are a Democrat with the con men in charge, you are a fool. Can I prove it? Of course. All you have to do is open your ears and hear, open your eyes and read Wikileaks and your desire to be a Democrat should instantly and permanently dissipate.

I'm sure there will be books with opposing points of view to this one, and those books will have PR budgets and will be embraced by corrupt gatekeepers. Tom Brokaw and Chris Cuomo will like those other books, saying the right things, written by the right people. But those books will be bullshit. In terms of facts and logic, they won't be honest and consistent.

Why? The mainstream media and the Democratic and Republican single party offer layer upon layer of false assumptions. Trump offers hyperbole. The truth is that only the Bernie Sanders ninety-niners have a coherent vision for making America a better place for working people. Everyone else is just spinning and creating narratives divorced from basic reality.

There are matters of fact in dispute. The way to settle those concerns is not to intimidate one side with a show of power, or to silence one side with innuendo and personal attack. When I say the leadership of the Democratic party is entirely responsible for Trump and have no substantial accomplishments despite two generations of power, I intend to prove both propositions. You can't tell me I'm wrong just because these statements upset your worldview. You have to respond on the evidential level, something Blue Dog Democrats have steadfastly refused to do.

**FACT ONE**: John Podesta's Pied Piper strategy played an essential role in the primary victory of Trump. Without the Pied Piper strategy, Trump would not have gotten the Republican nomination.

**FACT TWO**: The 2016 Democratic primary was fraudulent, including criminal voting fraud, criminal election law fraud pertaining to super pacs, and non-felony but still civilly actionable distortion of the calendar of states, the order of voting, the debates, the manipulation of the media, and a money laundering scheme in August 2015 involving 33 state parties. Given that one side could set the calendar, largely determine who was allowed to vote in many states, get as much money from big donors as they wanted and use it however they wanted in violation of the law, have the debates tailored to be as hard to watch and biased as possible, and receive more than 50 times as much television coverage early in the campaign, it's hard to believe that Bernie managed to get 46 percent of the popular vote in this undemocratic show election. Crimes were committed. The primary was a farce and no reforms have occurred since that disaster.

**FACT THREE**: The Democratic leadership refused to compromise with the left flank of its party, particularly in the vice president choice, but in every other way as well.

**FACT FOUR**: HRC was a terrible candidate. She was unlikable, unpopular, and ran a bad campaign. Hillary Clinton took bribes, flouted security rules, stole, played a key role in the rise of Isis that allowed the worst terrorist organization in history to take root in the Middle East, started wars, stole an election, and admitted in private to rich bankers that she lies to the people. She is likely a repeat felon.

**FACT FIVE**: The mainstream media was proven in 2016 to be partisan and biased. The United States does not in fact have a free press at the national level.

**FACT SIX**: The combination of money in politics, antiquated voting rules, biased press, power of lobbyists and manipulation of primaries mean the United States is not a democracy.

Advocates of real democracy remain deeply hostile to the Democratic party. Much of the rest of the populace is not attracted to the party. More than 40% of eligible voters are disengaged. Without a change in the Democratic party Trump can win again in 2020, unless he implodes. The refusal of the establishment Democrats to reconcile with the left means the disaster of July 25, 2016 is likely to repeat itself. Democrats have to stop denying the crime of 2016.

On one hand, the completely reactive, often alarmist and hysterical reactions to Trump actions of the leadership of the Democrats, responding with one fundraising email after another, was threatening to drown out their role in the rise of Trump. On the other hand, Trump's administration was doing some actually fairly alarming and disgusting things, which threaten to squash any discussion or even consideration of ways to actually improve the lives of Americans and effectively turn around this imperialist, over-extended, unfair, decrepit ship. In addition to reacting to each new Trump outrage, the anti-oligarchy faction needs to say what we are for. One thing we cannot be for is the Democratic party as long as they are heading nowhere.

I kick around some ideas to change the system. I provide long lists from Wikileaks that demonstrate the depth of what we learned about how a corrupt oligarchy pretending to be a democracy functions. This book offers a left wing approach to Pizzagate.

Trump only won because of Democratic crimes. If the laws around elections and election fundraising were enforced, if the DNC honored its charter to be neutral in primary races, if the mainstream press had not colluded with the DNC/HRC team, Bernie Sanders should have been elected president in 2016.

In no way does Trump represent America and it is wrong to blame the people for his presidency. 43.1 percent of eligible voters did not vote, 27.8 percent voted for Clinton, and 26.6 percent voted for Trump. America is not a democracy, so it is wrong to blame the concept of democracy for the rise of Trump. There was no democracy.

Republicans control every piece of Kentucky's government for the first time in its history, all branches of the federal government, two out of three states. It's embarrassing to be a Democrat in much of the country. Immediately after this disaster, after losing 1034 seats in six years, the Democrats appointed a Senator from New York City and a congresswoman from San Francisco to lead the party in the congress, both rich and White and from the two safest, richest, increasingly Whitest districts in the country. The Democrats have nothing other than rich, White, coastal, clueless, and stupid leadership; that's their answer to losing the working class, poor minority turnout, increased minority Republican vote and disaster in the Midwest.

There is too much to say for a blog post and it's too hard to get through to anyone with some kind of internet debate: those go nowhere. We need books. We'll get books. We'll get ghost writers throwing out statistics (all deceptive) peppered with charming or alarming mostly fake anecdotes about real people (who could write their own story and in fact do everyday on social media). When the book is done, they will decide whose name to put on the front as his or her "memoirs." Maybe they can get Eric Schmidt at Google to write an algorithm for apologies for oligarchy with liberal nice-nice talk so ghostwriters can partake of the wonders of Obamacare $800 a month premiums and $2400 annual deductibles without the distractions of work and pay. And I am one of the "lucky ones." Following these fake books, there will be fake interviews. And no one will ask Obama about the spreadsheet from Michael Froman or the drone strikes (not by anyone other than a sycophant and not with follow up anyway).

Some of the chapters in this book are meant to prove specific charges. In these evidence chapters, you will find long lists, citations to laws, articles, Wikileak ID numbers (Podesta release by default, otherwise Clinton or DNC as noted). These list chapters are really too boring to read. The point of listing almost every available case of, for example, illegal coordination between the HRC campaign and her super pacs is to establish a pattern of criminal behavior. If only half of the list are crimes, it's a lot of crime. Anyone who says I exaggerate or wants to defend the Clinton/Obama mafia, has to refute the whole list.

Other chapters are essays. I connect history to 2016. July 2016, right before the Democratic convention, was a pivotal moment in American history. The true depth of the betrayal of working people by an elite political/propaganda machine is clearer when we go back to 1919, or 1859, or up to 1971. So, often I write historical essays to help understand 2016.

Other essays are about what could be, ideas for the future.

The Democrats want to sell you some shoddy politics, just as Walmart sells you shoddy goods. Hillary Clinton said at Sanford Bernstein, a paid speech on May 29, 2013:

> *You know, it was a retail business obviously, and retailing is a lot like politics, you have very direct relationships with your customers or with your voters, we have to know what's on people's minds if you're going to sell them something or get their vote. And I learned a lot from, you know, watching how he managed this growing company, how he dealt with his associates, you know, they would have the annual meeting in the field house of the University of Arkansas basketball arena, so you have tens of thousands of people, you'd have entertainment and they'd bus in, you know, these men and women who worked at Walmarts from all over the country and build camaraderie and basically kind of you're on the Walmart team.*

Come on Democrats, we too can be the Walmart of politics, she cheerleads… And you call this resistance to Trump? Or you think Hillary is the only Democrat who thinks like this? Which is why they all endorsed her?

Wasserman Schultz: "This is a silly story. He isn't going to be president" (Wikileak ID 9999). Guess what Debbie? With that attitude, neither is Hillary. Hard to say I'm sorry about that, given what you did, Debbie. Wasserman Schultz on Bernie's suggestion that the party was not fair to him: "Spoken like someone who has never been a member of the Democratic Party and has no understanding of what we do" (ID 5477). So you don't want my vote, I see. Guess what? You didn't get it in 2016 and it looks like your crew won't get it in 2020 either. Unless you and your ilk resign, America is going to Trump. Put the country ahead of yourself for once. Obama, Schultz, Clinton, Schumer, Pelosi: the party of egomaniacs.

We had a choice in 2016, as in 1932, between fascist nonsense or a substantial correction to the capitalist system. Hillary Clinton did not figure in the calculation and she is nothing but a servant of the bankers who paid to hear her "speak."

Before I'm done I want to question all kinds of assumptions: what qualifies someone to lead? Everything we think about leadership is wrong. What is money, the market? Everything we think about the economy is wrong. We don't have to work long hours for a pittance. What is the role of a representative in a democracy? Everything we think about representation is wrong. We don't have to be mistreated by egomaniacs. How should we get information? Everything we think about the media and government information is wrong. The New York Times is giving you all the news between four and six on the dial but the dial goes from one to ten, so you are missing 80% of the story if you think that Marco Rubio and Barack Obama define the poles of debate. If you listen to NPR, you aren't aware of your real options. What we think about globalism is wrong. We can have international trade but only if we put workers and the environment above corporate profits. War? Sixteen years of constant war hasn't worked at all. Everything is fake and wrong and built on assumptions that don't appear to be true. We have a lot of questioning to do. Let's get started.

## Sources

Rather than copy links or provide excessive information in footnotes, in the body of the text I provide enough information for an interested party to look up the information using a search engine.

All Wikileaks releases are accurate reflections of what was emailed, as claimed. The HRC team tacitly acknowledges the legitimacy of all emails. First, the official campaign Twitter feed for HRC noted on October 7, 2016 that Hillary did not call Bernie Sanders supporters a "bucket of losers." However Wikileaks had already disavowed this fake news item previously. Thus, we know the campaign will disavow fake items when they find them, as will Wikileaks.

Secondly, in the presidential debate on October 8, 2016 Hillary Clinton verified that her comment as to her "public and private positions" was accurately reported in the Wikileaks. She blamed her own duplicity, strangely, on Abraham Lincoln. In these two instances, Respondents acknowledge the legitimacy of the Wikileaks information cited here.

Wikileaks released years of emails with attachments including an audit, memos, spreadsheets. This body of information is the basis for much of this book.

A book like Clinton, Inc. by Daniel Halper, published a year before Wikileaks dropped its bombshell leaks, relied on anonymous insiders, often people close to the Clintons who hated them. Staff, servants, secret service people all seem to have hated Hillary Clinton, Halpert reports. Gary Byrne reports that same in *Crisis of Character: A White House Secret Service Officer Discloses his Firsthand Experience with Hillary, Bill, and How They Operate.*

Obama and the Clintons don't get along, and the Clintons maintained an enemies list for people like George Stephanopoulos and Bill Richardson. Halper paints Chelsea as a monster and Doug Band as a thief. Also see, Politico's January 12, 2014 piece "Hillary's Hit List: The Clintons keep a favor file of saints and sinners, according to this excerpt from *HRC: State Secrets and the Rebirth of Hillary Clinton*."

An inside baseball personality driven work like *Clinton Inc.* could also come out of the Wikileaks releases of 2016, instead of relying on insider, anonymous, scuttlebutt. For example, Doug Band, Bill Clinton's only real friend (for awhile) and surrogate son, and Chelsea Clinton, hate each other and Chelsea insists on the audit of the foundation (big mistake!) that we cover here in this book.

In ID 11261, we see that Bill had a paid speech with Morgan Stanley scheduled for after Hillary announced her run for presidency. Hillary wanted Bill to do the speech anyway, breaking federal law to get one more paycheck from the banks, while Bill thought he should cancel. Huma Abedin had to inform Hillary that Bill cancelled the speech. The intermediaries between the two, Bill and Hillary, debate the issue over days, expressing what each Clinton thinks about the matter, but never is there any indication that Bill and Hillary might actually speak to each other directly. There is plenty of that kind of thing, gossip, and perhaps the unguarded emails of people close to the Clintons, and Hillary herself, are a better source of information than anonymous leaks.

But the personalities are not the driving issue in this book. The Clintons are central players here because, as we see in the reaction to Wikileaks and in books like *Clinton Inc.*, the Democratic party knew who the Clintons are and put them forward out of cowardice and venality anyway. I don't want to write an inside baseball book about horrible people simply to entertain but to provide work that can serve as a reference for anyone who favors the ninety-nine percenters over the oligarchs, a book useful as a reference guide to sham politics in America, an upclose look at the corruption in every part of government provided by Wikileaks that we may never get again.

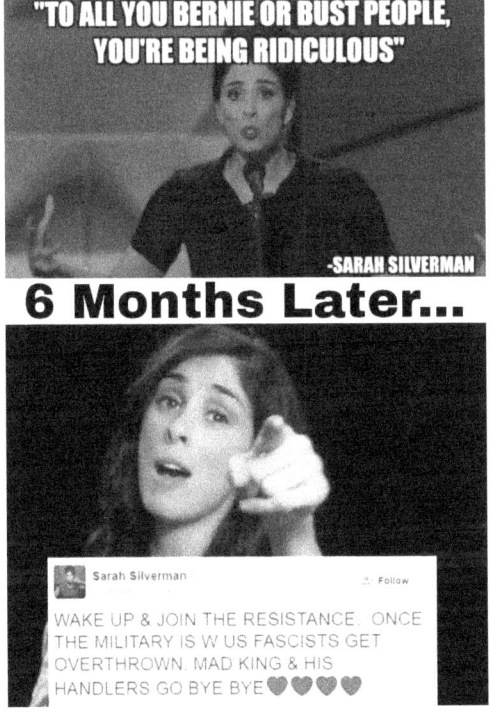

Clinton/Obama created Isis, destabilized Africa and made war crimes routine.

**WATERGATE ON STEROIDS, WITHOUT THE OUTRAGE.**

Inoculate yourself from MSM. It's a disease.

**DON'T BELIEVE THE HYPE.**

# THE DEMOCRATS' RAP SHEET

**Real Progressives**
4 hrs · 

"In the 2016 election, David Brock's Correct the Record spent $1 million berating Bernie Sanders and Jill Stein voters, as well as conservatives. To the Democratic establishment, "Bernie Bros" were just as dangerous as Trump voters, since complete loyalty demanded everyone fall in line behind Hillary Clinton. The Los Angeles Times explains the Democratic Party's view of unity in a piece titled Be nice to Hillary Clinton online — or risk a confrontation with her super PAC:

Hillary Clinton's well-heeled backers have opened a new frontier in digital campaigning, one that sec... have been inspired by some of the Internet's... instincts. Correct the Record, a super PAC coordinating with Clinton's campaign, is spen... some $1 million to find and confront social me... users who post unflattering messages about t... Democratic front-runner...

"That is what the Clinton campaign has always b... about," he said. "It runs the risk of being exactly... their opponents accuse them of being: a campaig... that appears to be populist but is a smokescreen... is paid and brought to you by lifetime political operatives and high-level consultants."

Throughout the Democratic primary race, Sanders has repeatedly said he wants to move the party to the left and has openly challenged the party to adopt his left-leaning policy platform in their July convention. This has led many pundits to suggest that very liberal voters would abandon the Democratic Party in November and it leads to the question of whether Sanders but not Clinton voters are mainly left-leaning liberals. Surprisingly, 57 percent of Sanders but not Clinton voters identify as moderates. This is a stark and surprising finding. It means that Sanders' margins over Trump are being driven by large numbers of moderate voters.

## Election Justice USA Study Find[s] that Without Election Fraud Sanders Would Have Won by Landslide

Interestingly, those who would vote for Sanders but not Clinton against Trump are evenly split when it comes to party identification – 35 percent identify as Republicans, 33 percent as Independents and 31 percent as Democrats. This is not particularly good news for Clinton as more than two-thirds of those who would support Sanders but not Clinton do not identify as Democrats. If the 31 percent who identify as Democrats vote in the general election, they will be much more likely to vote Democrat than Republican. But the likelihood that the 33 percent of Independents in this group would vote Democrat is unknown. And it is hard to believe that a large number of the 35 percent who identify as Republicans would be persuaded to support the Democratic nominee.

SOURCE: QUINNIPIAC UNIVERSITY POLL, APR. 27-MAY 8

### POTENTIAL GENERAL ELECTION MATCHUP

| FLORIDA | | OHIO | | PENNSYLVANIA | |
|---|---|---|---|---|---|
| HILLARY CLINTON | DONALD TRUMP | HILLARY CLINTON | DONALD TRUMP | HILLARY CLINTON | DONALD TRUMP |
| 43% | 42% | 39% | 43% | 43% | 42% |

CAMPAIGN 2016 ★
CBS THIS MORNING **CLOSING IN ON CLINTON**
POLL SHOWS TIGHT RACE WITH TRUMP IN SWING STATES

Wikileaks Proves Primary Was Rigged: DNC Undermined Democracy

# Philadelphia, the summer iceberg of July 25, 2016

All empirical evidence (favorability ratings, head-to-head polling, crowd size, etc.) through May, June and July of 2016 showed Bernie would almost certainly win and Hillary might well lose against Trump in a toss up or close race. By July 25, Trump had gone from a five point underdog against Clinton to a six point favorite. The rise of Trump and decline of Hillary was true before we could factor in the Wikileaks DNC release and the negative effect of Hillary picking Tim Kaine. If you are looking for a way to dig yourself a hole, the Democrats were offering a master class. They were losing, then doubled down on all the factors that were combining to make them lose.

Politifact rated the statement "Bernie Sanders says he polls better against Donald Trump than Hillary Clinton does" as "mostly true" at the time of the Democratic convention. The key question was the word "all" -- there was no doubt that almost all (and all the larger and national polls) showed significantly better results for Bernie, with an average of Bernie beating Trump by three times as much as Hillary. Politifact bent over backwards to not give Bernie a "true" but "mostly true" is good enough.

RealClearPolitics favorability average for the week before the election showed Clinton with a -12.8 and Trump with -21.0. Meanwhile, in April 2016, "Sen. Bernie Sanders (I-Vt.) is the best-liked presidential candidate from either party, according to a new poll. Forty eight percent of all Americans view the Democratic White House hopeful favorably in The Associated Press/GfK survey released Tuesday. Thirty nine percent view Sanders unfavorably, giving him the best net positive favorability rating." Over time, Bernie's numbers got better, as people got to know him. August

2016 NBC News/Wall Street Journal Survey, July 31 to August 3, (ID 201627 Hart Research) found Sanders with a +22. Around the time of the Democratic convention: FoxNews +26, The Economist +17, CNN/ORC +24.The Economist/YouGov Poll conducted October 7 - 8, 2016 showed Sanders with a +19. His average in this poll was +21 over the entire period of the election. He averaged about +10 in the spring, +20 in the summer and was still at about +20 when we were herded into the voting booth and instructed to vote for Clinton or get hammered with Trump.

One would ask, would one not, of the Democratic party: do you want to beat Trump or not? Why play chicken with fascism? Pick the better candidate, since, as we all know, there was no democratic primary to respect, as the Democratic primary was not democratic.

Huffington Post published an article on November 11, 2016 called "New Pre-Election Poll Suggests Bernie Sanders Could Have Trounced Donald Trump." Gravis Marketing, two days before the general election, found that Sanders would have received 56 percent of the vote while Trump would have won 44 percent. In May 2016, the RealClearPolitics average of polls had Bernie beating Trump by 12 and Hillary winning by three percent.

So, consistently over at least five months, one story emerges from the polls. FiveThirtyEight gave Trump a 33% chance of winning days before the election. If the Democrats wanted to play with fire, they should not be surprised when they got burned.

New York Magazine on July 7, 2016 said, "Like Hitler, Trump is a radical, authoritarian figure who lies outside the normal parameters of his country's conservative governing class." At the Emmy awards ceremony, Transparent creator Jill Soloway compared Donald Trump to Adolf Hitler. Others: the front page of the Philadelphia Daily News in December 2015; the Council on American-Islamic Relations; the Holocaust survivor Zeev Hod. Washington Post columnist Danielle Allen July 25, compared Trump to Hitler.  July 25, same day, the Post published a piece by Peter Ross Range titled "The theory of political leadership that Donald Trump shares with Adolf Hitler." On June 14, the newspaper featured left-leaning historian Eric Rauchway in an article linking Trump's "America First" theme to Hitler. MSNBC's Chris Matthews said that when Trump intoned "America first" during his inauguration speech Friday, it had a "Hitlerian background to it." Ashley Judd delivered a poem of sorts the next day at the Women's March that reached similar conclusions: "I didn't know devils could be resurrected, but I feel Hitler in these streets!"

Polls aren't perfect. They give probabilities. If you like a one third chance of fascism, you pick one candidate. If you want almost no chance of fascism, you pick another candidate with higher favorability ratings. If the future of the human race is at stake, as the alarmists in the Democratic party seem to think with their relentless Hitler analogies, which odds look better to you: 1:3 or 1:100?

Rally size did seem to matter a lot in 2016. We know that in rural counties in Pennsylvania and Ohio where Trump held rallies, he did better than previous Republicans even though he did not poll better than the Republicans generally in many of these same areas. If you compare areas where Trump did hold rallies to areas where he did not hold rallies, you see a difference. The same is not true for Hillary because no one but Blue Dogs and professional Democrats went to her rallies.

Bernie had the biggest rallies of all, often on short notice with no media hype. While I know (in person and online) tons of people who voted for Trump or stayed home or voted third party who would have voted for Bernie but not Hillary, I don't know anyone who convincingly says they would have voted for Trump or stayed home if Bernie had been the Democratic nominee. Even today Bernie has favorability ratings more than double those of Hillary. No FBI investigation, no embarrassing leaks, no bribes, no stealing, no pedophilia art collection (see Washington Post, "Married, With Art" September 23, 2004): Bernie was clean, popular, and it was an anti-establishment year.

Who was the better candidate could not have been clearer. Then, with all those factors in place, the DNC leaks broke right before the convention. The DNC leaks showed clearly that the primary was rigged. With the subsequent Podesta leaks, we now know that crimes were committed and that Hillary absolutely cheated. The more Democrats pretend that Hillary won the primary, the more people like me will not vote for Democrats. Lying about your previous cheating is not a good reconciliation strategy. Without reconciliation, Trump will have it easy. So, stop lying, Blue Dogs.

This combination of a weak candidate and an illegitimate election should have sent Obama and the Democrats into crisis mode. They should have taken a look at the possibility of a Trump victory and put their egos and personal interests aside in the interest of the country. Their chosen candidate was unlikable, unpopular, and just exposed as illegitimate. She was not up against some run of the mill Republican but a racist whack job.

If you were watching TV instead of following the live feeds of Bernie delegates in Philadelphia, you might not know that July 25, 2016 was a pivotal moment in US history. The Democratic convention was going to be a critical moment in the history of the

United States. Either the party would find a way to heal and get a good ticket out there or any minor swing in the news cycle could doom the nation to fascism, if the alarmists are to be believed about the magnitude of the Trump threat (nagging thought when you hear the alarm: if the alarm is legitimate, why didn't you nominated the better candidate to take him on?).

What did Obama and his party do? Shut the Bernie delegates down, suppress their voices, depend more than ever on the MSM and try to plow through with a strategy to get Hillary in the White House first hatched in 2008 or maybe 2012. Here are the things Team Hillary said at the time:

"Will he [Trump] have some appeal to working-class Dems in Levittown or Bristol? Sure," Former Pennsylvania governor Ed Rendell was quoted as saying. "For every one, he'll lose one and a half to two Republican women. Trump's comments like 'You can't be a 10 if you're flat-chested,' that'll come back to haunt him. There are probably more ugly women in America than attractive women. People take that stuff personally."

On July 27, 2016, as the Democratic party split into pieces, Chuck Schumer, true genius like his colleague Rendell, said, "The electorate is moving in a more Democratic direction. When middle class incomes decline, people tend to move in a more progressive direction… For every blue-collar Democrat we lose in western Pennsylvania, we will pick up two moderate Republicans in the suburbs in Philadelphia, and you can repeat that in Ohio and Illinois and Wisconsin."

Can I get a "Ha!" We have a sense of the spin from the Blue Dog side. We can find many more such quotes from the establishment Democrats. And why did Schumer think Illinois was a swing state? I mean, talk about bad leadership.

On July 25, 2016 the Washington Post published "90 percent of unwavering Sanders supporters plan to vote for Clinton in November." However, the original source was a single poll by Pew Research conducted in April to early June. This 90% figure was from before the DNC leaks published on Wikileaks. The Democrats were building themselves a house of illusion rather than dealing with the crisis of their party coming apart at the seams.

Where did the Washington Post get the term "unwavering" from for their headline? Their asses? A survey in April cannot indicate unwavering support in July. The way you would determine if the support is unwavering is to do another poll in August, then another in October. That's what you'd do if you really wanted to know if the support was "unwavering." If you are just spewing propaganda with no empirical basis, you would just assume the support is unwavering because you wish it to be the case and your bosses want it to be the case.

The support didn't sound too unwavering on July 25, 2016. Wayne Allyn Root in an article in The Blaze from July 26, 2016 said, "Hillary Clinton and the Democrats are melting down. Democrat National Committee Chairwoman Debbie Wasserman Schultz is despised and deposed – literally fired and booed off the stage. Hillary's coronation is in chaos and crisis. Julian Assange says he's releasing Hillary's personal emails next. Meanwhile, Donald Trump is surging in polls. Hillary is in a world of trouble. Then there's her vice president pick. It's the worst EVER. Hillary announced Tim Kaine to a soaring crescendo of… SILENCE. It was P.T. Barnum who once said the worst thing that can happen in business is…NOTHING. In business or politics, silence isn't golden, it's deafening."

Jacqueline Luqman said on July 25, it was becoming obvious Trump would win. Michael Moore published his article "Five reasons Trump is going to win"... any guess of the date? July 25. There is an article on the Advocate byline Sunnivie Brydum, "Nate Silver's Terrifying Prediction: Prepare for President Trump." Guess the date? July 25.

On my facebook feed, on July 25, I said: "...Trump lead will probably grow after we take the WikiLeaks situation into account. A negative convention which looks like what we will have may also hurt Hillary. Without getting overly emotional and angry we need to solve the situation or we're going to have Donald Trump as president. Simply telling the other people what they should think when it is not what they do think or what they will think is not going to work. I propose that a few democratic bigwigs including some progressives meet behind closed doors and come up with a new ticket...Thinking that somehow Hillary Clinton can get the job done is simply not the case. It's a risk we don't need to take." I think the discussion on my Facebook page that followed encapsulates the delusion of the Democrats and the rage of the Berniecrats perfectly.

Rather than be honest, apologize, and compromise, make Bernie VP or change their plan in some real way, like yanking Hillary out of there and putting in a fusion ticket, Obama and Clinton went straight ahead, pissed off their base, and nominated a widely despised candidate who had tons of baggage and secrets yet to reveal.

July 25, 2016 was a crisis and a test of the Democratic party. The party screwed up and now Trump is president. That the liberal echo-chamber MSM didn't even acknowledge that the ship of state was crashing into an iceberg should awaken you to the fact that the news is not the news and these millionaire talking heads on your screen are screening you from the truth.

I said all of this almost verbatim on July 25, 2016 on my Facebook page. This is not "hindsight is 20/20." We told you at the time. I could find 1,000 similar posts. We told you so. We told you so. We told you so. We are telling you so again now. The writing was on the wall. Obama was the only man who could have taken some lumps and turned that ship around. Instead, guess what: iceberg, crash, disaster.

Leadership? He can dance a mean tango, sing in a deep baritone, shoot a three point shot, write a legal brief, orate, act, slow jam the news but on Obama's tombstone you only really need one word: wimp.

## The Pied Piper strategy was key to Trump's nomination

A memo dated April 7, 2015 addressed to the DNC "outlining the strategy and goals of a potential Hillary Clinton presidential campaign would have..." regarding GOP opposition. "Most of the work contained in this memo is work the DNC is already doing. This exercise is intended to put those ideas on paper." The attachment of this email discusses their "Goals and Strategy" regarding GOP Candidates. I'm going to include the ending statement, but the language used in the attachment is surprisingly even worse. "We need to be elevating the Pied Piper candidates [Cruz, Trump, Carson] so that they are the leaders of the pack and tell the press to take them seriously" (Wikileak ID 1120, "Strategy on GOP 2016ers.PDF").

Podesta wrote the Pied Piper memo on April 7, 2015, and Donald Trump announced his run for president on June 16. The

Washington Post ran a story on August 5, 2015 called, "Donald Trump talked politics with Bill Clinton weeks before launching 2016 bid." Vanity Fair and CNN, plus others, ran similar stories.

So, Podesta came up with the strategy in April. The Clintons said, "Yes, that would be great. Trump would be perfect. He could get the Republican nod, and then we could beat him." Then, sometime in May, Bill called his pal Donald. Donald Trump and Bill Clinton played golf together at least 12 times and socialized on many other occasions, including Trump's third wedding. Step one: memo. Step two: phone call.

Now, step three: over the next few months, the DNC and HRC people encouraged the media to cover Donald and re-arranged the primary calendar (Wikileak IDs 28484, 19697, 1797, 40448, etc.) to make sure Donald got the nod from the Republicans. In ID 40448 HRC campaign chief Mook says, "The overall goal is to move the IL primary out of mid March, where they are currently a lifeline to a moderate Republican candidate after the mostly southern Super Tuesday. IL was a key early win for Romney in 12." That worked. It's the Pied Piper strategy being approved by the Illinois state legislature.

If Podesta can order the Illinois state legislature to change their primary calendar to reduce the leverage of the state of Illinois in the selection of presidential candidates, do you not think he can order up some coverage of Trump from CNN, Univision, New York Times and MSNBC, who routinely ask him what to ask Trump and provide debate questions in advance and other collaborative activities?

We know the Illinois state legislature did change the calendar after Podesta asked for the change. We do know that the HRC campaign and the media do conspire. We know that Trump got two billion dollars worth of free coverage in the early part of his campaign (see section on media collaboration from more exact links). The HRC/DNC people also liked to plant false information (ID 37259). The New York Times on March 15, 2016 headlines, "$2 Billion Worth of Free Media for Donald Trump."

This free time had nothing to do with promoting ratings. This was part of the Pied Piper strategy. You might also like to read "How the Hillary Clinton campaign deliberately "elevated" Donald Trump with its "pied piper" strategy" on Salon, November 9, 2016.

There does not seem to be any evidence that Podesta did not send Hillary the Pied Piper memo, that Bill Clinton did not call Trump, then Podesta fixed the primary calendar, and meanwhile the media did not give Trump two billion dollars worth of free media in the run up to the Republican primaries. Podesta created the possibility of a president Trump. No Pied Piper memo, no candidate Trump, no nominee Trump, no president Trump.

The legacy of corporate media was still powerful in 2016 and used their leverage to push Trump over the top in the Republican primary at Hillary's request.

More true statements ahead.

# The 2016 Democratic primary is a crime scene

Absent the criminal law violations that allowed Hillary to steal the 2016 nomination, Trump would not now be president. The cheating that was not at the felony level (rigging debate, skewing coverage, calendar manipulation, disingenuous superdelegate counts, closed primaries, the superdelegate system itself, the 2015 August money laundering scheme involving 33 state Democratic parties, etc.) should still be actionable legally in the civil court. These actions are also illegal, with possible civil remedies. The criminal activities of the Democrats include election law violations every week and criminal ballot tampering.

On June 15, 2016 the Inquisitr published an article stating, "A study done on the Democratic primary is pointing to signs of election fraud in multiple states. Two statisticians studied exit polls and other data and compared them to actual election results.

*Operationalizing the Strategy*

*Pied Piper Candidates*

"In 2015, Wall Street Bonuses —not regular compensation, bonuses— seven years after they were bailed out with the public purse, totaled $29.4 billion dollars. Total compensation paid to every single person in this country who makes minimum wage totaled $14 billion. I'll stop there."
~ Mark Blyth

There are two ways to approach the strategies mentioned above. Th[...]mage on itself similar to what happened to Mitt Romney in 2012. The variety of candidates is a positive here, and many of the lesser known can serve as a cudgel to move the more established candidates further to the right. In this scenario, we don't want to marginalize the more extreme candidates, but make them more "Pied Piper" candidates who actually represent the mainstream of the Republican Party. Pied Piper candidates include, but aren't limited to:

- Ted Cruz
- Donald Trump
- Ben Carson

We need to be elevating the Pied Piper candidates so that they are leaders of the pack and tell the press to them seriously.

Axel Geijsel of Tilburg University in The Netherlands and Rodolfo Cortes Barragan from Stanford University in California published the study on June 7, the day the last six states held their primaries and caucuses." The full title of the study is, "Are we witnessing a dishonest election? A between state comparison based on the used voting procedures of the 2016 Democratic Party Primary for the Presidency of the United States of America." The paper is a compelling statistical analysis. Read it.

Exit polls are reliable. Indeed, in new democracies as in Eastern Europe, foreign observers have mandated re-votes based on discrepancies between official totals and exit polls that are far less than the discrepancies we saw in the 2016 Democratic primary. While the Republican exit polls were almost perfect, no more than a couple percentage points difference at most across a long list of candidates and on many separate occasions, the exit polls were routinely wildly off on the Democratic side.

The response of the corporate media to this study which could, were we talking about a new democracy, nullify an election was to cancel exit polls in the last states. On primary election night in New York, a media outlet briefly flashed an exit poll showing Bernie getting 48 percent to Hillary's 50 percent, as I saw the screenshots on social media. And then the poll disappeared.

A memo entitled "Re: 2016 presidential candidates" from May 26, 2015, DNC leak, shows that everyone at the DNC already assumed the democratic candidate would be Clinton more than a year before the convention. The memo suggests, "use specific hits to muddy the waters around ethics, transparency and campaign finance on HRC."

DNC staff was also invited to join the Hillary For America team

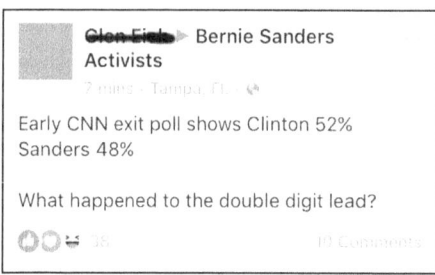

This exit poll flashed on screens, then disappeared.

on Slack around the same time, revealing that the DNC directly worked for the Clinton campaign before the Democratic primaries had ended (DNC ID 29412).

They knew she was dirty. They knew they were going to nominate her anyway. They planned a Pied Piper strategy to help her across the finish line. Now, they want to blame someone else for Trump assuming office.

The May 2015 "muddy waters" memo and the April 2015 Pied Piper memo were echoed in the mainstream media throughout 2016, as we can see that this was no accident. Trump got the coverage he needed to execute the Pied Piper strategy. The media did everything they could to in fact "muddy the waters." The line from the DNC memo to CNN, MSNBC, Washington Post, New York Times, CBS, ABC, NBC, Huffington Post, Politico is straight.

They knew she was going to win six months before anyone voted. In 2013, President Obama did everything but officially endorse Hillary with his sit-down CBS 60 minutes interview. No wonder so few candidates emerged to challenge her. The August 2015 33 state money laundering deal gave Hillary a 55 million dollar advantage and control of 33 state DNC parties.

In this environment of inevitability, Martin O'Malley and Bernie Sanders stepped up. Martin O'Malley, former Maryland governor, gained little traction in the primary, but he does show up twice in the Podesta Wikileaks. In ID 7131 O'Malley is quoted in the media saying, "There are not Wall Street CEOs banging down my door and trying to participate or help my campaign." Tony Carrk, Clinton campaign research director, ridiculed him for this assertion, saying "Exactly." Then in ID 2356, after he dropped out of the race, Podesta wrote to O'Malley, "Want to know how you are doing and interested to get your observations and advice. We would, of course, love to get your support."

O'Malley wrote back, "Thanks for reaching out. I'm good. No money, but no real debt. Good to be home again actually. I'm now looking for work. As far as observations -- when you think your country no longer works for you and your family, voting becomes solely an act of protest. Most Americans feel their own politicians have rigged the economic opportunity game against them. But you know all of that. HRC kindly called me a while back, very nice of her. Good luck to you both. Sent from my iPad."

The first part of O'Malley's email is telling: if Podesta write to him, he immediately discusses money. That's what Podesta is all about, as he knows.refused to endorse Hillary over Bernie. He tells Podesta, more or less, to buzz off. I don't know what to make of the "looking for a job" comment. If he wanted a job from Podesta, he would have had to endorse Hillary and he didn't. O'Malley then predicts Trump will win, in effect, through protest voting. And all that on iPad! And that's it for O'Malley for the 2016 primary campaign. From now on, It's all Bernie and Hillary.

Before this election, the Brennan Center for Justice report "Voter Purges" by Myrna Pérez concluded that "Far too frequently, however, eligible, registered citizens show up to vote and discover their names have been removed from the voter lists. States maintain voter rolls in an inconsistent and unaccountable manner.

Officials strike voters from the rolls in a process that is shrouded in secrecy, prone to error, and vulnerable to manipulation." This problem existed in 12 states as of 2008. And guess what actually happened?

**NEW YORK**: The Democratic Party engaged in election law violations, as reported on wnyc.org January 12, 2017 in an article headlined "Justice Department Says City Board of Elections Violated Federal Law in Brooklyn Voter Purge." We see statistical evidence of massive fraud. An election official was fired: Diane Haslett Rudiano. In September 2014, Rudiano sold a brownstone for $6.6 million to Holliswood 76, LLC, owned by Dana Lowey Luttway, a developer and daughter of U.S. Congresswoman Nita Lowey. We have Department of Justice confirmation.

Sara Latham wrote to Podesta (ID 11068) on February 22 that "I like our chances in Brooklyn!" months before the New York primary. Why? Did they plan the purge then, months before the primary?

**CALIFORNIA**: See The Young Turks "UNCOUNTED: The True Story of the California Primary." Judy Frankel for Huffington Post wrote, "The controversy stems from California's semi-open policy allowing voters who aren't registered Democrats to participate in the primary. Thousands of provisional ballots were cast, but these voters were not allowed to use the same ballot as Democrats—if they didn't obtain a special crossover ballot, their vote was nullified. Independent voters may have been disenfranchised during the June 7th primary because of unusual rules that don't apply to voters who register under a party. Independents, falling under the category of No Party Preference (NPP), needed to use special 'crossover' ballots in certain California counties – Los Angeles, San Francisco, and San Diego being among them – to vote for president."

NEVADA: There were issues around NGPVAN, including automated enrolling of voters, as reported in the Observer on September 16, 2016 in an article called, "Former Democratic Congressional Candidate Says Hillary Stole Nevada." Also see the Inquisitr of September 16, 2016, "The caucus results in February in Nevada were announced to the world before the votes were tabulated I can prove it from people on the ground."

A video shows election law violations during the Nevada caucus. A 30-second video uploaded to social media argues that Hillary Clinton supporters might have voted in the Nevada Caucus on Saturday without registering first. "They're letting into the caucus right now without registering them," a woman's voice can be heard on the video about potential voters bypassing the check-in desk. Another person says, "they will register after this."Register after getting in? Not allowed. See Nevada Statute NRS 193.135. On Reddit at r /politics under "hillary clinton supporters caught allowing" many Nevada voters reported similar incidents. "As a first time caucus goer in Nevada today, I could have gotten away with anything. No one knew what they were doing from start to finish." At the state convention, the last part of the three step caucus process, the Blue Dog democrats refused to give credentials to Bernie's delegates. Shaun King reported this event well. This was the event where California Senator Barbara Boxer gave Bernie's delegates the middle "FU" finger. A PBS reporter John Ralston falsely claimed a Bernie supporter threw a chair. Also see ID 5423.

RHODE ISLAND: DNC Deputy Communications Director Eric Walker (ID 6564) to several DNC staffers cites two news articles showing Sanders leading in Rhode Island and the limited number of polling locations in the state: "If she outperforms this polling, the Bernie camp will go nuts and allege misconduct. They'll probably complain regardless, actually." DNC leak ID 6564 further see an effort to front a fake investigation, as the governor and the attorney general are "one of ours" -- at a time when the DNC was supposed to be neutral between Hillary and Bernie.

ARIZONA: Salon article on March 24, 2016 notes "Polling places were cut by 70%, leading #Election Fraud to trend on Twitter & a petition to get 100,000 signatures… Phoenix Mayor Greg Stanton took a step further, writing a letter to Attorney General Loretta Lynch requesting a federal investigation into the allegations of misconduct, local media outlets reported."

KTAR news published "Arizona poll worker testifies incorrect ballots given to Democratic voters" on April 26, 2016. In "Arizona Poll Worker Testifies ONLY Democrats Were Given Wrong Ballots" published April 27, 2016 we read:

> "Diane Post, an attorney and Arizona poll worker, had to testify yesterday at a hearing on the election challenge that there were extensive voting problems with Democratic ballots during the recent presidential primary. She noted that at her location, 36 people failed to get the proper ballot. 'Every single time it happened to me it was a Democratic voter who wasn't able to access a Democratic ballot.' In addition, nearly two dozen people at the same location were listed as members of the wrong party. Post also said that at her polling place, they ran out of ballots for at least two congressional districts. One resident, Alisa Wolfe, noted that her registration was improperly changed from Democrat to Independent. She was able to vote provisionally after speaking to the Pima County recorder's office, which told her 'the problem was a computer glitch.' A couple of weeks ago, the Democratic Party and their candidates sued the state because some voters were in

*lines up to five hours and were never given a chance to vote: '…citing the alarmingly inadequate number of voting centers resulted in severe, inexcusable burdens on voters countywide, as well as the ultimate disenfranchisement of untold numbers of voters who were unable or unwilling to wait in intolerably long lines.' According to local news station KTAR News, budget cuts had slashed the number of polling places from 200 to 60 in the previous preference voting. Maricopa County Recorder Helen Purcell claimed cuts were due to funding problems. She did note the number will jump to 116 for a special statewide election in May.*

Also according to KTAR News: "The county has acknowledged it made mistakes in operating the primary by dramatically cutting the number of polling places and widely underestimating Election Day turnout." Ironically, this was not before Assistant Attorney General James Driscoll-MacEachron attempted to have the legal action dismissed because "the primary doesn't fall within the scope of what electors can challenge." Maricopa County Superior Court Judge David Cass denied the challenge and is allowing the case, which is expected to last a couple of days, to go forward.

The Court will also be hearing a separate case filed by Tucson resident John Blakely, who sued Arizona secretary of state Michele Reagan and all 15 counties after the March election, asking that "the results be decertified." Brakely's suit alleges that "long lines in Maricopa County suppressed the vote and statewide voter registrations problems led to illegal vote counts."

In acknowledging that reforms are needed, the Arizona State Attorney General claims the results can't be challenged because Brakey "can't show the result would change." We shall see, because Brakey is also getting his day in court as the Justice Department has launched its own inquiry into the problems.

The attempts at voter disenfranchisement in Arizona should surprise no one, as it is emblematic of a systemic problem in Republican-controlled states. A Republican operative, Todd Allbaugh recently announced he was leaving the Republican Party after 30 years because GOP state senators in Wisconsin were ecstatic that the Supreme Court ruling was allowing these new vote-suppressing laws to be implemented in advance of any preemptive challenge by the Justice Department – as a means merely to suppress Democratic voters. It's all they can do, since they can't win elections based on policy anymore.

IOWA: Sanders' supporters claim county caucus chair Drew Gentsch and precinct captain Elizabeth Buck did not count Sanders supporters at precinct #43." The video was live on C-SPAN and discussed more at length on Reddit.

MASSACHUSETTS: Bill Clinton stumped for his wife directly in front of the Buttonwood Park, New Bedford polling place. Mayor Mitchell of New Bedford endorsed Hillary in front of the doorway to the voting place. When Clinton arrived, the secret service prevented voters from accessing the poll for 28 minutes.  Bill Clinton continued his stops at polling places across Massachusetts, including one in Boston. The former president was spotted in the Newton Free Library in Newton, as well as the Holy Name gymnasium in West Roxbury—both polling locations. At Holy Name, he kissed an elderly woman on her head, and signed another voter's Hillary sign. The Boston Globe also reports Clinton told one voter, "Pull the lever for Hillary." He was joined by Boston Mayor Marty Walsh, a Clinton supporter.

Massachusetts election law is extremely clear about this: "Within 150 feet of a polling place...no person shall solicit votes for or against, or otherwise promote or oppose, any person or political party or position on a ballot question, to be voted on at the current election. No campaign material intended to influence the vote of a voter in the ongoing election, including campaign literature, buttons, signs, and ballot stickers, may be posted, exhibited, circulated, or distributed in the polling place, in the building where it is located, on the building walls, on the premises where the building stands, or within 150 feet of an entrance door to the building."

In an interview with the New York Times, William F. Galvin, the Massachusetts secretary of state said "We had to remind some of our poll workers that even a president can't go inside and work a polling place."

The mainstream media covered this as a humor item. This voter suppression strategy was blunt, probably not extremely effective, but clearly criminal and Bill Clinton should have been arrested.

KENTUCKY: A Pike County man has been indicted on multiple charges of election violations in connection with the recent statewide primary. Attorney General Andy Beshear announced Tuesday that a Franklin County grand jury has charged Keith Justice, 50, of Pikeville with four counts of intimidating an election officer and one count of interfering with an election involving a precinct in Pike County on May 17, 2016. The investigation began after a complaint was filed by the Pike County Clerk's office.

"The Attorney General is responsible for investigating and prosecuting election law violations," Beshear said. "We take seriously our duty to ensure honest and fair elections for all

Kentuckians." Justice is facing up to five years in prison for each felony charge.

In general, each county has a Republican and Democratic chair for its election commission. Thus, cheating in a primary is easier than it would be in a general election. And in court, the Democratic party of Arizona argued they are allowed to cheat, not that they did not cheat.

ILLINOIS: Jim Allen, Communications Director for the Chicago Board of Elections (BoE), acknowledges that "the numbers didn't match" initially in the legally mandated 5% audit of voting and tabulating machines after the recent Illinois Democratic primary between former Secretary of State Hillary Clinton and Vermont Senator Bernie Sanders. Allen, however, insists that this is simply a "perception issue" and that absolutely no election fraud took place.

Allen was responding to questions regarding allegations from citizen vote monitoring groups Who's Counting? – Chicago and the Illinois Ballot Integrity Project (IBIP). Dr. Lora Chamberlain is a leader of Who's Counting, which works with IBIP to credential election day monitors and joined them this year to audit the audit. IBIP was started in Illinois in the aftermath of the 2000 Al Gore versus George Bush Debacle. A total of six members of the two groups gave affidavit-based testimony at the April 5, 2016 Chicago Board of Elections meeting.

The testimony as to the admission of widespread, systemic cheating in the Illinois primary can be viewed in its entirety on the official Chicago Elections YouTube channel, beginning around the 24 minute mark of "Chicago Election Board Meeting - 2016-04-05."

CONCLUSION: The evidence of a pattern of multiple election law violations is compelling even if no serious criminal investigations are conducted. The reason this crime is so horrible is that this pattern of undermining democracy led to Trump becoming president.

A communication from late May laid out the pros and cons of DNC Chairwoman Debbie Wasserman Schultz accepting an invitation to CBS's 'Face the Nation', and indicated that the DNC was plotting its moves based on what would be amenable to Hillary Clinton's presidential campaign... "Clinton campaign is a mess, they're afraid of their own shadow and didn't like that we engaged," DNC communications director Luis Miranda wrote. "But they'll be unhappy regardless, so better to get out there and do some strong pivots and land good punches on Trump. They can't tell us NOT to do TV right now, we shouldn't pull ourselves out until they actually do... It's clear that Bernie messed up and that we're on the right side of history," Miranda wrote in another bullet point, referring to the Nevada convention.... "Let's take this offline," Wasserman Schultz said in response. "I basically agree with you" (ID 8253). The key points from 8253 are that 1) the DNC is obligated to be even

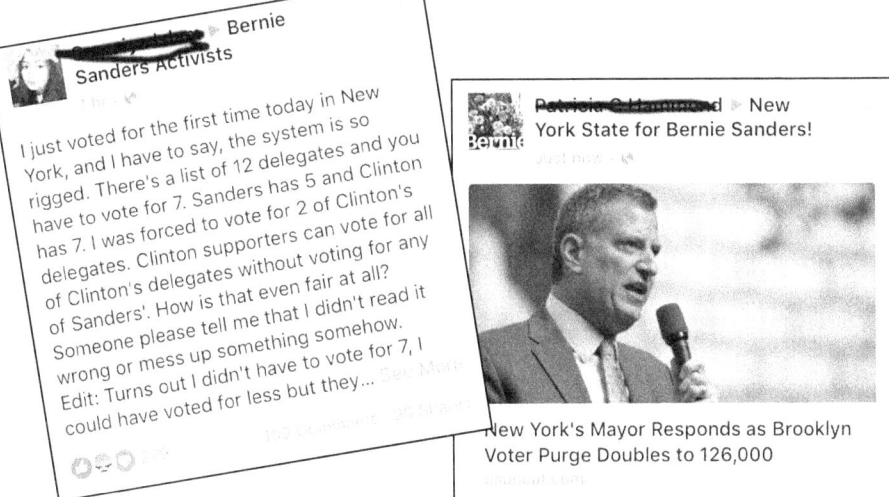

Bernie Sanders Activists

I just voted for the first time today in New York, and I have to say, the system is so rigged. There's a list of 12 delegates and you have to vote for 7. Sanders has 5 and Clinton has 7. I was forced to vote for 2 of Clinton's delegates. Clinton supporters can vote for all of Clinton's delegates without voting for any of Sanders'. How is that even fair at all? Someone please tell me that I didn't read it wrong or mess up something somehow. Edit: Turns out I didn't have to vote for 7, I could have voted for less but they... See More

Patricia ▸ New York State for Bernie Sanders!

New York's Mayor Responds as Brooklyn Voter Purge Doubles to 126,000 handed between candidates and they obviously were not; and 2) Schultz was aware that this was the rule and wanted to take the conversation offline to avoid leaving evidence of wrongdoing.

"Wondering if there's a good Bernie narrative for a story, which is that Bernie never ever had his act together, that his campaign was a mess," Paustenbach wrote in the May 21 message. "Specifically, [Debbie Wasserman Schultz] had to call Bernie directly in order to get the campaign to do things because they'd either ignored or forgotten to something critical" (ID 5423). Debbie Wasserman Schultz on Jeff Weaver, after suggesting Bernie continue to the Convention... "He [Weaver] is an ASS" (ID 10806). Again, if you hate one side and work to plant negative stories about that side, the DNC is not being fair to all candidates, as required by its charter.

Additional emails showed a discussion on how to frame Bernie's religious beliefs to weaken his appeal to religious groups, using anti semitic innuendo (ID 7643). Another held strategizing on how to help Clinton beat Bernie in Rhode Island with media (ID 6564). This one speaks for itself... "We have the Sanders folks admitting that they lost fair and square, not because we 'rigged' anything" (ID 5423). The DNC was aggressively trying to take one candidate down.

Donna Brazile, subsequently DNC chair, seven months before the end of the primary pledged to John Podesta that "as soon as (Hillary's) nomination is wrapped up. I will be your biggest surrogate… Look forward to working with you to elect the first woman President of the United States" says Podesta (ID 5616#efmACTADd).

Hillary Clinton's most trusted aide, Huma Abedin, wrote to Hillary's campaign chairman John Podesta and her campaign manager Robby Mook about receiving insider information about the DNC convention and organizing a private call with Debbie Wasserman Schultz (ID 7741).

**DEBATES**: Fox News leaked Town Hall questions to Clinton campaign (ID 21526#efmAJiAOE). Donna Brazile (CNN contributor at the time, and current DNC Chairman now) received Town Hall Debate questions from CNN before the debate... "From time to time I get the questions in advance" (ID 5205#efmAD-AMa).

Univision chairman (IDs 3782, 4553) Haim Saban sought to parlay his leverage with Hispanic voters through his network to influence Hillary Clinton's Israel policy. Univision hosted a debate in the Democratic primary that many found clearly biased against Bernie. "The Jerusalem Post recently rated Saban the most influential Jew in the world, partially due to his close relationship with Clinton," noted Rabbi Shmuley Boteach On October, 21 2016. I guess the Rabbi has never heard of some old Jew from Vermont. The owner of the largest Spanish-language network in America clearly cared more about Israel and his relationship with Clinton than he did about the conditions and interests of his Hispanic viewers.

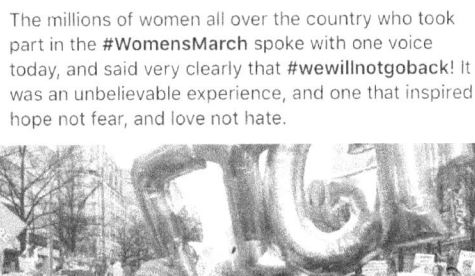

Rep. Debbie Wasserman Schultz added 6 new photos.

The millions of women all over the country who took part in the #WomensMarch spoke with one voice today, and said very clearly that #wewillnotgoback! It was an unbelievable experience, and one that inspired hope not fear, and love not hate.

~~Sadiq Samani~~ 🏛 Board of Elections.

1 hr · New York ·

I got my right to vote in New York motherfuckers!!! One more vote for #Bernie2016. I went to court, got in front judge, and he decided that I was credibl that I did register to change my party affiliation prior to the Oct 9, 2015 deadlin

If you are in New York and your party was switched or they are telling you that you can' vote, go to the Board of Elections and see a judge. Take any evidence you can. Also, if yo need legal advice and want to run your story through a lawyer, call Bernie's lawyer hotline NOW! (347) 379-4298

WIN New York!!!

 ~~Luis Cruz~~ ▶ Bernie Believers [Bernie Sanders]

7 mins ·

Saw a judge. And now I'm going to the polls to vote for Bernard sanders.

23 Comments 10 Shares

 ~~Kendall Nelson~~ ▶ Bernie Believers [Bernie Sanders]

32 mins ·

Am I the only one who had some insomnia last night because I'm so nervous about today's primary in NY? I feel so bad I can't join the fight because I didn't change my party from independent to democrat in October!

 Ben Casselman
@bencasselman

Two hours after polls are meant to open in #Brooklyn and our polling place isn't ready. #NYPrimary

 ~~Sheldon Calish~~ is Murdered Bernie Sanders Upstate Connect

3 hrs ·

Nobody can vote in Harlem . Everyone is being turned away. 100s couldn't vote. Only the out of ten people can find their area on 127th w in Harlem . Many have been to six different polling places and aren't on the list. Hundreds and hundreds of people being turned around. Even the poll people didn't get their paper to vote early. This is disgraceful. Who can I call ? Or is this just how this racist day is going to go down in history. I've never seen so many people that couldn't vote in my life ! Let along find their place if th... See More

 ~~Susan Murtha~~ ▶ New York State for Bernie Sanders!

30 mins ·

My usual voting place says my name is not on the list :/
I cannot get anyone to answer the phone at my county's Board Of Elections.
I asked someone I know if they might know what is going on, they told me I couldn't vote today because I'm in the Working Families Party?
Does anyone know if this is true?
Right on the Working Families page they say they are endorsing Bernie Sanders.
This is so frustrating! >:(

 8    30 Comments 3 Shares

she has successfully voted. Only took four hours.

5 minutes ago · Edited · Unlike · 3 · Reply

 Will Pflaum
Thank her for us all
8 minutes ago · Like · 1 · Reply

 Kat Anderson
This was her first election vote ever. What an initiation.
6 minutes ago · Like · Reply

 Sarah Simon Bianco
I'm sorry it was such an intense initiation but I bet because of what

**Will Pflaum**
But anyway, you win. From Bernie's lawyer in NY: "There was a lawsuit filed yesterday seeking an open primary. The application was denied. We should absolutely not be encouraging voters registered as independents to vote by affidavit ballot. If they registered Dem and show up as unaffiliated the we shoul encourage them. The Board of Elections told me that some districts are flooded with provisional ballots from registered independents. This will only slow down the count. They think the Sanders campaign is tellin independents to vote. This is from personally: don't do it."

**Will Pflaum**
So no, if you did not follow the ru you probably should not vote. If do vote, I have an argument ava

It's hard to maintain civility when so many aspects of the system encourage anything but. The primary system cultivates so much hostility because it repeatedly reminds individuals that "their" vote really doesn't matter. 3 million registered independents were denied their say in choosing the candidate they feel most confident in, so it's hard to just accept that and not want to lash out. The divisiveness is carved out by those who have co-opted a process which is supposed to produce a candidate who represents the people, and when you deny those people an opportunity to speak, they tend to do so in more volatile and less rational forms....

**Bernie Believers [Bernie Sanders]**

Hey guys.. I have been a registered Democrat since I was 18. I am now 37. Today at 6pm I went to place my vote and was told I was registered as a Republican. I have never attempted to change my voter status and I have never in my life voted Republican. I am at my county's board of electrons waiting to see a judge, conveniently he is on dinner break until 8. I am hoping I am able to get back to my polling location in the 27th district in time. When I explained the issue to the volunteers at the polling location, they told me to "just vote Republican" it was only because of **Citizen Action of New York - Southern Tier Chapter**, this Facebook page and others devoted to **U.S. Senator Bernie Sanders** that I knew my rights. Sharing so that others will know **The People For Berni**
~~~~~~~~~~~~~~~~ **~mton for Bernie Ber~**
Sanders 201

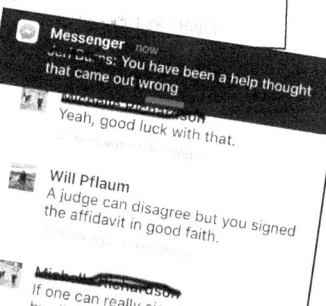

**Messenger** now
~~Jon Burns:~~ You have been a help thought that came out wrong
Yeah, good luck with that.

**Will Pflaum**
A judge can disagree but you signed the affidavit in good faith.

If one can really sign it in good faith, by all means do so. If it were me, I could not.

Or you do it as an act of civil disobedience. The ethics of which, are basically saying 'I knowingly break the law and will accept charges/punishment for my crime of perjury.'

# Violations of FEC laws

Breaking election laws are, like sharing classified information and election law violations, crimes. Campaigns are required to comply with Federal Election Campaign Act and are required to comply with the federal campaign finance law, in particular sections of FEC Regulation 11 CFR 110.11(c)(3)(ii)(A) and (B), also 2 U.S.C. §§ 441a(a) and (f), 11 C.F.R. §§ 110.1(b),110.9,114.2(d) (2006) §109.20 (a) (b), Federal Election Act, Title 52, United States Code 30101, et seq.

Under the Federal Election Act, Title 52, United States Code 30101, et seq., there are several provisions that define the relationship between a candidate's official campaign and an independent political action committee. Under the Act, expenditures by a person or organization in cooperation, consultation, or concert with, or at the request or suggestion of, the agents of a federal candidate or that candidate's authorized committee are deemed a contribution to the candidate's campaign, and, thus, subject to the contribution limits imposed by federal law on donors to federal campaigns.

Tyler Harber pleaded guilty in Federal District Court on February 12, 2015, to one count of illegal coordination of spending under campaign finance law and one count of false statements to the FBI. The Harber matter pertains to the instant matter of Clinton coordination with PACs.

Here are the violations of law pertaining to Jose H. Villarreal, treasurer; John Podesta, chairman; Robby Mook, campaign manager; Charlie Baker, Chief Administrative Officer; Hillary Clinton, candidate for president; Dennis Cheng, campaign national finance director 2016 (HILLARY FOR AMERICA); Jim Messina,

Co-Chair of Priorities USA, Jonathan Mantz, advisory board
for Priorities USA, Paul Begala, Senior Advisor/ Principal Paul
Begala (PRIORITIES USA (P-USA)); David Brock, chair, Elizabeth
Cohen, treasurer (Correct the Record) and other super pacs who
routinely violated federal law by coordinating activities with the HRC
campaign.

ID 27167 of May 3, 2015 includes Hillary Clinton herself
stating, "I agree with you, John. I think we focus hard on raising
as much as we can and then throw the kitchen sink at everyone
who we believe steps over the line, understanding that has
limited impact." This comment was in response to John Podesta's
comment, "I have no magic solutions other than execution. Elias
may have some legal ideas to slow them down. We have 3 things
we have to do. Raise the primary $ by expanding the bundler
network. Get Priorities functional. Use this to scare our people into
giving bigger sums. We may need to get WJC into the mix sooner.
We should also ask BHO to do more in light of this, although
they are kind of prissy about how they approach this." Here we
see that 1) Barack Obama (BHO) was aware that the activities
of HRC campaign skirted the law and reluctant to participate; 2)
Priorities USA was a campaign instrument from the first day; 3)
the campaign, as personified by Podesta, was not merely standing
aside and letting Priorities USA conduct independent fundraising
but using leverage from the campaign, including Clinton herself, to
"scare" donors into giving larger sums to the PAC; 4) Hillary herself
was part of this illegal scheme to mix PAC money and campaign
money.

The subject header for ID 27167 is "F.E.C. Can't Curb 2016
Election Abuse, Commission Chief Says There is a stalemate
among the agency's six commissioners, who are perpetually

locked in 3-to-3 ties along party lines because of a fundamental disagreement over the commission's mandate." In other words, the FEC is incapable of enforcing the law and the HRC campaign need not worry about complying with the law. In Wikileaks ID 14580 from campaign manager Robby Mook makes a similar point.

ID 29206 of October 25, 2013 shows a pattern of coordination which became illegal after the presidential campaign began but did not stop as required by law. Clearly, the PACs and the campaign were tied at the hip from before the time the campaign officially began.

To wit, in a July 2015 memo addressed to Clinton herself, her campaign laid out plans for working with the Democratic National Committee and Correct the Record, a Super PAC. Correct the Record was created by David Brock, a longtime Clinton ally and the founder of Media Matters for America. One section of the memo instructed: "Work with CTR and DNC to publicize specific GOP candidate vulnerabilities." This coordination violates laws prohibiting the coordination between PACs and the campaign. See document "3125946-Strategic-Imperatives-Memo" and IDs 5267, 16024 and 16970.

In October 2015, several Clinton staffers strategized over ways to attack author Ed Klein for attributing an apparently fake quote to former President Bill Clinton in his book. "I'm sure Brock and team would love to go at him. Nick, want me to put you in touch with them?" Clinton campaign communications staffer Christina Reynolds, wrote, referring to Clinton's press secretary Nick Merrill. "I can reach out to David," volunteered Karen Finney, another Clinton staffer on the email chain. This coordination violates laws prohibiting the coordination between PACs and the campaign (ID 6119).

A month later, Reynolds emailed a list of agenda items for an upcoming campaign meeting. High on the list: determining how to frame Bernie Sanders, and whether attacks on Republicans "should go through HRC, surrogates, DNC, CTR," another reference to Correct the Record. This coordination violates laws prohibiting the coordination between PACs and the campaign (ID 5267).

In another email that month, Bonner requested Podesta speak to an adviser to Jim Simons, a hedge fund manager who was considering donating to Correct the Record. "He told me he is intending to call you on Monday to discuss the importance of CTR and their donation," Bonner wrote. "He is interested in the fact that CTR is a coordinated PAC that does not do any paid communication." (Simons has not donated to CTR.) This coordination violates laws prohibiting the coordination between PACs and the campaign (ID 6700).

In February 2016, Dennis Cheng, the lead fundraiser for the Clinton campaign, emailed other staffers to recommend that Podesta call certain donors to Priorities USA Action, the largest pro-Clinton Super PAC, to thank them for their six- and seven-figure donations. Cheng flagged three donor names, telling a colleague they were "very important Priorities USA calls that ideally John can make." This coordination violates laws prohibiting the coordination between PACs and the campaign (9358 and document "Podesta-Priorities-Calls").

In a separate email, Guy Cecil, an official from Priorities USA, apologizes to Podesta for sending him to the wrong address for a meeting. Podesta noted it had been raining and quipped, "Priorities owes me a pair of shoes." Routine contact between PACs and the Campaign violates the spirit of the regulations. Also, no debts, even shoes, should be passed between the PAC and the campaign.

In email ID 5332 members of the campaign are asked to provide suggestions for a PAC board, "Please think of people who would be good and send me suggestions by Monday." This coordination violates laws prohibiting the coordination between PACs and the campaign.

Charles Baker, Chief Administrative Officer, wrote: "I explored with Marc what the limitations would be on HFA's use of Governor Granholm if she were paid by Correct the Record. As a threshold matter we could not call her a spokesman for the campaign or schedule her directly. We would be able to refer groups or media to her if they are looking for a non-campaign, third part surrogate, the same way we might refer them to the DNC Chair or Stephanie Schriock. For example this weekend she spoke at the Ohio State Party dinner. If she were at Correct the Record we could at least make sure her speaking and media opportunities met our needs/requests. Finally, as a person paid by CTR she could not solicit donations for the campaign. She could be at CTR for a period and move to some other vehicle (New York - or Michigan- state party, DNC, HFA) at any point (i.e. there is no waiting period)." This coordination violates laws prohibiting the coordination between PACs and the campaign (ID 16024).

In the email, Marc E. Elias of Perkins Coie LLP 700 13th St, NW Washington, DC 20005, writing a legal opinion for Respondents, notes: "Per John's question below — there is one legal tool we could use that might slow them down. The law has a little noticed or used provision that says that if a complaint has been filed and it is either dismissed or not acted upon within 120 days the entity that filed the complaint can sue the FEC to force it to proceed with enforcement. If the FEC fails to move forward, then the complainant is permitted to bring their own lawsuit to enforce the law directly. IF it were announced that this was the path we intended to take, it would both make news and perhaps give pause to the groups. Is this something we want to push forward? If so, would we want the DNC to do it? The campaign? Or would we prefer it be done externally? It would be hailed by the reform groups, but is a significant step in legal escalation and will certainly result in similar action against Priorities et al. Let me know if you want to discuss any of these options." Clearly, Respondents understand the law and simply wish to skirt FEC regulations.

Campaign chair refers to "best of hits for both Correct the Record and American Bridge on the Presidential..." In December 2015, a fundraiser for multiple pro-Clinton Super PACs emailed John Podesta, the campaign's chairman, with a suggested seating chart for an event with Super PAC donors. "John, Below is the seating chart for this evening and attached is a best of hits for both Correct the Record and American Bridge on the Presidential," Mary Pat Bonner, the fundraiser, wrote. Campaign finance records show four donors on Bonner's list have given $725,000 to American Bridge 21st Century, which conducts opposition research against Republicans. One donor on the list has contributed $125,000 to Correct the Record. Bonner included a document highlighting the work done by Correct the Record. The paper asserts the group may "coordinate directly and strategically with the Hillary campaign." This coordination is a clear violation of FEC regulations with the force of law (ID 5636 and "CTR-Update").

ID 2638 shows coordination between PACs and the campaign. It has the subject line "Organizations that can help with turnout." Email 1293 includes a PowerPoint list attachment. This shows coordination.

ID 31968 of March 16, 2015 includes a PDF file called

"Alternative Approach to Super Pacs" from Marc E. Elias of law firm Perkins Coie, LLP to John Podesta offers legal advice to the candidate on how to coordinate with Super Pacs without leaving evidence of soliciting funds for the Super Pac by the candidate or her campaign staff. Clearly, Podesta's own lawyer would prefer that HRC and her campaign staff not attend Super Pac events but the HRC team insisted on doing so and looked for advice on how to skirt the law.

ID 17720 of December 17, 2015 shows the scheduling of an illegal coordination meeting between Podesta and Priorities USA and HVF (Hillary Victory Fund).

**Conclusion**: The HRC campaign routinely violated Federal Election law, did so thinking they could get away with it due to gridlock in the FEC, and Hillary herself was aware of this pattern of criminal activity.

But we continue with truth.

# Anyone could have hacked Podesta's accounts

I must make an important point: John Podesta, former chief of staff to Bill Clinton and Hillary Clinton's top campaign official, transition chair for Obama, has the brains of a boiled potato. John responded to a phishing email in late March 2016. He was apparently hacked twice, fell for a phishing email twice, and never put on two step verification. Wikileak Podesta ID 36355: look that one up as per his digital carelessness.

America is a great place. Even a person with almost no IQ who believes that UFOs have landed in America can become one of the most powerful people in our country. Children, being as dumb as shit and having no idea what is a true threat and what is baffling idiotic nonsense is no impediment to your rise to greatness, as long as you remember this one lesson: do as the big guy says and obey.

To wit, **after** (the word there is after), after (again in case you thought it was a typo), Wikileaks released thousands of his emails, John Podesta still did not install two step verification on his iCloud account. He did not change his password. His gmail password, which resulted in the hack, was *Hillary2016* (I saw this on 4chan and then it disappeared, for what that's worth) and his iCloud password was *podesta1234* (according to the threads on 4chan before they disappeared). He still had that as his password after (did you read that word before?) his emails were the talk of the universe.

Now, an anonymous post on 4chan would not be a reliable source of information, if I did not also see Podesta's Twitter account get hacked with a pro-Trump message on the same evening as his password was published on 4chan. And if there were any doubt that a hack occurred, CNN ran a story about it the next day. The claim on 4chan was that the hackers broke into Podesta's iCloud account as well as Twitter. Screenshots were posted showing the location of John Podesta's ipad under "find my device."

Apparently the person who hacked the Twitter account got the password from the same post I was looking at, as the hacker put "hi /pol" in the tweet… so quite likely those passwords were the actual passwords at the time.

On Wednesday October 12, /pol/ posted his hacking activities on Podesta's phone. Then CNN reported on October 13, "Hackers breach Clinton campaign chairman's Twitter account." So, /pol/ is confirmed. Now, /pol/ says Podesta has podesta1234 as his password. We know /pol/ posted this on 4chan. We know someone used that information and broke into Podesta's Twitter feed.

Hillary Clinton takes American security seriously?

Obama himself, out of his own presidential mouth, blamed Russia for interfering with our elections. Yet, at the same time, Podesta left his phone in a cab (ID 7155). He had no protection on his phone and a password that is easy to guess. And he didn't fix any of it even after Obama ran his august mouth about crap with no evidence.

Obama, maybe you should tell your people to change their passwords and shut up about Russia? /pol/ is not Russia. Any fool can read Podesta's emails, get his iCloud contacts, and set his phone to factory settings.

Craig Murray, Wikileaks associate and former UK ambassador, says that the DNC and Podesta releases did not come from a Russian source. You can read his blog (craigmurray.org. uk) particularly, "The CIA's Absence of Conviction." He says he personally knows who the source was. Julian Assange says the same thing.

If Russia had nothing to do with the leaks, and if Podesta was careless with his digital information, then all discussion of the Russian role in the 2016 election seems silly. Global Research, July 31, 2016 published, "Israeli Intelligence Debunks Notion of Russia Hacking DNC Emails." Many more such articles have followed this initial report.

And what if Russia did interfere with the US election? Humans Are Free published, "CIA Has Interfered With Over 81 Foreign Elections in the Past Century" and the other sources will confirm this list. Then there are the articles from 1996 about the US helping Boris Yeltsin win in the race for president of Russia: "Moscow Journal; The Americans Who Saved Yeltsin (Or Did They?)" in the New York Times is one. Democratic donor George Soros, a frequent flyer in the Podesta email leaks, supported "civil society" programs all over Eastern Europe in order to elect governments to his liking and openly bragged about his efforts in the pages of the New York Review of Books.

Wikileaks (cia-france-elections-2012/releases/) exposed documents from 2012 showing the CIA intending to influence the election in France. The 7 pages of documents reveal that all major French political parties "were targeted for infiltration by the CIA's human ("HUMINT") and electronic ("SIGINT") spies in the seven months leading up to France's 2012 presidential election."

Now, Trump may well have financial ties to Putin. There is evidence that Trump is willing to abandon the Ukraine and let Russia sanctions lapse in exchange for money for himself, in the form of shares in a Russian oil company. If true, these links would be outrageous and impeachable offenses.

Trump's national security adviser, Michael Flynn, resigned amid a flow of intelligence leaks that he had secretly discussed sanctions with the Russian ambassador to Washington and then tried to cover up the conversations. All of a sudden, Democrats loved the CIA and leaks.

Funny that, hun? You'd think a consistent position in favor of a free flow of information, or a bias toward leaks in the public interest showing criminal behavior by the US government, as in the cases of Snowden and Manning, would be more noble than a partisan abuse of Deep State super power. Not if you're a chicken little Democrat scurrying around with no sense of morality or if you're a megalomaniac like Trump, who can't see he should pardon Snowden and Assange, assuming the US government has an actual charge against Julian Assange of Wikileaks.

But even if Trump collaborated with Putin during the election, even if Russia in fact played a role in the Wikileaks releases, the American public is better off knowing what we now know.

Russia didn't tell MSNBC and CNN to cover Trump in late 2015 and early 2016 to help him win the Republican nomination, Podesta arranged that. Russia didn't pick Tim Kaine as a running mate. Russia didn't blow off Michigan and Wisconsin. Russia didn't disenfranchise hundreds of thousands of voters in Brooklyn or let people who weren't registered to vote into the caucuses in Nevada.

Tom Brokaw Unwittingly Reveals Whats Wrong With Corporate Journalists

The Jimmy Dore Show 69,237 views

3K 51

Caitlin Johnstone ✓

Follow

## Rachel Maddow Is An Asshole

#RachelMaddow #JillStein #GreenParty #RedBaiting #MSM

 Follow

David Hildenbrand

Again I don't care who you are voting for. If you live on earth this should make you sick. #HillaryClinton #DonaldTrump #PodestaEmails3

Wikileaks

50% of Clinton voters state that Russia tampered with vote counting, despite no evidence that it did #FakeNews

The Guardian's Summary of Julian Assange's Interview Went Viral and Was Completely False

Another season of John Oliver, shameless pro-establishment shill

John Harwood

a Dad who covers Washington, the economy and national politics for CNBC and the New York Times. Find my speakeasy interviews at cnbc.com Speakeasy

Washington, DC

what should I ask Jeb...

From: john.harwood@nbcuni.com
To: john.podesta@gmail.com
Date: 2015-09-21 16:54
Subject: what should I ask Jeb...

John Harwood
CNBC/NYT
202 359 8751

https: wik

# The mainstream media is propaganda

In 2015, I thought there was bias in the media. I suspected that some elite journalists hung around with politicians, favoring some, sharing an insulated world view, but that there was no "mainstream media" as right wingers used the term.

ID 59125, from 2007 to Sara Ehrman, includes a memo written to "Memo To: George and Jonathan Soros, Peter and Jonathan Lewis, Herb and Marion Sandler, Steve Bing, John Sperling, Michael Vachon" from John Podesta called "COMBINED FUNDRAISING, MESSAGING AND MOBILIZATION PLAN." This memo outlines plans to turn the already power deferential corporate media into a liberal echo chamber, as the right has on Fox and talk radio.

Tin foils hats, wild conspiracies, George Soros, yeah, shadow government... all nuts... but wait! It's all true! Go read the memo! It's been online since October 2016 and have you heard about it in the MSM? Why not? BECAUSE IT'S ALL TRUE. The media is lying to you every day, all day, and doing nothing else. If that were not the case, they would have reported on this memo and reformed their ways. Instead, they don't want you to know the memo exists and continue to soak up their propaganda. Wake up! I just gave you the ID number.

I used to laugh when Jon Stewart poked his finger in Fox News' eye. Then I thought there was a substantial difference between the propaganda of Fox and the real, if biased, news of the other traditional outlets, like the New York Times, CBS, NBC, and CNN.

Blackout. No news about people coming together to stand up to the oligarchy. That was no coincidence, not driven by

**The New York Times**

## SECURITY; Increase in Electronic Attacks Leads to Warning on Iraqi Hackers and U.S. Safety

By ERIC LICHTBLAU
JANUARY 17, 2003

Intelligence officials are concerned that a recent rise in electronic attacks against government and military computer networks in the United States may be the work of pro-Iraqi hackers and could signal a "potential crisis" in national security, according to a classified F.B.I. assessment.

The assessment, prepared last week by the National Infrastructure Protection Center at the Federal Bureau of Investigation, warned intelligence officials that the attacks, which have been relatively limited, are likely to grow more

**REDS TRY TO STIR NEGROES TO REVOLT**

Widespread Propaganda on Foot Urging Them to Join I. W. W. and 'Left Wing' Socialists.

**ATTACK COLORED LEADERS**

Publications Circulated Among Uneducated Classes In Southern States.

civilized nations. * * * The best and bravest, the noblest and most courageous, are in the dark and cavernous prison cells of this country. * * * We must give more consideration to those men who will face jails and cells for a principle, and less to the smug, sleek leaders who swerve, compromise, and equivocate for soft berths, fat salaries, and slothful ease."

"The situation created as a result of this agitation," said a Federal official, "is one that deserves the consideration of all right-thinking people, white and black. It is an agitation which involves the I. W. W., Bolshevism and the worst features of other extreme radical movements. It appeals to the ignorant and seeks openly to create a feeling of resentment among certain negro elements that may lead to results that all good citizens will deplore unless it is stopped. That the movement is making headway there is no doubt. Reports from all parts of the country show this to be the case."

ratings. The corporate interests behind big media do not want an awake citizenry. So, they lied, distorted, omitted: every outlet who coordinated with Podesta should be considered fake news. You don't give a political operative control over your story and call yourself a journalist. What the New York Times and their ilk is doing is pure propaganda. Now, let's prove that proposition.

Let's start with this, an interview from November 29, 2016:

*AMY GOODMAN: March 15th, Super Tuesday III, was the night when Rubio gave his speech, and Ted Cruz gave his speech, Clinton gave her speech, and Donald Trump, they waited for half an hour for him to give his speech and showed the open podium, as they often did. They showed more of the open podium waiting for Donald Trump than ever playing your speeches. That's what—those were all the candidates that night. And they played all their full speeches. They did not play one word of your speech. You were speaking in Phoenix, Arizona, to the largest rally of any of those people that night. They didn't even speculate where you were.*

*SEN. BERNIE SANDERS: I wish I could disagree with you. No, no, no, Amy is raising a very—and we go into it in the book. I was stunned. I mean, you know, in the middle of the campaign, you're not figuring out this stuff or thinking about it. Turns out that from January 1st, 2015, I think, through November 2015, ABC Evening News had us on for 20 seconds.*

**PARTIES**: Clinton Staff hosts private "off-the-record cocktail party" with 38 "influential" reporters, journalists, editors, and anchors (from 16 different mainstream media outlets including CNN, NBC, CBS, NYT, MSNBC, & more) with the stated goal of "framing the race" (ID 5953 see attachment).

John Podesta hosts a dinner with reporters: I'm "Cooking for 30 of your reporter friends" (ID 4543#efmAAGABu. Full list of media guests (ID 12063).

MSNBC's Meet The Press host and Political Director for NBC News, Chuck Todd, hosted a dinner party in 2015 for Clinton Campaign communications director Jennifer Palmieri (ID 13686).

**MSNBC/NBC**: Another chain (ID 5508) reveals MSNBC's Chuck Todd and DNC staff members discussing how to discredit Sanders.

MSNBC's Mika Brzezinski's call for Wasserman Schultz to resign. Schultz tells Todd to behave (ID 4025) and he does.

Hillary Clinton reads directly from script during Phone Interview with MSNBC's Chris Hayes (ID 4274#efmAEcAWc).

Video at twitter.com/wikileaks/status/786158412119707648. CNBC panelist colluding with John Podesta on what to ask Trump when he calls in for an interview (ID 7710#efmAakAd6AjgAIR).

Wasserman Schultz sent an email to NBC anchor Chuck Todd with the subject line "Chuck, this must stop," and set up a time for the two to talk about MSNBC's "Morning Joe" co-host Mika Brzezinski calling on Wasserman Schultz to step down (ID 10945).

AMAZON/CIA/THE WASHINGTON POST: The Washington Post took money from the CIA. The Nation reported, "[Jeff Bezos, owner of Amazon.com and the Washington Post] recently secured a $600 million contract from the CIA. That's at least twice what Bezos paid for the Post this year. Bezos recently disclosed that the company's Web-services business is building a 'private cloud' for the CIA to use for its data needs." Also see, "IBM Concedes $600M CIA Cloud Deal To Amazon" on Cruxialcio.com, October 30, 2013.

Washington Post columnist Dana Milbank asked the DNC to do research for a negative column he wrote about Donald Trump in April 2016. Milbank's column was titled, "The Ten Plagues of Trump," and featured a list of "outrageous things" said by Trump. Internal DNC emails suggest Milbank's asked for — and then leaned heavily on — DNC opposition research on Trump for the article (DNC IDs 5531, 8993).

On December 18, 2015, Amazon sent an email to all US customers, even those who declined to receive advertising and newsletters, with the headline, "Most Read from The Washington Post: DNC: Sanders campaign improperly accessed Clinton voter data... Please enjoy this complimentary daily newsletter from The Washington Post, an award-winning news leader, brought to you by Amazon, working to be Earth's most customer-centric company."

Google, Facebook and Amazon used every resource they could to help Hillary cheat.

FACEBOOK: In ID 15092#efmARfAUUAZpAd9AfGAf6, Podesta is invited to meet Mark Zuckerberg to discuss "political operations to advance public policy goals on social oriented objectives (like immigration, education or basic scientific research)." Facebook COO Sheryl Sandberg, said in ID 19070#efmACIAD6 "I still want HRC [Hillary Rodham Clinton] to win badly," she wrote. "I am still here to help as I can. She came over and was magical with my kids."

THE NEW YORK TIMES: Clinton campaign and the New York Times coordinating attack strategy against Trump (ID 4664). New York Times reporter Mark Leibovich gives Hillary veto power over his story (ID 4213#efmDV1DWd).

John Podesta receiving drafts of New York Times articles before they're published (ID 844). New York Times and AP "helpful" to Clinton campaign, says Podesta (ID 5502).

Clinton staff "Placing a story" with Politico / New York Times "place a story with a friendly journalist" "we have a very good relationship with Maggie Haberman of Politico" "we should shape likely leaks in the best light for HRC" (ID 7524#efmA14A2IA3AA36A9fA-kA-6BAICwpCx4). Coordinating against Trump with the New York Times (ID 4664).

Neera Tanden on the New York Times and Associated Press being helpful to the Clinton Campaign... (ID 5502).

Cheryl Mills on "placing a story" with a "friendly journalist [Maggi Haberman of Politico]"... We have had her tee up stories for us before and have never been disappointed" (ID 7524#efmA14A2IA3AA36A9fA-kA-6BAICwpCx4).

Nick Merrill "I've spoken to both [New York Times and Wall Street Journal] to steer them towards progressive names," regarding Hillary Clinton's approach to economic policy (ID 9007#efmAcTAdS).

In ID 1542, Lynn Rothschild sent a 16 page paper to the New York Times' Amy Chozik to influence her reporting. Doc leaked to Podesta and crew from "one of our friends."

In an article called "On WikiLeaks, Journalism, and Privacy: Reporting on the Podesta Archive Is an Easy Call" Glenn Greenwald noted that The New York Times' David Barstow said he does not care who leaked us Trump's tax return, or what the motivation was. Yet, CNN's Chris Cuomo said that it was illegal to read Wikileaks.

**truthdig**

Beware of the World
Mark Zuckerberg and
Facebook Are Making,
The Observer Warns

Sent from my iPhone

On Apr 19, 2015, at 4:28 PM, John Podesta <john.podesta@gmail.com> wrote:

I know she has begun to hate everyday Americans, but I think we should use it once the first time she says I'm running for president because you and everyday Americans need a champion.

I think if she doesn't say it once, people will notice and say we false started in Iowa.

**BOSTON GLOBE:** The Boston Globe colludes with Clinton campaign to give Hillary a "big presence" (ID 4180#efmAJhALE). Ad for Hillary Clinton secretly pitched by 'right-leaning' Heat Street 'journalist' Louise Mensch (ID 5740#efmAMvAUe).

**HUFFINGTON POST AND THE HILL**: Brent Budowsky (writer for The Hill and Huffington Post) warns John Podesta about possible Hillary attacks and that not talking to the press is killing her support: "I'm not going to raise this publicly, but.." (ID 6453#efmARBAUVAVJAXBAfNAhWAkaAl4).

Huffington Post contributor Frank Islam writes to John Podesta in email titled "My blogs in the Huffington Post", says "I am committed to make sure she is elected the next president." "Please let me know if I can be of any service to you" (ID 5988#efmADmAE6AF-AG1).

Nevertheless, despite (or because of) the clear bias of the Huffington Post, the DNC granted a debate to the organization of DNC chair January 2017.

**ASSOCIATED PRESS**: Clinton staff "placing a story with a friendly at the AP (Matt Lee or Bradley Klapper)" (ID 9272#efmBKsBMU). Clinton staff appearing to control the release times of Associated Press articles (ID 8460). The Associated Press openly collaborates to write positive HRC stories and negative Bernie stories. Podesta and other campaign staff discussing options regarding the release of an Associated Press story about the deletion of Clinton server emails, and how to proceed with a statement on publication implying that they have some amount of control over when the story is released.

**POLITICO**: Kenneth Vogel of Politico forwards a pending story to DNC for review, as "per agreement". It is worth pointing out he sent this before his own editors saw it (Wikileak ID 10808).

Glenn Thrush, Politico's chief political correspondent and senior staff writer for Politico Magazine, sends John Podesta an article for his approval. Writes: "Please don't share or tell anyone I did this. Tell me if I fucked up anything" (ID 12681#efmAByAEV).

**CNN**: Phil Mudd, a former CIA counterterrorism official, appeared on CNN and he claimed Wikileaks founder Julian Assange is a "pedophile." CNN later had to retract the statement. Wolf Blitzer plans his Trump interview with Podesta (ID 23554). Donna Brazile famously gave the questions for a CNN debate to Clinton in advance.  The links between the DNC and CNN are almost too numerous to detail.

**CONCLUSION**: The mainstream media (MSM) was down (and still is) with the DNC and HRC. One team: MSM-DNC-HRC.

So, in addition to **closed primaries**, which are an abomination to democracy that disenfranchised as many as 42% of eligible voters who identify as independent, **superdelegates**, which are an abomination to democracy  , media collaboration with one candidate and an enforced, near complete **blackout** on the other candidate for months, clearly not by any stretch of the imagination a free press, **rigged debates**, utterly disgraceful, and a calendar of primary states chosen specifically to favor one candidate, the Sanders campaign also had to contend with criminal fraud, FEC violations, money laundering, and criminal voter suppression.

# Obama knew

In ID 27167 we see that Obama knew that HRC was breaking election law by coordinating with her super pacs. He begged off participating himself but did nothing to stop team Hillary from routinely breaking the law.

On December 12, 2008, the Clinton Foundation signed a memorandum of understanding with the White House. The signed agreement was obtained by Judicial Watch and is available on their website. Bruce Lindsey, chairman of the Clinton Foundation, and Valerie Jarrett, Obama's top aide, signed the document. Why did Obama make Hillary sign this memo of understanding? Because he knew The Foundation was not legitimate.

Chelsea pushed for an audit in 2012. BKD Ltd. produced an audit dated September 28, 2012 with the document title "Audited Financials and 990." This audit showed "significant deficiencies and material weaknesses… in internal control over financial reporting… internal control." In short, the Foundation was still a mess. The report noted that most of the Foundation money was kept in foreign bank accounts. The audit noted, "The financial statements for 2011 are consolidated and include the accounts of the Foundation, CGI and CHAI. All significant intercompany accounts and transactions have been eliminated in consolidation." This is important as the MOU notes CGI and the Foundation. Basically, they are all the same entity.

"Interim.Report.Nov.10.doc" sent on December 6, 2008 refers to Executive Order 13476 of October 9, 2008. The agreement says, "In particular, a government employee may not allow the improper use of non-public information to further his own private interest or that of another by knowing unauthorized disclosure. 5 C.F.R.

§ 2640." On December 6, 2012 Lindsay received an audit from Kumiki Gibson. One of it's prominent conclusions:

"Specifically, as a not-for-profit organization, which enjoys tax exempt status under Section 501c(3) of the Internal Revenue Code and which solicits funds from third parties, the Foundation is subject to a number of Federal and State laws governing such organizations... No matter what the leadership decides about the larger, over-arching question, it must act immediately to bring the Foundation into compliance with the law and standards that govern not-for-profits, and must create strong legal and HR offices so to prevent any lapses in the future."

There is no way to read this document other than to conclude that Lindsay knew that the Clinton Foundation was operating outside the law for 501c3 entities. Earlier, he signed an agreement with the White House committing himself and the Foundation to taking no foreign contributions.

The memo garauntees "the Parties also seek to ensure that the activities of the Foundation, however beneficial, do not create conflicts or the appearance of conflicts for Senator Clinton as secretary of state." The memo states that "President Clinton will not solicit funds... he will not send sponsorship letters... will not accept contributions from foreign governments... suspend events outside the United States."

No foreign donors. No conflict of interest. Yet Isis funder Qatar gave Hillary $1 million in her pocket, as reported by Reuters on November 4, 2016. The Washington Post article of February 25, 2015 reads, "Foreign governments gave millions to foundation while Clinton was at State Department."

# Worse than Watergate

The 2014 Snowden files, the 2016 Podesta and DNC Wikileaks releases and the 2017 Vault 7 publications show corruption far worse than anything in the Watergate era.

Here is the short version of what the Watergate scandal was about: In 1972, the Committee to Re-elect the President hired former FBI and CIA agents to break in the DNC to steal information that would hurt Nixon's opponents. This same group attempted to steal notes from Daniel Ellsberg's psychiatrist to embarrass the man who reveal the Pentagon papers showing that government pronouncements on the Vietnam war were dishonest. They also tapped phones illegally. In addition, the Nixon team conspired and tried to turn the FBI and the IRS into instruments to attack their political opponents but did not get very far with this effort. The other perhaps more significant but unrelated scandal of that era was COINTELPRO. The FBI undermined and eliminated political movements J. Edgar Hoover disagreed with, including framing and assassinating activists. While Nixon was power-hungry and paranoid, he did not attempt to enrich himself from his government roles. The Clintons, on the other hand, did enrich themselves by selling access to government power.

Republicans of the era quickly abandoned Nixon and did not circle the wagon. Now, the Democrats steadfastly refuse to make any changes despite vast evidence of criminal activity at the DNC, as noted in this book. The Democrats did not insist Obama get congressional approval to overthrow Gaddafi. The Democrats did not call for hearings on emails showing US involvement in the creation of Isis, or undue influence of CitiGroup in TARP funding.

The press aggressively pursued the president and followed the evidence wherever it went. Now, CNN, MSNBC and the New York Times collaborated with John Podesta to execute the Pied

Piper strategy to help Clinton win the White House. They distorted and ignored evidence that the CIA is conducting false flag attacks, even as they ginned up this "Blame Russia" DNC-MSM strategy. The Washington Post, unlike in the 1970s, is actually owned indirectly by the CIA and cannot report the news in any realistic way. Again, the CIA paid Amazon 600 million apparently for cloud computing services, although they clearly overpaid and likely did not really need any cloud computing outsourcing. Jeff Bezos, founder of Amazon, bought the Washington Post with the money at about the same time. The Washington Post is effectively owned by the CIA through Bezos.

In the 1970s, information that was stolen, such as pertaining to COINTELPRO, was printed in the media and lead to changes in government, although not enough changes, obviously. Today, the way that Wikileaks got the the Podesta and DNC releases is the subject of pointless congressional hearings while the actual details of multiple felonies in those emails is ignored.

While Nixon's team illegally wiretapped and read the correspondence of a small number of people, under Obama the NSA read everyone in the country's correspondence and had the capacity, through the CIA, to listen to and record anyone's private conversation, through Samsung TVs, and may have done so.

There is no comparison. Watergate is less of a scandal than just one Clinton scandal-- take the UBS scandal as an example. As Secretary of State, Clinton agreed to allows tens of thousands of American tax cheats avoid millions in tax payments in exchange for a direct payment from UBS to her husband of 1.5 million dollars. The Abu Dhabi airport scandal is bigger than Watergate. The funding of Isis through Saudi Arabia and Qatar in the "congrats" email is bigger. The Froman spreadsheet is bigger. And the fact that these were not major stories is the biggest scandal of all.

# The Clintons took bribes

T he New York Times reported on February 2, 2017 that, "No evidence emerged of a quid pro quo while Mrs. Clinton served as secretary of state." Emerged? Was there an investigation? Or do you mean emerged in the media also controlled by and allied with the Clinton faction of the DNC?

I can point out several clear examples of quid pro quo right here. After you read this chapter, you will know, if you choose to know it, that the New York Times is a spin factory, not a legitimate source of news.

In ID 17343#efmARzATdAeFAfj her own campaign said that strengthening bribery laws is 'really dicey territory' for her. Why do they think bribery might be dicey if there is no "evidence of a quid pro quo" as the New York Times puts it?

Bill Clinton took one million dollars from Qatar for his birthday (ID 8396#efmAEOAGW). Morocco paid 12 million to meet with Hillary (ID 22030#efmABAADKADLADiAEeAExAFbAH_ AJwAKXAOWAO2). Bill will only talk to the King Of Saudi Arabia for six million dollars (ID 6775#efmACoADwAIqAJzAOXASM). John Podesta owns $75,000 in shares in a Russian oil company (ID 4635#efmAFyAGUAWLAYP).

Clinton Foundation Executive, Doug Band says the Clintons have over '500 Different' conflicts of interests (ID 21978#efmAALABKAD5AGdAGfAHV). No one is closer to Bill Clinton than Doug Band. He says they have hundreds of conflicts of interest. Is that not evidence of conflicts of interest? Is not the whole Band TENEO operation a quid pro quo?

Before Hillary became secretary of state, Bill averaged

$150,000 per speech. After she took office, he made $500,000 per speech, as reported by Jim Young of Reuters with David A. Graham, published in the Atlantic on April 23, 2015. Bill was just as much a compelling speaker and just as famous before his wife became secretary of state. Is not the increase in fees evidence that those paying the fees were expecting something other than a speech?

The Abu Dhabi government paid Bill Clinton directly, personally (also Clinton Foundation tens of millions in donations) two million dollars and Hillary Clinton arranged for the Abu Dhabi airport to have unprecedented pre-clearance of customs for flights to the US. See Politifact article "Fact-checking 'Clinton Cash' author on claim about Bill Clinton's speaking fees" rated "true," and the Wall Street Journal, "Speaking Fees Meet Politics for Clintons" December 30, 2015 and the Daily Mail on December 31, 2015, "Bill Clinton's speaking fees draw new attention as they line up with actions his wife's State Department took between 2009 and 2013." These articles correlate fees paid to favors received, such as customs clearance in the Abu Dhabi airport. Other than the bribes paid to the Clintons, why did Abu Dhabi get customs clearance on the departing end when no other airport has this service?

Doug Band's infamous memo, in response to Chelsea Clinton's queries about his enormous fees to the Clinton Foundation (ID 2874), means, according to the Washington Post (by Rosalind S. Helderman and Tom Hamburger October 26, 2016), "When top Bill Clinton aide Doug Band wrote the memo, he was a central player at the Clinton Foundation and president of his own corporate consulting firm. Over the course of 13 pages, he made a case that his multiple roles had served the interests of the Clinton family and its charity. In doing so, Band also detailed a circle of enrichment in which he raised money for the Clinton Foundation from top-tier corporations such as Dow Chemical and Coca-Cola that were clients of his firm, Teneo, while pressing many of those same donors to provide personal income to the former president."

The government of the poorest country in the world paid Bill Clinton $650,000 to speak, for sure, and the mining company The Lundin Group probably donated to the Clinton Foundation while removing whole villages in the Congo to mine. See Forbes April 17, 2016 "Why Did Congo Offer Clinton $650,000 For Two Pics And A Speech?" and similar articles.

Free Beacon, on October 19, 2015 in "Emails: Clinton Foundation Donor Lobbied State Department for Haiti Hotels: Foundation donor emailed State Department Chief of Staff Cheryl Mills" reported:

> "Richard L. Friedman, a Boston hotel developer emailed Cheryl Mills, Clinton's chief of staff, to tout the [Haiti Hotel] project on May 17, 2011. "We had a good meeting with Jean-Louis, Marriott executives, [the Overseas Private Investment Corporation], etc regarding building hotels in Haiti—I am pursuing this vigorously and hope to be able to develop 2 to 3 hotels with Marriott as manager," wrote Friedman. "I am talking with Commerce and Export/Import Bank today." Friedman said he recently had a discussion with Hillary Clinton at the White House and asked Mills to forward her a note for him. It is unclear what he and Clinton discussed, and portions of his email have been redacted by the State Department due to "personal private interests." The note he asked Mills to send to Clinton is also redacted. "I will keep you informed about our progress in Haiti—we are going to need all the help we can get,"

*Friedman wrote Mills. Mills forwarded Friedman's full email to Clinton and her scheduler, Lona Valmoro, on June 7 with the note "See highlight—resending." The copy released by the State Department does not indicate which portion of the email Mills highlighted. Friedman contributed between $1,000 and $5,000 to the Clinton Foundation and gave $2,300 to Clinton's presidential campaign in 2008, records show. He is not the only Clinton donor associated with Marriott's efforts in Haiti. The company Digicel Group teamed up with Marriott International in 2011 in Port-au-Prince to build a luxury hotel, which opened earlier this year. Digicel has contributed between $25,000 and $50,000 to the Clinton Foundation, and its owner, the Irish billionaire Denis O'Brien, has donated between $5 million and $10 million. Unigestion Holdings, a subsidiary of Digicel that was reportedly tasked with managing the hotel project, gave between $10,000 and $25,000. Marriott International is also a hefty donor to the Clinton Foundation, contributing between $50,000 and $100,000. According to a Marriott press release on Nov. 28, 2011, the Clinton Foundation helped arrange the partnership between the hotel group and Digicel."*

Hillary and Bill Clinton made 153 million almost entirely (more than 80%) in speaking fees from sources that also lobbied the US government at the same time yet have only 60 million in net worth (assets) as of 2015. The Clintons do have four mansions: a $5.7 million "embassy estate," a $1.7 million "country-side cottage," an $11 million "Hampton's hideaway," and a $13 million "beachside bungalow." They also have other assets… still the Forbes figures suggest the Clintons either spent five million dollars every year or are hiding their money. Sources: Forbes, September 29, 2015 "The mystery of the Clinton's missing millions" and AP, April 21, 2016,

"Firms that paid for Clinton speeches have US gov't interests" and CNN, February 6, 2016, "$153 million in Bill and Hillary Clinton speaking fees, documented."

**TRIPLE DIP**: The Clintons got speaking fees, campaign contributions and foundation contributions from the same organizations most of the time, see Wall Street Journal, May 7, 2015, "How the Clintons Get Away With It: The Clintons are protected from charges of corruption by their reputation for corruption." Doug Band explains this to Chelsea Clinton in the famous memo released by Wikileaks. Add in "investments" with Hillary's son-in-law and you can quadruple dip.

**HUMA ABEDIN**: Clinton right-hand woman Abedin worked for the Clinton Foundation and an associated consulting firm while at the State Department (New York Times, "Questions on the Dual Role of a Clinton Aide Persist" August. 18, 2013).

**UBS SCANDAL**: Bill Clinton received 1.5 million from Swiss bank UBS and Hillary arranged for the bank to only release only a small fraction of the original list of tens of thousands of multimillionaires with Swiss bank accounts in exchange for Switzerland accepting a couple Weger prisoners from Guantanamo Bay, see the Atlantic "Hillary Helps a Bank—and Then It Funnels Millions to the Clintons" from July 31, 2015.

Keystone pipeline Canadian backers paid Clinton Foundation a million (Wikileak DNC ID 1950) while she was secretary of state and the New York Times suppressed the story.

A memo entitled "Re: 2016 presidential candidates" from May 26, 2015, DNC leak, shows that everyone at the DNC already assumed the democratic candidate would be Clinton. The memo suggests, "use specific hits to muddy the waters around ethics, transparency and campaign finance on HCR." The DNC clearly knew Hillary was dirty before they nominated her.

RAJIV FERNANDO SCANDAL: Hillary put a wealthy donor with no relevant experience on a committee to address nuclear arms. "ISAB Board (board Raj wanted) now has an opening" (ID 4838 Clinton leak). It literally says "board Raj wanted." Also, ABC, June 10, 2016, "How Clinton Donor Got on Sensitive Intelligence Board."

URANIUM SCANDAL: Hillary and Bill Clinton and their foundation took money from Russian owned Canadian company and then allowed them to control much of US Uranium market, see New York Times, "Cash Flowed to Clinton Foundation Amid Russian Uranium Deal" April 23, 2015.

Billionaire with ties to Nigerian dictator donates to Clinton Foundation and receives access to policy makers pertaining to Lebanon, see Los Angeles Times, August 28, 2016, "He was a billionaire who donated to the Clinton Foundation. Last year, he was denied entry into the U.S."

Hillary Clinton dramatically increased arms sales to the Middle East from the Bush Administration as secretary of state and donors to the Clinton Foundation got the majority of the weapons. Both defense contractors and foreign governments contributed and paid for speeches by Bill, see Mother Jones, May 28, 2015: "An investigation finds that countries that gave to the foundation saw an increase in State Department-approved arms sales."

If you are nominating a candidate who takes bribes, you lose your credibility to criticize a president, such as Trump, who appears to have made a deal with Vladimir Putin that may involve a transfer of shares of an oil company to Trump in exchange for an end to sanctions and allowing Russia to be more assertive in the Ukraine. That's a very dirty deal on Trump's part, if true. But Hillary was (is or would be) just as bad.

CONCLUSION: This is your standard bearer, Democrats? You gotta be kidding. No quid pro quo? Who are you kidding, New York Times?

Meanwhile, Angela Merkel lives in the same apartment she had before she was chancellor and her husband walks to the supermarket to do the shopping, Pepe Mujica, former president of Uruguay, lives in a little shack and has an old gas cookstove and some pots he had for years, Bernie Sanders lives in a normal suburban subdivision, and Dilma Rousseff, former president of Brazil, lives in her mother's apartment, and buys her own groceries at the local supermarket. Think of those famous pictures of Bernie walking to work or shopping as Cosco: he's really one of us.

Harry S Truman said, "You can't get rich in politics unless you're a crook."

# The Clintons stole

A gold mining concession in Haiti went to a company where Hillary Clinton's brother sat on the board of directors. Donor money disappeared from the Haitian rebuilding project. Promised elections were cancelled in Haiti, along with massive interference in the 2011 election that did occur. See the Daily Mail, March 16, 2015, "Hillary Clinton's brother landed lucrative gold-mining permit in Haiti after Bill Clinton helped country recover from earthquake devastation" and the New York Times "High Hopes for Hillary Clinton, Then Disappointment in Haiti" on March 14, 2016, and "Red Cross Built Exactly 6 Homes For Haiti With Nearly Half A Billion Dollars In Donations" in Huffington Post, June 30, 2016.

Published in the Guardian, "Trump and Clinton share Delaware tax 'loophole' address with 285,000 firms, 1209 North Orange Street in Wilmington is a nondescript two-story building yet is home to Apple, American Airlines, Walmart and presidential candidates."

Shell companies may play a role in what happened to the 153 to 160 million they made between 2000 and 2016, since their net worth was only 60 million on their official disclosures for the election of 2016. How is it that they made so much but only so few assets on their financial disclosures? Did they spend the rest, about 5 million a year? Talk about a lavish lifestyle. John and Tony Podesta show up in the Panama papers, as in the Observer April 7, 2016, "Panama Papers Reveal Clinton's Kremlin Connection." Maybe the shell companies funnelled money to tax havens through lawyers like the firm revealed in the Panama papers.

Doug Band, Bill Clinton's closest advisor, reports that Chelsea Clinton stole three million dollars for her wedding (see Wikileaks, search Doug Band. The Inquisitr said, "Hillary Clinton's daughter, Chelsea, allegedly used Clinton Foundation money and other charity resources to fund her wedding to Marc Mezvinsky. This was discovered through a new batch of WikiLeaks emails from top Bill Clinton aide,

I'd give you more, but I'm using a million dollars of your money on my wedding

Doug Band. On January 4, 2012, Band wrote in an email that Chelsea used Foundation resources 'for her wedding and life for a decade.' He also alleged a top Foundation donor was responsible for "killing" unfavorable press coverage."

If she didn't steal the money, why did Doug Band say she did? He would have known. Shouldn't the IRS look into whether or not she reported the money as income?

Hillary's son-in-law Marc Mezvinsky and Trump's son-in-law Jared Kushner, like Ivanka Trump and Chelsea Clinton, are almost twin couples. "Chelsea Clinton's Husband Closes His Hedge Fund" Bloomberg reported on February 8, 2017. Hillary loses and three months later, millions in "investments" get yanked from Mezvinsky. So, therefore, the investors in his hedge fund, Eaglevale, were not actually investing so much as buying influence with the next president.

This relationship could be as big a scandal as Michael Flynn talking to the Russians and having to resign from the Trump administration. We're so inured to Clinton cheating and oligarchic control that it's hum hum news… oh well, some more rich people who don't mind sinking 50 million in a fake hedge fund to twist the government to their will… campaign contributions, speaking fees, donations to a foundation, investments in a hedge fund… so many ways for a Democrat to get rich by selling the working person out to the rich man, you can't be surprised they refuse to resign, although they don't deserve jobs mucking manure out of my barn. Too dumb to use a pitch fork. Too weak to finish the job. Too crooked to be trusted and you'd have to watch them the whole time so they don't pinch the tools, slip some drill bits in their pockets if they find out where you keep your stuff. That's Obama's clean Democratic, all White party. It's a fun party, if you're invited.

Chuck Schumer: the stealing the Clintons did, you did too. Nancy Pelosi: you are an accessory to a crime. Barack Obama: you might as well have stolen my silver when I invited you to dinner. I worked for your campaign and you gave me Eaglevale, Trump and Obamacare. Go get your check from CitiGroup. It's waiting for you.

# Team Hillary slandered Bernie Sanders

The oligarch-owned, CIA funded, complicit in DNC scheming as revealed in Wikileaks Washington Post published an article "What Bernie Sanders still doesn't get about arguing with Hillary Clinton" on March 7, 2016. On March 6, New York Magazine published "Sanders Tells Clinton: 'Excuse Me, I'm Talking' is Arguably Sexist." CNN, complicit in rigging debates against Bernie asked, "Is Sanders' 'Excuse me, I'm talking' line sexist?" on March 8, 2016. The New York Times wrote on March 7, "Was Bernie Sanders' snap at Hillary Clinton sexist?"

DNC ID 11604 reveals DNC communications strategist Deshundra Jackson had a mole contact in the Sanders campaign to provide her staff with information. "I pinged my friend on his campaign but she was let go a few days ago. I don't have any other leads," wrote Jackson in regards to what Sanders would be discussing at a press conference.

We now know, thanks to Wikileaks, that the media blackout on Bernie Sanders was coordinated between the DNC, the HRC campaign and the media. The debates were rigged, with Hillary getting the questions in advance, the location and times designed to favor Hillary, and every single journalist allowed to ask questions was a partisan of Hillary asking questions favorable to her and hostile to Bernie.

Bernie got less airtime. He was not allowed to speak in the debate. He did get the questions he wanted. He didn't know what the questions would be in advance. He got no coverage in the media due to the orders of Debbie Wasserman Schultz. And when he said, "Let me speak!" they pounced on him as sexist. People enriching themselves off of their office should not slander an honest man without consequences.

Have these august media outlets gone back and apologized for these misleading and terrible articles slandering a man with a 100% feminist voting record in congress? A man who was for gay rights since 1972? A man who worked tirelessly for equal pay for women his entire career? And in slandering him, they helped elect a man with three wives (one gets old, divorce her and buy another) and an actual rapist in the White House, Trump?

Is Bernie Sanders sexist? Of course not. We now know the DNC, while obligated to be neutral between the candidates by law, were in fact willing to use anti-semitism against Bernie, a Jew (DNC ID 11508). In DNC ID 4476 DNC an employee called Sander's campaign manager and Bernie supporters "scummy… violent and threatening…" Washington Times, October 2, 2016: "Hillary Clinton privately slams Bernie Sanders' supporters as 'basement dwellers.'" Yeah, nice. When they Slandered Bernie, they slandered us, the people.

# Hillary participated in multiple imperialistic wars, assassinations and coups

Hillary Clinton supported a coup that ousted a democratically elected government and led to chaos, as per Truthout "Here's Why Activists Don't Buy Hillary Clinton's Justification for the Honduras Coup" July 17, 2016. Also, the cables leaked by Chelsea Manning reveal that the State Department knew the coup was "illegal and unconstitutional."

Berta Caceres, activist, subsequently murdered, said, "We're coming out of a coup that we can't put behind us. We can't reverse it. It just kept going. And after, there was the issue of the elections. The same Hillary Clinton, in her book, Hard Choices, practically said what was going to happen in Honduras. This demonstrates the meddling of North Americans in our country. The return of the president, Mel Zelaya, became a secondary issue. There were going to be elections in Honduras. And here she [Clinton] recognized that they didn't permit Mel Zelaya's return to the presidency."

Hillary says that her no fly zone proposition would "kill a whole lot of Syrians" (ID 927#attachments). As noted below, her rush to war in Libya was shocking to many in her own administration. The results of that disaster compare with the fiasco in Iraq in 2003.

A quote from a paid speech For Deutsche Bank, April 24, 2013:

> AUDIENCE MEMBER: Secretary Clinton -- Madam Secretary, if there was indisputable evidence that the Syrian government used chemical weapons on its people,

*would you be in favor of armed American intervention in the form of air strikes or boots on the ground?*

*SECRETARY CLINTON: ...That requires not just boots on the ground, it requires, you know, being able to, in effect, liberate such a depot or such a convoy from those who are currently in charge of it. And then it requires managing the material so it doesn't have disastrous consequences. And then it requires bringing in and protecting the experts long enough that they can take hold of and, in effect, disarm the weaponry... So yes.*

While she favored boots on the ground in Syria, she only wanted to bomb Iran from the air. She told Goldman Sachs at the 2013 IBD Ceo Annual Conference, June 4, 2013, "Well, you up the pain on Iran that they have to endure by not in any way occupying or invading them but by bombing their facilities. I mean, that is the option. It is not as, we like to say these days, boots on the ground."

Boots on the ground in Syria and bombs from the air in Iran? What she promised for the future was more of what she did as secretary of state. The story of her warmongering was a story even in the mainstream media in the New York Times Magazine piece, April 21, 2016, "How Hillary Clinton Became a Hawk: Throughout her career she has displayed instincts on foreign policy that are more aggressive than those of President Obama — and most Democrats."

Clinton met with staff on Tuesday November 23, 2010 shortly after 8 AM on Mahogany Row at the State Department to attempt to formulate a strategy to avert Assange's plans to release an enormous batch of 250,000 secret cables, dating from 1966 to 2010.

"Can't we just drone this guy?" Clinton openly inquired, offering a simple remedy to silence Assange and smother Wikileaks via a planned military drone strike, according to State Department sources. The statement drew laughter from the room which quickly died off when the Secretary kept talking in a terse manner, sources said. Clinton said Assange, after all, was a relatively soft target, "walking around" freely and thumbing his nose without any fear of reprisals from the United States.

Speaking to CBS News, Hillary says, referring to the recently murdered head of state of Libya, "We came. We saw. He died." She then laughs.

Hillary Clinton foreign policy advisors, as reported in the Intercept on September 8, 2016, and likely leaders of her administration had she won, in an article "Hillary Clinton's National Security Advisers Are a "Who's Who" of the Warfare State," include: David Petraeus, Iraq war architect. Michael Chertoff, head of Homeland Security under Bush, then went on to make big money as a consultant on security in the "private sector." Mike Morell, former head of the CIA, says the US should kill Iranians and Russians in Syria. Jim Stavridis, favors US ground war in Syria. They all have cash ties to defense contractors (military-industrial complex) and many participated in the series of terrible decisions around Iraq.

Hillary Clinton voted to invade Iraq, aggressive war, a violation of international law.

# The Clinton Foundation was a slush fund

The Clintons enriched themselves on the public purse and took bribes in two ways: through speaking fees and the foundation. Hillary's campaign manager, Robby Mook, said "it's a little troubling" that meeting of Clinton Foundation was held at Goldman Sachs HQ (ID 1381#efmAAwACA).

Anyone who thought the Clinton Foundation was a charity now can know, if they want to know, that it was a fraudulent con money laundering operation. If you look at the pattern and timing of speaking fees, there is no doubt that they were not speaking fees but bribes.

The Clinton Foundation has been a flop on the ground, helping almost no one. Please see Politico's "There's no country that more clearly illustrates the confusing nexus of Hillary Clinton's State Department and Bill Clinton's foundation than Haiti—America's poorest neighbor" from May 4, 2015 for example.

Email ID 46848 includes an attachment, an audit of the Clinton Foundation. This audit and the fact that the Clinton Global Initiative had to shut its doors and close up immediately after Hillary lost prove that Hillary rose to dominate the Democratic party and establishment politics in general by throwing money around. She operated a slush fund and was no better than a gangster.

They spent 255 million in one year, but only 18 million of it on programs. In fact, they spent about as much on parties and other get togethers called "trainings" as on charity (18 for charity 14+ 3 for parties). Those are millions. Consulting, $9 million. Yes, Doug Band got most of it, to cover his uncharged expenses at Teneo for setting up speeches for Bill. So that's mostly what that is about.

Page 28 of the audit:

*Significant deficiency(ies)? Yes*

*Material weakness(es)? Yes*

Page 27:

*This report is intended solely for the information and use of the governing body, management, others within the Foundation, federal awarding agencies and pass-through entities and is not intended to be, and should not be, used by anyone other than these specified parties.*

Whoops!

UNITAID got 108 million of the 255 spent on expenses other than programs. UNITAID is an AIDs related UN program. This might be charity work, except that UNITAID gave the money right back to the Clintons, as reported by Ken Silverstein on October 26, 2015 and Jerome Corsi on April 23, 2105. "To be fairly precise, UNITAID alone reported donations to the Clinton Foundation of about $341.5 million during that period while the Clinton Foundation claims it spent about $215.4 million" we read in Byline. That $215.4 figure for the Clinton Foundation to UNITAID is in line with the audit noted here, over 2011 and 2012.

To make the big drug companies happy, the Clinton Foundation worked to keep the price of AIDS drugs high in Africa (ID 36248). In the April 14, 2016 Counterpunch article, "Tough Questions About Haiti for Hillary Clinton" and in ID emailid/25770#efmADXAFGAHrAJq, we see the Clintons looking at the Haitian earthquake as a business opportunity.

"However, as discussed in the accompanying schedule of findings and questioned costs, we identified certain deficiencies in internal control over financial reporting that we consider to be material weaknesses and other deficiencies that we consider to be significant deficiencies... A deficiency in internal control exists when the design or operation of a control does not allow management or employees, in the normal course of performing their assigned functions, to prevent or detect and correct misstatements on a timely basis....We consider the deficiency described in the accompanying schedule of findings and responses as item 11-01 to be a material weakness... We consider the deficiencies described in the accompanying schedule of findings and responses as items 11–02 and 11–03 to be significant deficiencies."

The other important document on the foundation we get from Wikileaks is the famous Teneo/Band Clinton Inc. memo (ID 2874). This is where we hear that Chelsea Clinton helped herself to three million dollars for her wedding, clearly tax fraud if true.

When Hillary was a senator, the Clinton Foundation limped along with an endowment of a couple of million and Bill was getting about $150,000 for a speech. When she became secretary of state, Bill's speaking fees tripled and the Foundation raised close to 3 billion dollars, according to the Atlantic "A Quick Guide to the Questions About Clinton Cash" from April 23, 2015.

After 2008, Hillary's campaign manager Debbie Wasserman Schultz was the head of the DNC. In any sane world, Wasserman Schultz would have stepped down from her DNC position for the duration of the primary. Even if she was a saint, and she is far from that, there's no way you can go from being someone's campaign manager to being "neutral and impartial" about their next campaign.

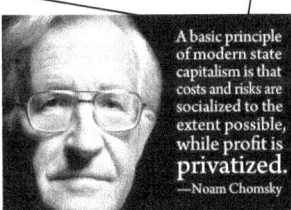

Hillary was set to be the heir apparent to the presidency. Democrats had won the popular vote in 5 out of the last 6 presidential races, with 2004 being a post 9–11 exception. With Hillary as the next president and the current secretary of state, Clinton Inc. seemed like a very good bet. You can get favors now, and get access later. It looked like a good deal to Google, UBS bank, the government of Kuwait, Dow Chemical, Saudi Arabia, Qatar, and everyone else.

Doug Band is exceedingly clear that the donors (like Saudi Arabia) do not care about women's health in Niger. But the Clinton Foundation did almost no charity anyway, and the donors knew that too. The only one on the inside who didn't know was Chelsea Clinton, and so we got this audit. They didn't just use the slush fund to buy support. They also skimmed off plenty for themselves, from the speeches, from the Foundation.

In speech income, there is potential tax fraud liability. Speeches were personal income sometimes, and Foundation income at other times. Because personal income is theoretically taxable, while charitable contributions are not, Clinton can't simply make a call willy-nilly on each speech. In other words, the nature of the income should be definitional, not a decision made by the recipient. Anyone else would worry about these issues and be more careful than were the Clintons.

And then Hillary lost. And all the money dried up right away. The Clinton Initiative closed in late 2016. Unbelievable corruption, and completely obvious. The New York Times, still working for John Podesta, in "Soul-Searching at Clinton Foundation in Trump Era" makes the laughable claim that the steep drop in donations following the loss in November, from millions per week to almost zero immediately after the election, is an indicator of "the energy, passion, desire and the good health" of Bill Clinton, as if his health and energy dramatically changed between November 8th and November 9th.

CONCLUSION: The Clinton Foundation was never a charity and always a slush fund. The New York Times is about as reliable as Fox News. Both spin for their teams.

## In private or with donors, Team Hillary freely admit that they are operators in an oligarchic system of fake democracy

The transcripts of Hillary Clinton's speeches to Goldman Sachs was a major issue in the Democratic primary. We finally got the transcripts in October 2016 from Wikileaks.

In the speeches we hear Hillary Clinton speaking in private to rich bankers. It's quite important to pay attention to the releases from Wikileaks in 2016 because we may never have a better look behind the scenes of how corruption works.

The comment about her "public and private positions" got the most attention, and well it should. In fact, "we have a public and a private position" could well be the motto of both the Democratic and Republican parties. This is another key passage, from the Goldman Sachs Builders And Innovators Summit, October 29, 2013:

> *HILLARY: I want to get back to having a two-party system that can have an adult conversation and a real debate about the future.*

*MR. BLANKFEIN (CEO of Goldman Sachs): Yeah, and one thing, I'm glad—I'm proud that the financial services industry has been the one unifying theme that binds everybody together in common. (Laughter.)"*

This exchange is similar to an exchange at Xerox, March 18, 2014:

*URSULA BURNS: Yeah, we do need two parties.*

*SECRETARY CLINTON: Two sensible, moderate, pragmatic parties.*

For Clinton, and her donors, we should have two basically similar parties and a fake debate limited to a narrow range of topics, as we have had in the past.

Or consider Wikileak ID 23756, on the 2014 Princeton Study "Testing Theories of American Politics: Elites, Interest Groups, and Average Citizens." The Podesta team says, "I guess it takes a study to point out the obvious."

And, my friends, there you have it. Right from the horse's mouth. If there were any doubt about the conclusion of the 2014 Princeton Study, those doubts have been obliterated by John Podesta. If his team says it's obvious that the US is not a democracy, and they should know, then it's true.

Don't believe politicians when they spin. Don't believe the MSM. Believe what they say behind closed doors to bankers and among themselves in their private emails. What they say is that the bankers run the government, that we do not live in a democracy, and that every word they say to us in speeches is a lie. Believe them. They just told you the truth (in private).

I could cite more examples of this kind of admission when they thought no one was listening but these few examples should suffice. The cat is out of the bag. No more discussion needed. America is not a democracy or a truly representative republic: the people who keep it that way know it and know why it is undemocratic and freely acknowledge the fact in private.

We all should simply stop referring to America as a democracy or representative republic, as we have definitive proof that the system does not work for the working people but does work well for a small group of connected oligarchs. Just wipe the phrase "American democracy" from your vocabulary the way we stopped saying "police man" and now say "police officer" or stop referring to African Americans as did Martin Luther King, "negro," and use the terms "Black" or "African American." Fix the language to reflect reality. Never say we live in a democracy as a short hand. We don't.

## Negative comments about the Clintons from insiders and friends

There are many books that contribute hundreds of quotes from people who know the Clinton's well and hate them, including *Clinton Inc.*

The Telegraph published a prophetic article back in November 22, 2008: "Barack Obama's aides believe he has made a mistake in hiring Hillary Clinton." The article says:

> *"They can't help themselves," the Obama aide told his friend, a fellow Democrat strategist. "Every event is a potential ladder up or a bullet to be dodged. They're positioning and spinning all the time. They lost. Now we seem to be handing them the farm."*

*Most shocking to Mr Obama's team is the loss of discipline and control that they have experienced since coming to Washington.*

*The President-elect's campaign was tightly controlled, with very few uncoordinated leaks. The candidate was known as "No Drama Obama." David Corn, Washington Bureau Chief of the left of centre magazine Mother Jones, summed up the problem: "The presidential transition of no-drama Obama became infected by the never-ending soap opera of the Clintons. And it really is time to turn that programme off."*

*The Washington Post columnist and Clinton sceptic, David Ignatius, added: "The idea of subcontracting foreign policy to Clinton, a big, hungry, needy ego surrounded by a team that's hungrier and needier still, strikes me as a mistake of potentially enormous proportions." It is a view that many around the President-elect now share.*

In ID 35921, consummate Hillary insider Neera Tanden, who has known Hillary well for years, said "sometimes HRC/WJC have the worst judgement." She also said, "Brock/Bonner Are a nightmare: Really, Suzie Buell isn't giving to the super pac? I wonder how that got in this story." Tanden expresses concern that the Correct The Record superpac is pushing its legal boundaries and may be colluding directly with the campaign (ID 10068#efmAAGAA4AEFAFn): "this does seem shady." Tanden further notes, "She may be so tainted she's really vulnerable" (ID 17343#efmAFHAHJARzATdAeFAfj).

Clinton campaign scrambled to escape "calls for transparency" on Hillary's health and taxes. Campaign manager Robby Mook said to chairman John Podesta, Hillary's health and taxes are "hyper sensitive topics" (ID 11563#efmAAqAEB). Clinton campaign insiders feared Bill's sex life could sink Hillary. Podesta says they should "shut the hell up about this" (ID 2301#efmAPjARK).

Top Clinton aide Doug Band details how Clinton Foundation Chief Laura Graham nearly committed suicide by plunging her car into ocean depths because of treatment from Bill & Chelsea Clinton. Staffers write each other about how Chelsea wouldn't care if she died (ID 3332#efmAdAAmB).

A journalist we will meet again in this book, Brent Budowsky, the webtv email address guy, a man who regularly emailed Podesta wise ideas, pointed out major concerns over Hillary's shady financing. It can "bring down a Hillary Clinton candidacy" (ID 6900#efmAAGAD3ALmASb). However, Podesta never seems to write back to Budowsky. Brent never published his concerns in the Hill or the Huffington Post. Budowsky warned Podesta to "be very very careful" of the "intense antipathy" being created by Team Hillary.

"Many Bernie supporters and younger women will not vote for her in November…. The daughter of a Democrat who has worked for senior Democrats told me 'I just hate her so much I might even vote for a Republican but I will never vote for her.'" (ID 11580#efmAAGAPF).

DNC ID 23855 is a compendium of quotes from newspapers that endorsed Hillary in 2016 sent by DNC staffer L. Hendricks.

> One year after announcing, her endorsers have called her "polarizing," "fiercely disliked," "extreme flip-flopping," "a taste for expediency," "has a trust deficit," "way too

*secretive," "almost paranoid," "a tone-deaf approach," "hardly lovable and certainly flawed," "plays fast and loose with the truth," and "a politician with so much baggage that even Southwest Airlines would start charging fees," are just some of the attributes highlighted by Clinton's "endorsers."*

*The most persistent problem identified was Clinton's use of a secret server that has sparked an FBI investigation, with The Free Lance-Star editorial board declaring that "it's anyone's guess when the probe will end and whether there will be an indictment." The Detroit News led the charge in questioning Clinton's trustworthiness saying that "even a disingenuous capitalist is preferable to a genuine socialist," as the Minneapolis Star Tribune cited a "disturbingly high level of mistrust" of Clinton. The Des Moines Register highlighted her shifting positions noting that "her changing stance on gay marriage, immigration and other issues has invited accusations that she is guided less by personal conviction than by political calculations." These half-hearted "endorsements" typify Clinton's problems with trust, ethics and character that have dogged her throughout this campaign, and led to legions' of Democrats grudging, unenthusiastic support.*

These are her friends.

In ID 9637 a lawyer tells John Podesta, "The one thing I heard in her super Tuesday speech that I thought that I would avoid is that she said: "whether we like it or not, we are in this all together…" I would advise eliminating the "like it or not" part and just say that "in order to make America whole we must be in this altogether."

That's funny. Hillary clearly wishes she could be president without having to pretend like she wants to be together with us regular folk. Her staff has to stop her from saying, you know, that we're deporables or basement-dwellers... oh wait, she did call us that.

Can anyone who has read the transcripts of her speeches to Goldman Sachs doubt that Hillary hates working people and loves rich bankers?

A U.S. diplomatic cable made public by WikiLeaks provides evidence that U.S. troops executed at least 10 Iraqi civilians, including a woman in her 70s and a 5-month-old infant then called in an airstrike to destroy the evidence, during a controversial 2006 incident in the central Iraqi town of Ishaqi.

The unclassified cable, which was posted on WikiLeaks' website last week, contained questions from a United Nations investigator about the incident, which had angered local Iraqi officials, who demanded some kind of action from their government. U.S. officials denied at the time that anything inappropriate had occurred.

But Philip Alston, the U.N.'s special rapporteur on extrajudicial, summary or arbitrary executions, said in a communication to American officials dated 12 days after the March 1! 2006, incident that autopsies performed in the Iraqi city of Tikrit showed that all the dead had been handcuffed and shot in the head. Among the dead were four women and five children. The children were all 5 years old or younger.

# DNC/HRC staff never say anything alturistic in any one of the more than 30,000 pages worth of documents released by Wikileaks

**H**ere, in this chapter, I provide the results of a crowd-sourced attempt to find any example of altruistic sentiment expressed by anyone in the inner circle of the DNC or the Clinton Campaign. This study asks: do the important people in the structure, when speaking in an unguarded way among themselves, ever express sympathy or interest in politics in any other way than the search for personal and party advantage?

The study considered more than 70,000 possible emails and attachments released in the summer of 2016 (DNC) or in October 2016 (Podesta). The total number of pages of material is vast but not calculated. The period covered includes emails going back to 2008 and involves many hundreds of people who would qualify were they to make an altruistic utterance.

CONCLUSION:

Insiders made numerous statements about ways to move the primary to cheat Bernie Sanders, referred to freely taking money at will from the Clinton Foundation, conferred with super pacs and coordinated strategy, planted Donald Trump as a candidate, collaborated with MSM, sent lists of pro-bank appointees who in fact were appointed and wrote the bank bailout bill, collaborated with banks to undermine regulation, supported extraction industries, etc. Statements outside of those necessary for work were also included, not an insignificant subset of the utterances: problems with Amtrak tickets, family events, alluded to racial and religious prejudices, time of arrival home, sports, holiday wishes, dinner plans, personality dynamics, media preferences, etc. In all of these many million of statements by more than 100 potential insiders, over many years, only one single statement qualifies as an expression of genuine altruism by an insider. This study found a single insider made only one single altruistic comment was verified. It was mildly altruistic in sentiment by a low ranking staffer, and it was only made once, briefly, in passing. Other than this offhand comment, there is no evidence that DNC/HRC insiders have any real concern for any matter of public policy other than how discussion of that policy might benefit them as ambitious politicians.

## DEFINITIONS:

**Leaked emails** may include any comment in any of DNC Leaks from the summer of 2016, include 19,252 emails and 8,034 attachments or in any of the approximately 30,000 or so emails and 10,000 attachments in the Podesta leaks.

**Altruistic comment** is an expression that reflects a writer's belief, hope or aspiration for any good outcome that would be shared by the broader public in any way with no addition and specific benefit to the writer him/herself and no reference to political calculation.

**Inner circle** means someone who regularly sends and receives response from paid employees or is a paid employee him or herself.

## METHOD:

This study leverages the power of crowdsourcing. The efficacy of crowdsourcing is the subject of scientific research (see

"Crowdsourcing as a Model for Problem Solving: An Introduction and Cases," Daren C. Brabham, February 1, 2008 and similar). While crowdsourcing is clearly effective in some areas and less effective in others, there is no research suggesting that relying on professional journalists is actually a superior means of arriving at truth.

Researcher posted a request of altruistic examples on Reddit in the DNCLeaks subreddit. As of the date of the experiment, there are 14,971 subscribers. 170 people upvoted the request. 84 comments have been submitted to date. Anyone can subscribe and post to this site, regardless of political beliefs.

## RESULTS

Contributors offered possible suggestions of altruism. Not all comments included nomination for the prize for examples of altruism. The suggested nominations on Reddit included links to original leaks were genuine attempts to find altruistic comments.

**IRSizone** suggested the tag line "Please consider the environment before printing this e-mail" in the context of an email noting that Chelsea Clinton is stealing from the Clinton Foundation. lgraham@clintonfoundation.org used this tag line 49 times. This might have served as an example of an insider altruistic statement if the submitting party had not admitted that this nomination was a joke.

Several statements by Brent Budowsky were submitted. However, there is no evidence that any insider ever wrote him back. And he said, "I will play the bad guy here because I do not want her money and because she needs to hear this from her friends." He is not an insider and his statements were not accepted on that basis.

**outbackdude** offered the example of John Podesta's son Gabe. Gabe appears to make many genuine and altruistic comments in emails to his father. "I've learned, are horrible officers motivated solely by what they have to gain personally with no regard to the country they ostensibly serve..." Gabe is in the Air Force and not connected to the campaign. What William Shakespeare would have made of such a noble son having no clue about his evil, Machiavellian father, we will never know.

**buttaholic** suggested comments denigrating Catholicism. These had no positive public policy implications and were not accepted into consideration.

**LOLELECTRONICS** reported, "I'm going on 3 hours. To be fair, this is the campaign manager's email box and any communication that isn't about strategy probably wouldn't exist at the highest level of political operations."

**Aaron 215** said, "it's mind boggling how hard it is... I'm agreeing with the people above..." His example only involved someone thanking someone for meeting for dinner, which has no public policy implications.

The example of Amitabh Desai was offered: Director of Foreign Policy at The Clinton Foundation, former JP Morgan analyst, concerned that the "islands project" (electric projects on small Pacific island) was being undermined by Ira Magaziner. Desai qualifies as an insider, the email is from the set considered. Would Desai benefit from the islands project? We know his former employer is financing energy projects (ID 1321) like the island project. Please note that this possible example of altruism includes complaints about looting of development funds by Ira Magaziner.

User **Berningforchange** offered example of Clinton herself telling environmental activists to "get a life." This suggestion was indeed by an insider, was from the set of included leaks, but was deemed not to be altruistic, given that the comment was made in the context of a paid speech of rich bankers whose interests are opposed to the environmentalists in the statement, as are Hillary's interests herself. Thus this nomination was rejected.

**LOL ELECTRONICS** Found this: "Nick Merrill is her press secretary and, among other things, he provides internal reports back to the rest of the staff whenever Hillary's on the campaign trail."

> *Flint was quite moving. When we walked in the church and the water fountains were covered and marked "out of order," all we've read and seen in the news suddenly became much more real. HRC met with mayor and an usher briefly, and she said that she fight to keep the lights from dimming on this.*

This appears to be the only statement by an insider where there is no evidence of any financial, political, or other self/party interest.

I have offered LOL ELECTRONICS prize money donated to Wikileaks in lieu of direct payment and have not had a response as of this publication.

That's it. They don't really seem to give a shit.

# Hillary Clinton and Barack Obama helped create Isis

Obama and Clinton knew the USA government was indirectly funding a terrorist organization that killed Americans, Europeans and Middle Easterners, Turks, as well as torture, rape and slavery in Iraq and Syria, but continued for years to fund Daesh/Isis through Saudi Arabia and Qatar, right through the end of the administration.

In the very first batch of Podesta Wikileak releases, there was ID 3774 sent from John Podesta to Hillary Clinton with the odd subject header "Congrats!"Hillary receives the email through her illegal email address "hrod17@clintonemail.com."

When I read this email, I went immediately to DNC Leaks to post a link. This seems like classified information that Podesta should not have on his computer, plus what it says is so outrageous that in my mind, Hillary would have to step down as the Democratic candidate for president. This one email would then be the top story in the mainstream media, I assumed. Security breach, funding Isis: she has to go now. Top stories tomorrow.

The parties mentioned below are right now still fighting to gain control of Mosul. I would not want Assad or Isis to know the information in this email, with specific operational details of an ongoing battle sent from an insecure server to a political operative, now released on the internet as the battle for Mosul continues. That the information could or did leak to Isis is obvious: if I can read it, so can Isis. Here is some of what we read in the "congrats" email:

> *Armed with proper equipment, and working with U.S.*
> *advisors, the Peshmerga can attack the ISIL with a*

*coordinated assault supported from the air. This effort will come as a surprise to the ISIL, whose leaders believe we will always stop with targeted bombing, and weaken them both in Iraq and inside of Syria. At the same time we should return to plans to provide the FSA, or some group of moderate forces, with equipment that will allow them to deal with a weakened ISIL, and stepped up operations against the Syrian regime. This entire effort should be done with a low profile, avoiding the massive traditional military operations that are at best temporary solutions. It is important to keep in mind that as a result of this policy there probably will be concern in the Sunni regions of Iraq and the Central Government regarding the possible expansion of KRG controlled territory. With advisors in the Peshmerga command we can reassure the concerned parties that, in return for increased autonomy, the KRG will not exclude the Iraqi Government from participation in the management of the oil fields around Kirkuk, and the Mosul Dam hydroelectric facility. At the same time we will be able to work with the Peshmerga as they pursue ISIL into disputed areas of Eastern Syria, coordinating with FSA troops who can move against ISIL from the North. This will make certain Bashar al Assad does not gain an advantage from these operations. Finally, as it now appears the U.S. is considering a plan to offer contractors as advisors to the Iraqi Ministry of Defense, we will be in a position to coordinate more effectively between the Peshmerga and the Iraqi Army.*

Okay, that doesn't seem like Podesta should know that, nor should he leave information like that in a cab. But worse:

*While this military/paramilitary operation is moving forward, we need to use our diplomatic and more traditional intelligence assets to bring pressure on the governments of Qatar and Saudi Arabia, which are providing clandestine financial and logistic support to ISIL and other radical Sunni groups in the region. This effort will be enhanced by the stepped up commitment in the KRG. The Qataris and Saudis will be put in a position of balancing policy between their ongoing competition to dominate the Sunni world and the consequences of serious U.S. pressure. By the same token, the threat of similar, realistic U.S. operations will serve to assist moderate forces in Libya, Lebanon, and even Jordan, where insurgents are increasingly fascinated by the ISIL success in Iraq.*

The statement that Qatar and Saudi Arabia are "providing clandestine financial and logistic support to ISIL" is the biggie. How is it that these monsters were able to roll into Mosul with so much equipment, seemingly out of nowhere, in the Fall of Mosul between 4–10 June 2014?

Meanwhile, in the New York Times article "Sale of U.S. Arms Fuels the Wars of Arab States" from April 18, 2015, reports that in the same year that Daesh took Mosul, "Saudi Arabia spent more than $80 billion on weapons last year [2014]...The Emirates spent nearly $23 billion last year, more than three times what they spent in 2006. Qatar, another gulf country with bulging coffers and a desire to assert its influence around the Middle East, is on a shopping spree. Last year, Qatar signed an $11 billion deal with the Pentagon...American defense firms are following the money."

Reuters reported, "Clinton's charity confirms Qatar's $1 million gift while she was at State Department" on November 4, 2016. Mother Jones reported May 28, 2015 that "Hillary Clinton Oversaw

US Arms Deals to Clinton Foundation Donors." Essentially, Hillary increased sales to Qatar and Saudi Arabia by many times over the figures under Bush while receiving money through the Foundation and paid speeches to Bill Clinton.

This email should have been a big story. When this email was released publicly, Hillary should have been forced to step down as a candidate for president of the United States. Anyone who would tolerate arms sales ending up in the hands of Isis should not be leading the country.

I told a friend who happened to be visiting at the time that I thought there was an email released on Wikileaks showing something so horrible that Hillary would have to step down. She got angry and said, "I don't care what she did!" She was visibly angry. She said I was guilty of male privilege. Somehow, if I were female I would accept that it's normal or okay or no big deal for the US government to provide arms to the most vicious terrorist organization in the history of the world and that the mainstream media is covering it up.

If there are enough Blue Dog Democrats out there, rank and file, to allow the mainstream media and team Hillary, including Obama, to hide behind partisanship, to be shielded behind a veil, and no discussion allowed, even of something as important as Wikileak ID 3774, when the truth is obvious to millions, what you will have is an end to gate keeping.

In the Independent we find, "Erdogan says he has evidence US-led coalition has given support to Isis," from December 27, 2016. The leader of Turkey has information, presumably beyond the publicly available Wikileak, that confirms the fact that Obama and Clinton armed Isis.

If the gate keepers use their position to bury one of the biggest stories in many years, the gatekeepers should and did lose credibility. And if you arm Isis, you shouldn't be president.

The Daily News reported on December 28, 2016, "Nearly 50% of Donald Trump voters believe Hillary Clinton is involved in pedophilia ring: poll." Democrats, before you get excited about the irrationality of Trump supporters, a YouGov poll published on December 26, 2016 found that "52% of Democrats believe Russia tampered with the vote totals to get Trump elected president."

No one has specifically alleged that Russia hacked voting machines. Matt Taibbi in Rolling Stone article, December 30, 2016, "Something About This Russia Story Stinks: Nearly a decade and a half after the Iraq-WMD faceplant, the American press is again asked to cosign a dubious intelligence assessment" points to examples of Democrats using the phrase "hacked the election." It's intentionally leading people to think that Russia flipped votes, when the actually unsubstantiated charge is meeting with Trump's people and leaking information to Wikileaks.

The right has a different way of spreading a story without openly stating a claim. Online, Pizzagate spread like wildfire, with no gatekeepers to credibly explain what evidence does and doesn't exist and what charges might and are unlikely to be true.

In any event, Pizzagate is more substantiated than is the charge of Russian hacking into US systems, as the CIA-funded Washington Post's story "Russian operation hacked a Vermont utility, showing risk to U.S. electrical grid security, officials say" has been retracted as false while no such determination has been made as to Pizzagate. So, next up, Pizzagate.

# Pizzagate, Wikileaks and MSM

Should Wikileaks have edited the Podesta leaks? Should the media have reported Wikileaks better? Is the MSM trying to debunk a fake story or cover up a real one? A serious charge, circumstantial evidence, some unverified, but not yet truly debunked. A vaguely sourced rumor not yet truly debunked.

Long before the term "Pizzagate" existed, Glenn Greenwald of the Intercept said that "you would have to be a sociopath" to indiscriminately release information on the internet, as Wikileaks has done in the John Podesta/DNC release of documents. See "Glenn Greenwald weighs in on WikiLeaks data dump on Clinton" October 22, 2016, CBC News. Greenwald expressed concern that innocent people might be hurt if a media outlet throws information out there to let people draw their own conclusions.

Greenwald raises a legitimate point. On the other hand, Wikileaks has opened the door to how politics really works in America as has no other publication in history. We need to know how our government works and maybe we have to grow up a bit on how we, the public, interpret information. Or maybe that's asking too much. And there will always be cranks…

The Podesta emails on Wikileaks were certainly released fairly indiscriminately. Spam is included in the database, things like special offers from the Sports Authority. We also learn that John Podesta believes that aliens from other planets have landed on earth (ID 1802, 45274, etc.). More at "The long, strange history of John Podesta's space alien obsession" in the Washington Post, April 8, 2016. The inclusion of these strange emails is evidence that the collection was not "curated" or edited, as DNC head Donna Brazil claimed.

When Greenwald made his "sociopath" comment, before Pizzagate, I thought about John Podesta's son, Gabe, an officer in the Air Force. Gabe seems to have absolutely no connection to his father's political work and to be a decent person, unlike almost everyone who actually works for the DNC or HRC.Gabe was serving in the Air Force and seems committed to doing his duty.

In one email, however, he complains about his co-workers. It's the kind of thing a lot of us have done in a private email to a friend or family member. I thought of Greenwald's warning and imagined trouble among the people Gabe works with as an example of "damage" done by the lack of editing in the Wikileaks releases.

A gun incident occurred at Comet Pizza on December 5, 2016. Harassment of the people associated with pizza restaurants mentioned in some Pizzagate related publications seems to have been intense. With these two types of aggression, we now have a more serious example of harm, as per the Greenwald "sociopath" comment above. See "Fake News Onslaught Targets Pizzeria as Nest of Child-Trafficking" in the New York times on November 21, 2016. The BBC also ran a story with "fake" in the headline prior to the shooting, "The saga of 'Pizzagate': The fake story that shows how conspiracy theories spread" on December 2, 2016.

Shooting up a restaurant, or whatever happened, and harassing people based on innuendo on the internet are despicable. People are being harassed and their lives upended completely unjustly.

While Pizzagate is certainly a rumor, an unconfirmed set of coincidences, the scandal has not been debunked by the New York Times or the BBC or anyone else. It could be debunked, assuming there is no merit to the actual evidence. Pizzagate is not yet "fake" news. A blog called "aceloewgold" has a discussion I found useful.

"Aliens" is fake news. Podesta believes aliens have landed on earth. That is fake. There is no basis for the idea that aliens have been on earth. No reasonable person can find any credible reason to accept the idea. Aliens do not occasionally land on earth. If they did, we'd likely know about it. You don't need to debunk the claim. The New York Times and the BBC did not debunk this idea. Like many crazy ideas out there, the alien idea is simply baseless.

Pedophile rings do exist, unlike alien visitors. The vatican (Wikipedia "Catholic Church sexual abuse cases"), Belgium (Reuters: "275,000 in Belgium Protest Handling of Child Sex Scandal" October 21, 1996), Norway ("Massive paedophile ring uncovered by police in Norway after arrest of 51 men" The Independent, November 23, 2016), Canada ("Alleged pedophile ring busted by police in Quebec, Toronto: 7 cities involved, including Montreal, Quebec City, Toronto, after 3-year probe of online activities" CBC News January 27, 2016), the BBC (Wikipedia "BBC sexual abuse cases"): pedophilia rings happen. An inquiry in Australia found that 7% of Catholic Church staff were child rapists for a number of decades. Connected, prestigious people have been involved in all of the abuse networks cited above.

While Pizzagate is a rumor, the routine violations of election law are facts. While the pedophilia story is very weak in terms of evidence, the idea that Google would try to sway an election is absolutely terrifying. A memorandum against conflict of interest has the force of law and Hillary Clinton broke her agreement. Clinton helped create Isis. If the media did not cover up the career-ending nature of these and other facts, they would now have the credibility to debunk Pizzagate. If the media did not collude in fixing an election, or attempting to, they would have the credibility to write off a story as "fake" and people would believe it.

What did or did not happen at Comet Pizza or whether Hillary Clinton knew about whatever happened in any place are not central to the rumor. Hillary is a bit player in Pizzagate and the restaurant site as such is not necessarily central either.

What does Pizzagate allege? At a minimum, that there is something mildly creepy about James Alefantis and John and Tony Podesta. The scandal, if it's anything at all, might not involve any violations of law or might not involve many people. It might be some people who have some strange sexual proclivities that they share in ways that are not illegal, as sort of a low end "scandal" emerging from the coincidences that build up to Pizzagate. At most, on the high end, you might have something like a pedophile ring. Those do exist.

The "evidence" for Pizzagate is all circumstantial. Most people on any board talking about this agree that there is no evidence to indict let alone convict anyone. Mostly, the rumor is a set of questions.

Comet Pizza and Besta Pizza had logos that appear to resemble symbols used by pedophiles. See Slate "The Pedophile's Secret Code" December 3, 2007 for a discussion of the FBI symbol information sheet or Wikileaks for a copy of the original FBI publication. Both Podestas, Tony and John, have pedophilia-related art collections.

The screen shots from Alefantis' Instagram page can be seen as controversial by interpreting the comments and context. No one has claimed the screenshots are fake, as far as I can tell. Look up "Alefantis screenshots." Even with comments most are not obscene or explicit, although the innuendos do seem disturbing. There is one of a girl "tied up." There is one referring to John Podesta's odd art collection. The term "chickenlover" appears in a comment next to what might be an innocent photo posted by Alefantis: is it a tasteless joke? The term refers to a man who has sex with very young children.

The trigger for the controversy were pizza-themed emails sent by or to Podesta in Wikileaks. Those emails are clearly real and not fake. To debunk those, you would need to explain what appears to be pizza code language and something other than pedophile double speak. If Pizzagate is "fake" let's get rid of it and cover the real news in Wikileaks. Here's how you get rid of it, to debunk Pizzagate, you could do any of the following:

Find out if the archived Instagram account, now on the web as screen shots, really belonged to James Alefantis. Alefantis posted the picture. He may have taken the picture. If those screenshots are fake, that would put a huge dent in Pizzagate. The screenshots should be part of any story claiming to debunk Pizzagate.

Is Australian citizen Michael Quinn, convicted pedophile, one of the shirtless, bearded men in a picture posted by James Alefantis? Does the t-shirt in the picture say, "I love children" in French or does it refer to a neighbor or cafe in Washington? There can be no guilt by association, but Michael Quinn was convicted of purchasing access to a child to rape, a contact made online.

Did Tony and John Podesta socialize frequently with James Alefantis? Was James Alefantis the former boyfriend of Clinton confidant David Brock? If Alefantis has no significant connection to Clinton, then his sexual proclivities may be a scandal, but not a political one. So, ask them. Tony Podesta celebrated his birthday at Alefantis' restaurant? Once? Often?

What do the references to pizza in the Wikileak emails mean? Clearly not pizza. You can visit on Reddit r/WikiLeaks you might

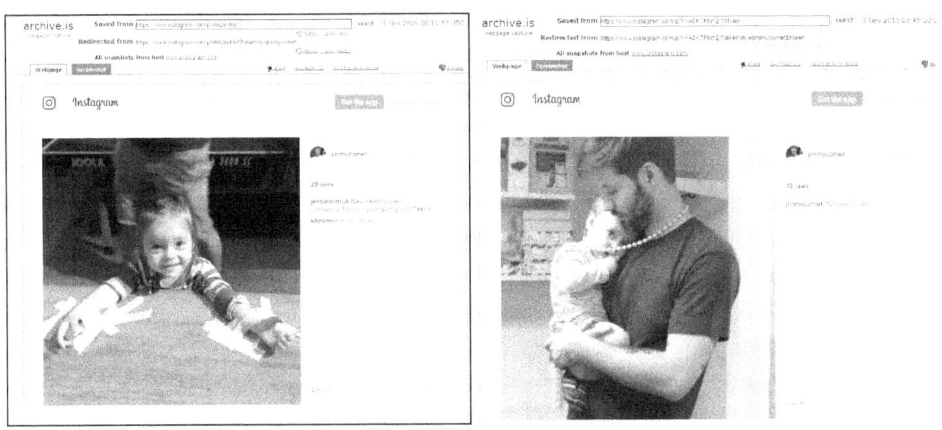

John Alefantis' Instagram account above, Podesta art collection below

still be able to track down "official_thread_for_leaks_and_evidence" for much discussion of the pizza comments in the Podesta emails. Someone could ask John Podesta. If he has a credible answer, then that would solve that problem.

It really does sound like code for something. What? I don't talk about pizza as something that is a matter of time, an hour, or a date coming up. In fact, although I eat pizza, I rarely talk about it. Podesta is usually quite taciturn and clearly quite busy in these emails. Yet he has time to talk about pizza.

The weirdest emails are the "handkerchief... map that seems pizza-related" (ID 32795) and the "pool party" emails (ID 10052). Do people normally enjoy watching children they don't know swim in a pool? John Podesta seems to.

Did Bill Clinton ditch his secret service detail to fly on Jeffrey Epstein's plane (Lolita Express) 12 times? 26 times? See "Flight logs show Bill Clinton flew on sex offender's jet much more than previously known" on Fox News May 13, 2016. Where did he go? Why? As far as I'm concerned, if Bill admitted to sex with adult prostitutes, that would be no big scandal. If the implication is sex with underage sex slaves, well, that's worse. Why not find out? Ask him. I don't expect him to admit to a crime, but he should be able to say yes or no to questions about flying on the plane and visiting the island. If he was not on the island for sex, why was he there? Was he there? If he was there for sex, it may be a private matter, depending on the kind of sex. This should have been a bigger story for some time.

Dennis Hastert (ID 48488 and 3664), Republican former speaker of the House, convicted pedophile, knew the Podesta brothers for 40 years. Emails pertaining to his arrest suggest concern for him on the part of John Podesta but not for his victims. However, John Podesta may have expressed concern for the victims in another forum. The issue here, as far as debunking the Pizzagate story, would be to re-open Hastert's history. Was he a life-long pedophile, even when sharing an apartment with Tony

"Do you think I'll do better playing dominos on cheese than on pasta?"

https://wikileaks.org/podesta-emails/emailid/30613

At this point, anyone doubting that they are using code for **something** is burying their head in the sand so deep they'll soon shit glass. Or they're a shill. So if you're going to try to dress me down with a long post basically saying the talk about pasta and pizza is innocent. Please. Start the post by telling me if you are on the blue pill or if you're payed to write that shit.

Because if you look at all this evidence (albeit circumstantial) along with the fact that a lot of high ranking people has been caught in rings like this before should mandate a thorough investigation on it's own. Sure, it *could be false*, but what if it's true? Even if there's just a small chance of it being true it should be taken serious. Because if it's true there are lives at stake here.

The fact that there is such massive backlash against "fake news" and this story should be a huge warning sign. This is serious stuff. Also. Bernie guy. It's not just "alt-right" people are interested in this story. That's just probably h

Ironically the thing that makes #pizzagate most credible is how every time it comes up, you get the same F.U.D tactics *every single time.*

If it was just a crazy conspiracy, nobody would fucking care. No one brigades a post about chemtrails or Alex jones and his "MAKING THE FROGS GAY" stuff because it's not credible. You can chuckle and move on.

Yet here we have the same people who proclaim "Trump is working with Russia alt right nazis to use weaponized green frog memes to destroy our democracy!" turning around and casually dismissing a potential pedophilia ring.

Why? Is this so incredible? Just look at that shit from instagram if nothing else, it absolutely reeks of some creepy shit.

Seriously, **10 fucking days after weiner's laptop was seized, FBI busted a child trafficking ring rescuing Rescuing 82 Children And Arresting 239 Pimps.**

Just another coincidence, I'm sure.

Edit:

Oh yeah and haiti? yeah someone investigating the child trafficking there was fucking disappeared.

Image from John Alefantis' Instagram account. Bearded man may be Michael Quinn

Podesta? Was the extent of his criminal activity covered up in any way? This should have been a bigger story at the time.

Laura Silsby (Wikipedia), was convicted of child trafficking children from Haiti. Her lawyer in that case was himself convicted of sex trafficking of minors, Jorge Puello Torres. Clinton aide Huma Abedin kept Hillary posted on Silsby's activities for many years prior to the conviction (ID Clinton 2772). Clinton ID 3741 includes "Transportation of the Children: $1800 to charter a bus in the DR to bring 100 children" by Silsby, a request for funding from Clinton. Others in Clinton Wikileaks relating to Silsby: ID 3741, 3465, 3539, Did Hillary Clinton intervene personally to reduce the charges when Silsby was on trial in Haiti? Also see Daily Mail, February 8, 2010, "The child snatchers: Special report from Haiti on the U.S. missionaries accused of 'stealing orphans' and why - most shockingly of all - their parents say they would give them away again."

We have five convicted pedophiles and child traffickers possibly in this story: Hastert, Epstein, Silsby, Torres and Quinn. Hastert is a long time friend of the Podestas. Epstein is friends with Bill Clinton. Silsby knows Huma Abedin and Hillary Clinton is concerned about her fate. Torres works for Silsby. Quinn may or may not know Alefantis.

These connections can be debunked but have not been. For example: It's not Quinn in the photo with Alefantis. The Podestas have nothing to do with and were unaware of Hastert's pedophilia. Bill did not fly on Epstein's plane and/or did not have sex with underage children on his island in the Virgin Islands. Hillary did not intervene on Silsby's behalf and/or did not know what she was really up to. I don't know any convicted pedophiles while four are poking around the Clinton circle. But their circle is wider than mine. Maybe it's a coincidence.

There are many ways for a journalist with access to these people or, certainly, an investigator with a badge, to clear this up. Unfortunately, the MSM has ignored a series of major scandals and has no credibility to simply write off Pizzagate as entirely fake. It's a rumor. It's not a wacko aliens area 51 story. There are pieces of evidence. Some of them could be fake. Are they? Vigilante harassment is terrible. I know that Wikileaks has revealed profound corruption at the heart of government that has nothing to do with this rumor. I know that I don't believe the hype when it comes to the MSM.

## Murder?

As long as we've discussed Pizzagate, we might as well touch on the rumors that the Clintons sometimes have people killed who get in their way. The FBI released a report on the suicide of Vince Foster suicide, for example, at vault.fbi. gov/vincent-foster. The New York Times article "Hillary Clinton's Fingerprints Among Those Found on Papers" from June 5, 1996 reads like a mystery novel.

You can look up the many murder rumors on the internet and evaluate them as you choose, if you want to. I would only point out a few comments in the Wikileaks releases of this year that might suggest paid hits, if you have a conspiratorial mind. Even if you dismiss these rumors, it's worth knowing that the "Arkansas Flu" and jokes about fake suicides are commonly accepted by many people as true (Vince Foster, Ron Brown, Ed Willey, James Mcdougal, Seth Rich, Don Adam, John Ashe, and on and on).

On Tuesday, February 9, 2016 at 4:36 PM, Podesta emailed (ID 6008) Steve Elmendorf, "Didn't think wet works meant pool parties at the Vineyard." Four hours later, Elmendorf emailed back, "I am all in. Sounds like it will be a bad nite, we all need to buckle up and double down."

Elmendorf claims to be "one of D.C.'s preeminent political strategists," a frequent guest on CNN, MSNBC, listed among the most influential leaders in Washington by Politico, The Hill.

The reason this is interesting is that Wikipedia says "wetworks" means "a euphemism for murder or assassination, alluding to spilling blood." Who did Podesta kill on February 9? No one, it seems. Antonin Scalia died four days later, but that would not make for a "bad nite" on the 9th as Elmendorf says. If ID 6008 refers to a murder, it would have to be on or about February 9, 2016.

In ID 36082, Podesta tells Mook, "I'm definitely for making an example of a suspected leaker whether or not we have any real basis for it." Mook responds, "I agree--when we have press staff, this will be MUCH easier. And I would love an example being made." That exchange was way back on February 22, 2015.

Seth Rich, the 27-year-old DNC staffer murdered in Washington, in an unsolved murder, was killed on July 10, 2016 at 4 AM. The email thread possibly suggesting a plan to kill or otherwise punish someone for leaking to present an example and scare other insiders is 36082. Podesta said he wanted punishment "that goes beyond internal discipline."

I'm just adding this in for interest. Also, we really need to know who killed Seth Rich and why. There have been hints from Wikileaks insiders that he may have been the person Craig Murray met in Washington and from whom he received a thumb drive.

**EXCLUSIVE: Illegal fundraiser for the Clintons made secret tape because he feared being ASSASSINATED over what he knew - and used it to reveal Democrats'**

Katie's Post

# CitiGroup vetted Obama's cabinet in 2008

ID 8190 from Michael Froman to John Podesta on October 6, 2008 is among the most important emails released by Wikileaks. Froman was then an executive at CitiGroup and sent the spreadsheet to Podesta from "fromanm@citi.com" -- a Citibank email address.

In the attached spreadsheet, Froman offers lists of people Obama can appoint to some of the 4000 political offices available to him. He offers undersecretaries grouped by ethnicity. And here is the cabinet:

### Cabinet Example

| Position | Candidate Examples | Diversity Probability | Example of Choice |
|---|---|---|---|
| WH COS | Daschle/Emanuel | | |
| WH Counsel | Kagen/Holder | 1 | Holder |
| NSC | Jones/Steinberg | | |
| State | Kerry/Dod | | |
| Defense | Gates/Reed | | |
| DHS | Napolitano/Bacerra | 1 | Napolitano |
| DNI | Steinberg/Blair | | |
| CIA | Blair/Steinberg | | |
| USUN | Rice | 1 | Rice |
| Justice | K. Salaza/Holder | 1 | Salazar |
| NEC | Tarullo/Schlosstein/Sperling | | |
| Treasury | Rubin/Geithner/Summers | | |

| | | | |
|---|---|---|---|
| OMB | Orszag/Spratt/Pryce/Sperling | | |
| CEA | Goolsbee/Henry/Collins/Farrell | .5 | |
| Commerce | Pritzker/Mulcahey/Parsons/Williams | 1 | Pritzker |
| USTR | Tysons/Parsons | 1 | Tysons |
| Labor | Sebelius/Gephardt/Cisneros | .5 | Sebelius |
| USDA | Clyburn/Nelson/Schwietzer/J. Salazar | .5 | |
| SBA | Hightower/Fong/Nesbitt | 1 | Fong |
| Performance | Farrell/Gupta | 1 | Farrell |
| EnergyCouncil | Steyer/Inslee | | |
| Energy | Rogers/Bryson/Harris | .5 | |
| EPA | Adams/Nichols | 1 | Adams |
| Interior | Browner/Richardson/J. Salazar | 1 | Richardson |
| DPC | Barnes/Jarrett | 1 | Barnes |
| Transportation | Kirk/Sims/Ford | 1 | Kirk |
| HUD | N. Rice/Sims/Cisneros/Booker/Jarrett | 1 | N. Rice |
| Education | Powell/Simmons/Reich/Duncan | .5 | Powell |
| HHS | Gayle/Sebelius/Dean | .5 | Gayle |
| VA | Duckworth/Shinseki | 1 | Duckworth |
| Urban Affairs | Jarrett/Canada | 1 | Jarrett |

| | |
|---|---|
| **Total** | 31 |
| Non-Hispanic White Men | 13 |
| Women | 11 |
| African American | 8 |
| Latino | 2 |
| Asian American | 2 |
| Native American | 0 |
| Disabled | 1 |

Look at the names on this list (one of three spreadsheets CitiBank sent to Podesta). It's the Obama cabinet. Do you think a CitiGroup executive would send his CitiBank employees to put together a list of people for the cabinet who were going to be hard on the big banks that caused the financial meltdown?

The three lists were certainly drawn up in a CitiBank office by bank employees and sent with a bank email account by a bank executive. Froman became an official member of Obama's transition team after the election. TARP was passed under Bush. The seamless transition from bank executive, to transition team member, back to bank executive, from Republican to Democratic administration really should stop you in your tracks.

New York Magazine published, "Citigroup Received More Bailout Money Than Any Other Bank" March 16, 2011. Total: $476.2 billion. If everyone around you says you have to bail out the banks and no one around you tells you to break them up, guess what happens?

Pew Research Center on December 12, 2014 published, "Wealth inequality has widened along racial, ethnic lines since end of Great Recession" and from August 30, 2013 "Black incomes are up, but wealth isn't." Here is a quote:

> *The Great Recession, fueled by the crises in the housing and financial markets, was universally hard on the net worth of American families. But even as the economic recovery has begun to mend asset prices, not all households have benefited alike, and wealth inequality has widened along racial and ethnic lines.*
>
> *The wealth of white households was 13 times the median wealth of black households in 2013, compared with eight times the wealth in 2010, according to a new Pew Research Center analysis of data from the Federal Reserve's Survey of Consumer Finances. Likewise, the wealth of white households is now more than 10 times the wealth of Hispanic households, compared with nine times the wealth in 2010. The current gap between blacks and whites has reached its highest point since 1989, when whites had 17 times the wealth of black households. The current white-to-Hispanic wealth ratio has reached a level not seen since 2001. (Asians and other racial groups are not separately identified in the public-use versions of the Fed's survey.)*

The study points to the loss of wealth in the housing crisis for those late to home ownership and in areas that did not recover. Black households were devastated by the banking crisis.

From 2009 on, Obama was president and had 57 Democratic senators and a majority in the house. The Democrats were completely in control of the government until 2010. The policies that gave money to CitiBank to bail them out and not to bail out Black homeowners, and others newer to home ownership in underwater mortgages, was all on the Democrats.

Why was TARP passed by Bush but administered by Obama without a hiccup? Maybe because, as Lloyd Blankfein, CEO of Goldman Sachs, said in the discussion after one of Hillary's paid speeches, "The financial services industry has been the one unifying theme that binds everybody together in common."

Both parties serve the same master. We only have the appearance of a two party system. This spreadsheet reveals the master behind the curtain.

American was in a financial crisis in 2009 when Obama took over. Did he consider breaking up the big banks to make sure "too big to fail" never happened again? Did he consider writing off all the debts of poorer homeowners to make sure Black households did not lose their life savings?

No. There was no one around him willing to speak truth to power, particularly the power of the banks. Everyone around Obama was vetted by CitiBank. Any freethinkers, anyone willing to question the absurdity of domination of the economy by six banks would not have gotten a seat at the table. No wonder they (the Republican-Democratic-CitiGroup establishment) let Obama win the 2008 primary but not Bernie in 2016.

At the Goldman Sachs AIMS Alternative Investments Symposium, October 24, 2013, Hillary was paid to speak. She blamed the 2008 crash on the government, not the banks:

> *I had great relations and worked so close together after 9/11 to rebuild downtown, and a lot of respect for the work you do and the people who do it, but I do -- I think that when we talk about the regulators and the politicians, the economic consequences of bad decisions back in '08, you know, were devastating, and they had repercussions throughout the world… You guys help us figure it out and let's make sure that we do it right this time. And I think that everybody was desperately trying to fend off the worst effects institutionally, governmentally, and there just wasn't that opportunity to try to sort this out, and that came later.*

That's the corporate Democrat point of view: more favors to Wall Street. The Froman spreadsheet, TARP funding article, and Pew Study of Black household wealth should doom Obama's legacy. Why doesn't he have to explain what he did?

## Obama Killed a 16-Year-Old American in Yemen. Trump Just Killed His 8-Year-Old Sister.

In 2010, President Obama directed the CIA to assassinate an American citizen in Yemen, Anwar al-Awlaki, despite the fact that he had never been charged with (let alone convicted of) any crime, and the agency successfully carried out that order a year later with a September, 2011 drone strike. While that assassination created widespread debate – the once-again-beloved ACLU sued Obama to restrain him from the assassination on the ground of due process and then, when that suit was dismissed, sued Obama again after the killing was carried out – another drone killing carried out shortly thereafter with perhaps even relatively little

**Julian Assange**
@JulianAssange

CIA plan to overthrow Syria by provoking sectarian tensions (1986)

Full doc (PDF): cia.gov/library/readin...

Me: Hillary oversaw a coup in Honduras which installed a regime that murders indigenous rights activists

Democrat: DO YOU WANT TRUMP TO WIN

KILL THEM, YES, BLOW UP THEIR NATIONS
BUT DO NOT YELL "FAKE NEWS" AT TV STATIONS

WORLD    THREATS AND RESPONSES   THE IRAQIS

### THREATS AND RESPONSES: THE IRAQIS; U.S. SAYS HUSSEIN INTENSIFIES QUEST FOR A-BOMB PARTS

By MICHAEL R. GORDON and JUDITH MILLER   SEPT 8, 2002

More than a decade after Saddam Hussein agreed to give up weapons of mass destruction, Iraq has stepped up its quest for nuclear weapons and has embarked on a worldwide hunt for materials to make an atomic bomb, Bush administration officials said today.

**theguardian**

OPINION

## The migrant slave trade is booming in Libya. Why is the world ignoring it?

I've seen the dangerous route to Europe through Libya, with thousands of people at the mercy of cruelty for profit. But we

In the lead-up to the Iraq war and its later conduct, I saw at a minimum, true dereliction, negligence and irresponsibility; at the worst, lying, incompetence and corruption.

— RETIRED GENERAL ANTHONY ZINNI
Former head of U.S. Central Command, in a new book, Battle Ready, about his military career, written in collaboration with Tom Clancy.

Jerad Miller or some Stolen The Front – photo

Its a shame our soldiers are being used as pawns to bring in the NWO

900 BASES IN 153 COUNTRIES
IS NOT FIGHTING FOR YOUR FREEDOM. IT IS AN EMPIRE

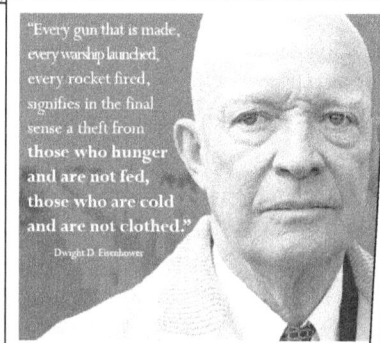

"Every gun that is made, every warship launched, every rocket fired, signifies in the final sense a theft from those who hunger and are not fed, those who are cold and are not clothed."

Dwight D. Eisenhower

# Obama/Clinton destabilized one third of Africa

When Obama won in 2008, a cheer went up across Africa that we could hear all the way over to America. But, unfortunately, Obama didn't care much for Africans. Ross Kemp in the Guardian on February 20, 2017 could compared the horror of the the migrant slave trade in Libya today to middle passage of slaves in the 18th century. Contributing to a horror of that magnitude is not a feather in your cap.

The Atlantic published, "The Legacy of Obama's 'Worst Mistake'" on April 15, 2016. The Obama administration overthrew the Gaddafi government, leaving Libya a failed state. Terrorists set up shop in Libya and weapons from the Gaddafi regime ended up in the hands of radicals. Based in Libya, the terrorists conducted raids in neighboring countries.

In April 2015, 21 Coptic Christians from Ethiopia were murdered by an Isis unit from Libya operating inside of Egypt. In November 2015, terrorists armed and trained in Libya attacked the Radisson hotel in the capital of Mali, killing 20 and upending the local economy. In June 2016, terrorists from Libya killed 38 foreigners in Tunisia, causing a collapse in the Tunisian tourist industry, to say nothing of the horrific loss of life. From his last day in office, January 19, 2017, in the Telegraph, "Barack Obama orders raid to kill 80 Islamic State terrorists in Libya who were 'plotting attacks in Europe.'" On March 13, 2016, three gunmen opened fire at a beach resort in Grand-Bassam, Ivory Coast, killing at least 19. Al-Queda in Libya accepted responsibility.

There was no reason to overthrow Gaddafi. He was willing to negotiate with the Obama administration. On January 28, 2015, the Washington Times reported that "Top Pentagon officials and a senior Democrat in Congress so distrusted secretary of state Hillary Rodham Clinton's 2011 march to war in Libya that they opened their own diplomatic channels with the Gadhafi regime in an effort to halt the escalating crisis, according to secret audio recordings recovered from Tripoli. The tapes, reviewed by The Washington Times and authenticated by the participants, chronicle U.S. officials' unfiltered conversations with Col. Moammar Gadhafi's son and a top Libyan leader, including criticisms that Mrs. Clinton had developed tunnel vision and led the U.S. into an unnecessary war without adequately weighing the intelligence community's concerns."

Former Ohio congressman Dennis Kucinich also attempted to negotiate with Gaddafi. He subsequently wrote an op-ed piece in the Guardian as the NATO war against Libya was still in progress. He said:

> ...the war against Libya has seen countless violations of United Nations security council resolutions (UNSCRs) by Nato and UN member states. The funnelling of weapons (now being air-dropped) to Libyan rebels was, from the beginning of the conflict, in clear violation of UNSCR 1970. The use of military force on behalf of the rebels, in an attempt to impose regime change, has undermined international law and damaged the credibility of the United Nations. Countless innocent civilians have been killed, and Nato airstrikes continue to place many at great risk. So much for the humanitarian-inspired UNSCR 1973 as a means to protect civilians. The people of Libya cannot take another month of such humanitarian intervention. The leading donor nations of Nato – the US, France and

*Great Britain – have been free to prosecute war under the cloak of this faceless, bureaucratic, alphabet security agency, now multinational war machine, which can violate UN resolutions and kill innocent civilians with impunity. War crimes trials are only for losers. The prospective conquerors, the western powers and their rebel proxies, will then expect to be able to assert control over Libya's vast oil and natural gas reserves. The US share of the war against Libya has probably exceeded the $1bn mark. This extraordinary amount of money for an intervention that Americans were told would last "days not weeks" could only be explained by looking at the war as an investment, and at control over Libya's wealth as an opportunity to make a return on that investment. Cynical? Then tell me why else we are at war in Libya. Viable peace proposals, such as the one put forward by the African Union (AU), have been quickly and summarily rejected. If there is going to be a peaceful resolution of the conflict, the US must work with and empower the AU to ensure regional security. The AU has proposed a peace plan that would facilitate an immediate ceasefire, the unhindered delivery of humanitarian aid, a dialogue between the Transitional National Council and the Gaddafi government, and the suspension of Nato strikes. … Continued military action promotes a cycle of violence that will persist whether Colonel Gaddafi is ousted or not. On 19 March 2003, the United States pursued regime change in Iraq. Eight years later, we're still wondering why the people of Iraq are not sufficiently grateful for our intervention, which has resulted in the death of over 1 million of their fellow countrymen and women. How can we expect this grim manifesto of* *interventionism to ever result in anything but tragedy? It's time to end the war against Libya.*

Sadly for the people of Libya and the rest of north and west Africa, the American establishment treat people like Dennis Kucinich as wild-eyed lefties, not to be taken seriously, and Hillary Clinton and Barack Obama as sober, realistic, professionals.

But if Kucinich had been in charge, Africa would be a safer, more prosperous place. Refugees would not now be using Libya as the principle launching pad into Europe.

## Obama is guilty of international and domestic war crimes

First, let's check the US Constitution: War Powers. Article I, Section 8, Clause 11 of the U.S. Constitution grants Congress the power to declare war. The President, meanwhile, derives the power to direct the military after a Congressional declaration of war from Article II, Section 2, which names the President Commander-in-Chief of the armed forces.

If the president is allowed to conduct an act of war without congressional approval, say, by killing a foreign head of state or bombing indiscriminately, then in fact, the President has the right to declare war. Any act of war is a potential war.

When did congress authorize the drone program in Somalia, Yemen, Pakistan, Syria, Libya, Iraq, and Afghanistan? The Guardian reported on January 8, 2017 that "In 2016, US special operators could be found in 70% of the world's nations, 138 countries – a staggering jump of 130% since the days of the Bush administration… President Obama has claimed that his overseas military adventures are legal under the 2001 and 2003 authorizations for the use of military force passed by Congress to go after al-Qaida." And Isis, of course, did not exist in 2001.

The Bureau of Investigative Journalism reported on July 1, 2016, "The US government today claimed it has killed between 64 and 116 "non-combatants" in 473 counter-terrorism strikes in Pakistan, Yemen, Somalia and Libya between January 2009 and the end of 2015. This is a fraction of the 380 to 801 civilian casualty range recorded by the Bureau of Investigative Journalism from reports by local and international journalists, NGO investigators, leaked government documents, court papers and the result of field investigations. While the number of civilian casualties recorded by the Bureau is six times higher than the US Government's figure, the assessments of the minimum total number of people killed were strikingly similar. The White House put this figure at 2,436, while the Bureau has recorded 2,753."

Each individual action, each expansion of forces to a new country, is an individual act of war; therefore, congress needs to have an individual and discrete oversight of each action. The strange thing is that Obama certainly could have gotten congressional approval for these actions. A system of committees to review evidence before a strike and the ability to discontinue the program would not have been hard to establish.

"That means taking strikes only when we face a continuing, imminent threat, and only where there is … near certainty of no civilian casualties," he told an audience at West Point in 2014. And yet Abdulrahman al-Awlaki was a 16-year-old American citizen with no criminal record, not charged with any crime, and was sitting in a cafe in Yemen when Obama killed him for secret reasons based on secret evidence.

In an armed conflict, under international law, the use of force must be limited to military targets, but these targets need not present an imminent threat to life at the time of the strike. But none of the U.S. drone strikes are part of an armed conflict, as there is not declaration of war. Obama understands these strikes as part of a non-international armed conflict against al-Qaeda and its affiliates ("non-international" meaning against non-state actors rather than another state). But Isis didn't exist at the time of the declaration of war in 2001 and some of the strikes clearly targeted Isis.

Obama wrongly applies the law of armed conflict to areas characterized by relative peace — where the rules of law enforcement should govern the use of force. An armed conflict against terrorist groups throughout the world with no clear geographic limits to the conflict, means the conditions of war can follow terrorists as they move, even into areas without active hostilities. Anywhere. Anytime. It's a "war" with no limit in time or space. No review domestically or internationally.

International oversight would also have been a good idea, if only after each action, in order to establish an international order for areas in failed states.  If there are places outside of state control, if non-state actors do in fact pose a significant threat to a given country, some way to engage in warfare against these non-state actors may be necessary and some of the drone program may have been effective. But as it stands, the entire campaign is illegal, even the parts of the campaign that may have been justified under international and domestic law.

We don't know why Obama killed Abdulrahman al-Awlaki, or any of the other 2,753 people (not including Libya). Maybe the king of Saudi Arabia asked Obama to kill a personal enemy in Yemen because he made a pass at his granddaughter. Maybe someone

Obama met when he was backpacking in Pakistan in the 1980s insulted him and owed him money and Obama decided to pay him back and blew his house up.

I doubt Obama did kill people for these reasons. But what about Trump? What are the limits of the program? Could he blow someone up in Turkey if they refuse to allow him to build another Trump tower in Istanbul? How would we know if he did?

In 1990, the Tamil Tigers attacked a police station in Sri Lanka, killing perhaps as many as 774 policemen. The strategic reason for the attack was to provoke an overreaction on the part of the government, which would involve atrocities against the Tamil population, thus pushing the Tamil people into the arms of the Tigers and making the logic of "us versus them" unavoidable. Up until this attack many or most Tamils did not support violence or the Tigers.

In 2001, Al Qaeda attacked New York, killing 2,996 people. Again, the purpose was to provoke an overreaction, and George Bush obliged by invading Iraq. While Al Qaeda and Osama bin Laden did not reap the benefits of the polarization, Daesh/Isis did. The strategy worked again, if you consider Jihadis in all their incarnations as a single force.

Donald Trump has very publicly imposed a travel ban. When the news of the ban reaches rural Yemen, it may be something like "Islam has been banned." People might get distorted news that Trump banned the religion itself in the United States. Now, Muslims have to gather their belongings and walk to Canada, expelled. News does not travel linearly to rural, isolated areas.

Even now most Afghanis have no idea why NATO invaded Afghanistan. A study of 1,000 Afghan men carried out by think tank the International Council on Security and Development in the

Southern districts of Kandahar and Helmand in 2011 found that most had never heard of 9/11 or Osama bin Laden. The Daily Mail reported "Afghan tribe so remote they didn't know about the Taliban or that the US had overthrown them is captured in stunning images" on October 9, 2016.

While starting up this stupid travel ban, in the most blunt, public way possible, Trump has not discontinued the equally stupid and counterproductive Obama era drone program. Now, when Trump bombs some location in Syria or Yemen, it will be pretty clear why he is doing it to those who have only word of mouth as a source of information: he wants to kill all the Muslims. He's forced the Muslims in America to leave, or something. People will believe the worst interpretation of the travel ban, even if the courts have in fact voided the ban. Then you look up (in Somalia, Yemen, Syria, Libya, etc.) and see an American plane or drone dropping a bomb. It's all very clear. The Americans are the new Rome, the great Satan, and they want to kill our children, every single one of them, or force us to convert to Christianity.

You live in a village. You know the Americans are attacking someone in the area. You know that America hates Muslims. So, reluctantly, you join the Jihadis to protect your religion, your land and your family. The more moderate people in the rural areas will have no case and have to shut up or flee. The cities will be burning wrecks and not the kind of place where a reasonable, educated, fact-based conversation can occur.

As Jihadis win among Sunnis in Syria, Yemen, Libya, etc. they will butt heads with the Shiites supported by Iran and Russia and get turned back. They will then have nowhere else to turn their increased energy and power than the Gulf States, including Saudi Arabia and Kuwait. A charismatic figure will unify the Jihadis who will be in position to do a pincer move on the Gulf, set up a Jihadi state that controls 50% of the world's oil and begin some kind of great war with America, settle their differences with the Shiites, and World War III will be under way.

The best way to avoid this possibility would be to end the drone program and other military strike campaigns that have little chance of changing anything on the ground but can help Jihadis tie together a misinterpretation of the travel ban and the clear evidence of war. So, it would be great if American presidents would stop taking the bait and stop interfering in Muslim countries. Trump's travel ban looks terrible. But it's only a potential catastrophe because of the history of intervention under Clinton/Obama.

The New York Review of Books published an article by David Cole on February 23, 2017 saying, "When Barack Obama became the forty-fourth president of the United States in 2009, he appointed Norman Eisen, a 'special counsel for ethics and government,' to ensure that he violated no prohibitions on conflicts of interest… Obama, in short, was punctilious about ethics, and his administration was almost entirely free of ethics scandals." Cole reaches this conclusion only because the Washington establishment and mainstream media has given up on controlling the imperial powers of the presidency to violate the war powers provisions of the constitution. Also, Cole seems not to have noticed that Hillary Clinton was openly selling access and favors to foreign and domestic oligarchs. If you let that go on, you are not punctilious.

Obama also had counselors write memos to justify his illegal war making. But memos don't count and Trump can wipe his ass with them. That's about all Obama's memos are good for now. Should have been more concerned with laws and power and gotten out of his seamless bubble of internal memos that don't mean anything. Ego playtime in the legal office.

# Obama and the democrats let Google become dangerously powerful in exchange for favors and donations

Google is the one of the most powerful organizations ever to have existed. They not only deliver the mail, they can read it. They control what people know through the search engine.

Europe has been more aggressive in constraining tech giants than America: antitrust actions, famously against Microsoft, or constraining Google through "right to be forgotten" court rulings.

The Intercept published "Google's Remarkably Close Relationship With the Obama White House, in Two Charts" on April 22, 2016. "In just the past few years, Google has provided diplomatic assistance to the administration through expanding internet access in Cuba; collaborated with the Department of Housing and Urban Development to bring Google Fiber into public housing; used Google resources to monitor droughts in real time; and even captured 360-degree views of White House interiors. But perhaps most salient here is the fact that modern life requires so much information technology support that a sprawling operation like the White House has turned to tech companies — often in the form of ex-Google employees — when faced with pressing IT needs… Somebody has to build and manage those projects, and Silicon Valley firms have the expertise needed to do that. White House officials have publicly asked Silicon Valley for aid in stopping terrorists from recruiting via social media, securing the internet of things, thwarting cyberattacks, modernizing the Defense Department, and generally updating all their technology. We can reasonably expect yet more things are being asked for behind closed doors."

Not only is Google ramping up its lobbying efforts, Wikileaks revealed that the company is actually trying to influence the results of the elections, to pick the candidates. The only logical, democratic response to Wikileak revelations is to break up Google, to separate the search engine from the rest of the company through anti-trust law.

United States antitrust law is a collection of federal and state government laws that regulates the conduct and organization of business corporations, generally to promote fair competition for the benefit of consumers. (The concept is called competition law in other English-speaking countries.) The main statutes are the Sherman Act 1890, the Clayton Act 1914 and the Federal Trade Commission Act 1914. These Acts, first, restrict the formation of cartels and prohibit other collusive practices regarded as being in restraint of trade. Second, they restrict the mergers and acquisitions of organizations that could substantially lessen competition. Third, they prohibit the creation of a monopoly and the abuse of monopoly power.

Consider these definitions in light of the markey position of Google. Eric Schmidt is executive chairman of Google (Alphabet). In the Podesta Wikileaks, he promises to help Clinton win. The emails between Clinton campaign chairman John Podesta and campaign manager Robby Mook show that Schmidt met with Podesta and was interested in assuming the role of "head outside advisor."

Then, Schmidt delivered. Crowdstrike, an internet security firm, is owned by Google. This is the company that outed your campaign for apparently breaking DNC Minivan rules. This same firm now says there are links between Russia and Wikileaks. (ID 37184)

Redacted Tonight produced a video called "Google Caught Rigging Search Results For Hillary Clinton!" Google, after offering to help the Clinton campaign, indeed helped in nefarious and unfair ways, as demonstrated in the video. Negative search terms for Clinton were replaced with positive options. Also, the Google delegate totals in the Democratic primary included superdelegates even after CNN had discontinued the deceptive practice.

Crowdstrike, search suggestions, and news reporting of the delegate totals are three areas of known collaboration between Google and the Clinton campaign. Here Google directly interfered with the election of the US President and compromised its search neutrality. The only logical response to Schmidt's offer in the emails release by Wikileaks is for the US government to break up this dangerous monopoly. We have seen time and again Google move into a sector and ruin existing companies by leveraging its search dominance. Mapquest was first in maps. They were squeezed out. This happens again and again.

Given this history of anti-competitive behavior, taking over the government is a step too far. Google is far too powerful already. With their finger in the White House, Google could render national sovereignty a quaint thing of the past. We would have no say at all in our future as a democratic people. Europe and America must work together on this. In the past, Europe has been much tougher than the US on enforcing antitrust laws in the tech sector.

The irony: Eric Schmidt sent evidence of his corrupting Google to rig an American election from a gmail account to another gmail account and it got hacked.

I love Google products. I also want to live in a democracy.

# Obama spent too much money on the military and not enough on the American people

The people of the United States have no significant foreign enemy. Russia, with a steadily declining defense budget about 1/10 the size of the US budget, has no ambition or reason to attack or undermine the interest of the people of America. Isis was born in the power vacuum created by American foolishness in Iraq and Syria and funded and armed by American allies, Qatar and Saudi Arabia. If not for our adventures in the Middle East, Isis would not exist and Jihadis would not put us, the people of America, as the top of their target list.

The Domino Theory was the express or official reason for the Vietnam war. As many as a million people died in that war but the Domino Theory was complete bullshit and it makes and made then zero difference to the people of the United States who controlled Vietnam.

The danger of weapons of mass destruction falling into the hands of terrorist was the stated rationale for the Iraq war, although geopolitical chess and control of oil was obviously the underlying reason. But Saddam Hussein was the enemy of the terrorist and had no WMDs. Again, another almost half million people died for nothing. We in America get nothing but hatred, dead soldiers, and poverty from these stupid wars and we would be far better off without them.

Defense One published "Obama's Trillion Dollar Nuclear Weapons Gamble" February 1, 2015. "In fact, the United States could maintain a fully capable deterrent without the unnecessary and redundant weapons or spending."

Reuters on September 15, 2016 published "U.S., Israel sign $38 billion military aid package." Meanwhile, Flint has not had clean drinking water since 2014.

WND and many other reported, "$6.5 trillion missing from defense department" on August 8, 2016, concluding "The fact the Pentagon can't account for how it spent money reveals a potentially far greater problem than theft"

From 2009 to 2015 Obama signed budgets with defense spending averaging just under 700 billion per year (2009: 693; 2010: 721; 2011: 717; 2012: 681; 2013: 610; 2014: 614; 2015: 637) for a grand total of about 5.3 trillion.

The Pew Research center said on July 14, 2015, "Overall, 20% of children in the U.S., or 14.7 million, lived in poverty in 2013 – down from 22%, or 16.3 million, in 2010. (Poverty in 2013 was defined as living in a household with an annual income below $23,624 for a family of four with two related children.) During this period, the poverty rate declined for Hispanic, white and Asian children. Among black children, however, the rate held steady at about 38%. Black children were almost four times as likely as white or Asian children to be living in poverty in 2013, and significantly more likely than Hispanic children."

Columbia University's Mailman School of Public Health published on February 8, 2017, "America's youngest children most likely to live in poor economic conditions. Report highlights severity of economic instability and disparity in the US: Out of all age groups, children are still most likely to live in poverty, according to new research from the National Center for Children in Poverty (NCCP) at Columbia University's Mailman School of Public Health. Using the latest available data from the American Community

Survey, NCCP researchers found that in 2015, while 30 percent of adults have low incomes, more than 40 percent of all children live in low-income families -- including 5.2 million infants and toddlers under 3. Despite significant gains in household income and reductions in the overall poverty rate in recent years, 43 percent (30.6 million) of America's children are living in families barely able to afford their most basic needs, according to Basic Facts about Low-Income Children, the center's annual series of profiles on child poverty in America."

Obama, you did this. You played footsy with the military industrial complex and the big banks and did nothing for the people. Feel safer yet? I don't. Can we please stop this?

## Obamacare is a failure

Hilllarycare failed. Hillary Clinton was secretive and ineffective and failed to get any meaningful, widespread reforms accomplished when tasked with reforming health care under Bill Clinton. Strike one. Now here comes Obama.

Brent Budowsky, later famous as the voice of reason in the Podesta Wikileaks, wrote "Does Obama have a secret deal with insurance companies?" in the Hill on September 30, 2009. On May 16, 2016, the CIA funded mouthpiece, the Washington Post, ran a story, "Poll: Most Americans want to replace Obamacare with single-payer — including many Republicans."

As the Budowsky shows, Obama, knowing the power of the insurance lobby, decided to cut a deal with the companies, whose stock prices rose under Obama. Rather than give the people a program that would work, cut costs, and be popular, as the poll reported in the Washington Post, Obama sided with the insider against the people.

Mitt Romney believes Obamacare was based on his program in Massachusetts (see "Romney: Without Romneycare, no Obamacare" October 23, 2015, Politico). The Commonwealth of Massachusetts passed a health care reform law in 2006 with the aim of providing health insurance to nearly all of its residents. The Patient Protection and Affordable Care Act (PPACA), commonly called the Affordable Care Act (ACA) and nicknamed Obamacare, is a United States federal statute enacted by President Barack Obama on March 23, 2010 about four years after the Massachusetts initiative.

Romneycare was less than five years old when Obama used it as his model for Obamacare. Obamacare was poorly designed based on an untried model from a small, unrepresentative, American state instead of looking at models that covered tens of millions for decades.

Germany has the world's oldest national social health insurance system, with origins dating back to Otto von Bismarck's Sickness Insurance Law of 1883. In Britain, the National Insurance Act 1911 included national social health insurance for primary care (not specialist or hospital care), initially for about one third of the population—employed working class wage earners, but not their dependents. This system of health insurance continued in force until the creation of the National Health Service in 1948 which created a universal service, funded out of general taxation rather than on an insurance basis, and providing health services to all legal residents.

Medicare is a term that refers to Canada's publicly funded health care system. Instead of having a single national plan, we have 13 provincial and territorial health care insurance plans. Under this system, all Canadian residents have reasonable access to medically necessary hospital and physician services without paying out-of-pocket. Canada current system dates to 1975.

In 2015 and 2016, my wife and I had Obamacare. We paid almost, later almost 800 a month to get insurance with a $2400 annual per person deductible. That means we'd have to spend $10,000 a year before the coverage kicked in. It's not reasonable and we opted out.

When the push for Obamacare happened back 2009, I remember Anthony Weiner of all people pushing the Medicare for all option. He made sense and this was long before his, er, picture twitters. I thought Medicare for all was simpler and certainly better, but then I assumed Obama was smarter than me and he understood the politics and had access to a whole bevy of health economists to plan his strategy, so Obama's plan, which I didn't really understand, must be kind of better, some kind of improvement, the best we can get. I was a Democrat and trusted by Democratic leaders to do something that worked, if not my first choice of what to do.

The law was upheld by the supreme court in 2012, which seemed like a good thing to me at the time, and went into effect in 2014. My kids had good health insurance the whole time through New York State, Child Health Plus. We adults had to scramble and figure out things with employers and employees and it was never good and always changing—filling out new forms every few months, starting over, paying through the nose, not having insurance for awhile. It just sucked.

Obama rolled out the program and the website crashed and stayed crashed for 6 months. That was embarrassing but I figured that was just the tech part of the program and that when the insurance kicked in, Obama's superior management style would assure that this program worked, like Social Security and Medicare work, I mean you can count on them.

I signed up for the cheapest policy, which wasn't cheap. Steady increases. I kind of skimmed the policy but there were only about five options from which to chose and none of them were great. We're both healthy, so the cheapest policy seemed like the best move.

Then I went dancing in December 2015 and screwed up my knee. It was the first time I needed any medical care (other than a tooth I had to pay for out of pocket) in probably 25 years. I went to urgent care—and only then did I realize that the 7000 dollars I was paying covered NOT ONE PENNY of the cost of seeing a doctor. I had a $2400 annual deductible.

I know people with pre-existing conditions like Obamacare. But those people are much more likely to use health care beyond what they pay in premiums. Insurance is about sharing risk. If the people with low risk at this time feel like they are getting screwed and leave the pool of people, then your insurance structure will fail, as there will be too much risk and not enough people to share it with. Also rich freelancers like Obamacare. $10,000 a year to avoid the risk of high bills seems like a good deal to them. But those with pre-existing conditions and rich freelancers is not a big enough pool to make the system work.

I want out of Obamacare personally. I want the Republicans to repeal it nationally. Obama made a serious political mistake: if 90% of the people who have personal experience with the program with your name on it (unofficially) that is your legacy and it doesn't work for them, they will blame you. It's nice to take care of the 10% who really need Obamacare, but politically it doesn't make a lot of sense. He watered down the plan to appeal to Republicans, modeling his program after Mitt Romney's plan in Massachusetts. But none of them did support his plan.

So you pissed off the electorate, or at least a big chunk of the electorate, in the name of bipartisanship which didn't happen, and worst of all, your program is not working. If you pass a big national program that affects a lot of people, it had better work.

Germany, the UK, Canada, Australia: there are a lot of models Obama could have considered. Some of these places are quite large with millions of residents and have had national health care for 60 years or more. Instead, he picked a ten-year-old program from tiny Massachusetts as his model.

How can you roll out a program this big and have it collapse? You can't blame the Republicans. Obama is supposed to be smart. maybe the problem is that you can "smart" you're way out of being screwed over by insurance companies, drug companies and a select group of specialists in medicine. You have to make them stand down and fight them and put in a plan that is proven to work, regardless of how the shareholders of CIGNA feel. Tough for them.

In 2009, Democrats had control of the House and Senate at the national level. The New York Times ran a story headlined "Reid's Big Gamble (or Is It?)" on October 27, 2009 claiming that the Democrats had no intention of passing a public option for health care, although they all claimed to be for such a policy. Phrases like "… NOT 60 Democratic votes to pass…" and "no filibuster proof majority…" peppered news reports. The reason the Democrats did not push through an aggressive progressive program with single-payer healthcare, higher minimum wage, trade deals that favor workers, reduce college costs, and redistribute the wealth was they did not have enough votes, not that they didn't want to do all that stuff, they tell us.

Obama blew his biggest domestic policy initiative by being

to political, trying to work around and with special interests and Republicans from the beginning instead of risking it all on something that might actually make millions of people's lives better and guarantee Democratic victories in the future by making it clear that the Democrats are for the people, not the special interests. That is far from clear.

## Under Obama, America made no progress on meaningful indicators of racial equality

Remember "too big to fail"? When banks were in trouble, the country stopped in its tracks and helped them out. What would happen if the banks failed? All hell would break out.

Meanwhile, Black household's are earning less as compared to White households in 2016 than in 1979. The average White household has more than 10 times the net worth of the average Black household. A crisis? Hardly. That's just the way it is, kind of like the weather. Eight years with a Black president: how is it that a handfull of rich White bankers matter so much more to the Obama administration?

Politifact, which, if that organization has any demonstrable bias, tended to be pro-Clinton, says that it is mostly true that Hillary called all black youth super predators. Mark Penn, 2008 campaign manager for Hillary, questioned Obama's "American" credentials. Factcheck.org thinks she did use a "he's a foreigner" strategy in 2008. She then insinuated that Obama was less than a real American in 2008, as also reported on PoliticalTicker from February 25, 2008.

There have been rumors Hillary spread the story that lead to the myth that Obama was not born in America; see the

Telegraph on April 27, 2011: "Birther row began with Hillary Clinton supporters." Obama believes Sid Bloomenthal started the birther rumors, according to a Politico article which Politico subsequently scrubbed from their website (/hillary clinton sidney blumenthal emails benghazi hearings 215083). Hillary was allowed to pick her own staff at the State Department, except for Bloomenthal.

Democrats have done so badly, that they can plausibly tell minorities, "vote for us or go back to the days of Jim Crow." A more uninspirational vision for America is hard to imagine. They also tell us that they have so 46 White Democrats and only one Black senator because the White voters won't vote for Black candidates. Right. The same White voters who elected Obama.

Shaun King wrote on November 30, 3016:

> "Democrats in the Senate use demographics as their excuse for the fact that they only have one African-American member in their ranks. They'll tell anyone who listens that they wish this wasn't the case and to the untrained ear, it sounds true. It isn't. The Senate looks just the way want it," the staffer told me. I must admit that I had also bought the lie — hook, line, and sinker — that only two current U.S. Senators out of 100, Cory Booker, a Democrat, and Tim Scott, a Republican, were black because state by state demographics just made it too hard for African-Americans to win statewide elections.

> "No, that's not it. Of course demographics are a factor in every election, but the Senate looks the way Senators want it to look. Let me prove it to you."

> "Do you know how many black Chiefs of Staff exist in the Senate? The whole Senate? One. Out of one hundred

*chances they had to hire a black chiefs of staff, they hired just one African-American," the staffer said in disgust.*

*"But hold up, hold up," the staffer continued. "I haven't even given you the punchline yet. Guess who the one black Chief of Staff works for?"*

*"Who?" I asked — having no idea what the answer was.*

*"Tim Scott," the staffer replied. "The lone black chief of staff in the entire United States Senate works for South Carolina Republican, Tim Scott. His office may be the most diverse in the entire Senate."*

King's phrase "soft racism" is right on.

On September 20, 2016, the day Black man, Terence Crutcher, was killed by the police because his car broke down, the Guardian reported on a study showing that the gap between Black and White Americans increased from 1979 to 2015. Here is one line from the article: "The median household income for white Americans in 2015 was $63,000. That's 70% more than the median household income of black Americans, which was $36,898." And this stat is worse than it was in 1979.

School segregation, housing discrimination, wage, representation in congress and wealth gap: where is the progress? In a 1955 speech by Martin Luther King during the bus boycott, keeping everyone together and focused, he said:

*And as we stand and sit here this evening and as we prepare ourselves for what lies ahead, let us go out with the grim and bold determination that we are going to stick together. We are going to work together. Right here in*

*Montgomery, when the history books are written in the future, somebody will have to say, "There lived a race of people, a black people, 'fleecy locks and black complexion', a people who had the moral courage to stand up for their rights. And thereby they injected a new meaning into the veins of history and of civilization." And we're going to do that. God grant that we will do it before it is too late. As we proceed with our program, let us think of these things.*

The history books have been written and they do say exactly what King predicted they would say, "new meaning" and "moral courage," all of that.

Legal discrimination in law is still around. Why do local school district boundaries matter more than access to a decent education for all citizens? School districts are laws, just as Jim Crow separation was law. The government could change what school district means and end segregation. But most people are white and most white people don't want to do it. That's all that's holding that problem up.Trump is the racism that you can see that has been around a long time.

Of course there is the racism that is harder to see, type B, or as Shaun King says "soft" racism. Letter from a Birmingham Jail in 1963 is one of America's great documents. In it, MLK said:

*I have almost reached the regrettable conclusion that the Negro's great stumbling block in his stride toward freedom is not the White Citizen's Counciler or the Ku Klux Klanner, but the white moderate, who is more devoted to "order" than to justice; who prefers a negative peace which is the absence of tension to a positive peace which is the presence of justice; who constantly says: "I agree with you in the goal you seek, but I cannot agree with your methods of direct action"; who paternalistically believes he can set the timetable for another man's freedom; who lives by a mythical concept of time and who constantly advises the Negro to wait for a "more convenient season." Shallow understanding from people of goodwill is more frustrating than absolute misunderstanding from people of ill will. Lukewarm acceptance is much more bewildering than outright rejection.*

He called it again. Exactly. Negative peace. I gave racism A to Trump and I'm giving racism B, "lukewarm acceptance is much more bewildering than outright rejection" to the Democratic National Committee. Right in their laps with this leaked memo. Released with the DNC leaks in July 2016, the memo is titled "Memorandum to DNCC Staff" dated November 19, 2015 from Troy Perry.

In the memo, DNC staff are to "meet with Black Lives Matter activists… invited BLM activists should be limited" and "listen to their concerns" but should never "offer support for concrete proposals." Campaigns should have a designated point person to meet with and finesse BLM activists.

# Hillary Clinton broke laws by using and lying about the use of her private email server

In a New York Times article from April 22, 2017— "Comey Tried to Shield the F.B.I. From Politics. Then He Shaped an Election."— we read that Russia agents had emails from Hillary Clinton that are still not released to the public. For this, she definitely should serve at least ten years in jail.

On June 17, 2011, Clinton encouraged aide Jake Sullivan to remove the identifying heading "classified" from a secure fax and "send nonsecure." She became impatient as she waited for "talking points" about a sensitive matter. Sullivan emails her, "They say they've had issues sending secure fax. They're working on it." Then Clinton emailed him, "If they can't, turn into nonpaper w no identifying heading and send nonsecure." (US Department of State, January 7, 2016)

Hillary Clinton received a top secret email on July 3, 2009 through an insecure server from Shelby Smith-Wilson about North Korea. Sid Blumenthal sent an email to Clinton that apparently names a secret US intelligence official on August 28, 2009 and only redacted versions of this correspondence are available publicly, presumably because the contents remain classified. On October 3, 2009, Clinton wrote an email to former senator George J. Mitchell (D), US Special Envoy for Middle East Peace at the time, subject heading is "Phone call report." The opening word "George-" was later unredacted while the rest of about seven or eight lines of text written by Clinton was redacted, due to containing "foreign government information" and "foreign relations or foreign activities of the United States, including confidential sources." (US Department of State, October 30, 2015) On November 10, 2009, Clinton emailed Sid Blumenthal, "Berlin was terrific. Lots of good exchanges [with] leaders." Then the next four and a half lines of Clinton's reply are completely redacted in the version that will be made public in 2015. (US Department of State, June 30, 2015) On November 21, 2009, Clinton and Matthew Gould, who is an aide to David Miliband, Britain's secretary of state, exchanged classified information on an insecure server. Blumenthal June 8, 2011: another classified email. June 9, 2011: from Clinton to Blumenthal. Although Blumenthal is a private citizen, he marked the top of the email "CONFIDENTIAL" and mentioned getting intelligence from a "particularly sensitive source" in Sudan who is speaking in "strict confidence." There are many more examples at Thompson Timeline. If any one of these emails were classified, Clinton would be guilty of violating government secrecy laws.

From May 21, 2010 to October 21, 2010, computer records suggest Clinton's private server could be located at the Clinton Foundation's headquarters. The result of an IP location look up of where Clinton's private server was in mid-2010 appears to indicate the middle of Manhattan, New York. (Credit: IP Finder / Google Maps)

According to publicly available computer records, the IP [Internet Protocol] address for the mail.presidentclinton.com server is 24.187.234.187 from at least 2009 to 2011. Records also show that mail.clintonemail.com server has the same exact IP address, 24.187.234.187, from at least May 21, 2010 to October 21, 2010. That means the two servers must have been in the same location for that overlapping time period.

Computer records can also indicate where the IP addresses are physically located, and that IP address at that time is somewhere in the middle of Manhattan, New York City. That makes sense for presidentclinton.com, since former President Bill Clinton's offices are there, and the Clinton Foundation headquarters is also there. But that would suggest that Hillary Clinton's clintonemail.com server used for all her secretary of state work is also based in Manhattan and not Chappaqua, New York, for at least part of 2010. (DNS History, 9/7/2015) (DNS History, 9/7/2015) (IP Tracker, 9/3/2015)

The US Code of federal regulations on handling electronic

records "allow employees to send and receive official electronic mail messages using a system not operated by the agency must ensure that Federal records sent or received on such systems are preserved in the appropriate agency recordkeeping system." (The Washington Post, March 10, 2015)

In 2015, Jason Baron, former director of litigation at the National Archives and Records Administration (NARA), commented that, "the use of a private [email] account was to be rare and occasional, and not to be the norm." Using a private account "without using an official account is inconsistent with the Federal Records Act." He added, "To solely use a personal e-mail for four years [as Clinton did] is something that is highly unusual." (Bloomberg News, March 3, 2015)

Clinton lied under oath about the date she started using her home brew server. January 28, 2009: Clinton exchanged 19 emails with Army General David Petraeus, chief of the US Central Command at the time. In August 2015, in a sworn deposition to a federal court, Clinton claimed: "I, Hillary Rodham Clinton, declare under penalty of perjury that the following is true and correct: While I do not know what information may be 'responsive' for purposes of this lawsuit, I have directed that all my emails on clintonemail. com in my custody that were or potentially were federal records be provided to the Department of State, and on information and belief, this has been done." (Judicial Watch, August 10, 2015). The 19 emails between Clinton and Petraeus from January 2009 were discovered by the Defense Department in September 2015, one month after Clinton's sworn deposition. Presumably, they come from Petraeus' email account. (Reuters, September 26, 2016)

Clinton began sending emails using the server by January 28, 2009, but will later claim she didn't start using it until March 18,

2009—a two-month gap similar to the two-month gap the server apparently wasn't properly protected. Apparently, she has not given investigators any of her emails from before March 18. (The New York Times, September 25, 2015)

Newsweek reported on May 25, 2016 that Clinton's sloppy security habits may have compromised anti-terrorism efforts. Bill Johnson, who was the State Department's political adviser to the special operations section of the U.S. Pacific Command, or PACOM, in 2010 and 2011, says secret plans to eliminate the leader of a Filipino Islamist separatist group and intercept Chinese-made weapons components being smuggled into Iraq were repeatedly foiled. Johnson says he and his team eliminated the possibility of other security leaks before settling on the unprotected telephone calls of the secretary of state and her aides as the likely source—though he quickly adds they have "no proof." Johnson, who voted for Barack Obama in 2008 and now supports Senator Bernie Sanders, says he had previously witnessed the lax communications habits of Clinton and her aides.

In January 2010, Clinton was in Honolulu to give a speech on the administration's "pivot" to Asia when news of the Haiti earthquake broke. She retreated to the secure communications facility in the basement of Pacific Command headquarters to make calls to various military officials and humanitarian groups to help organize a response to the catastrophe. But she also "needed to talk to her senior staff on Mahogany Row," her seventh-floor executive suite back in Washington, Johnson recalls. All of which disturbs Bill Johnson, now retired in Florida after nearly 40 years of military and State Department service.

Johnson's story jibes with what is known about Clinton's Blackberry use. Clinton's office in State Department headquarters is a SCIF, which means a secure room, and she's not allowed to bring her BlackBerry into it. Also, Clinton is unwilling to use a computer to check her emails. But around this time, security officials create a space where she can check her BlackBerry. In 2016, a State Department official will explain, "There is an area dedicated to supporting the secretary outside but in the immediate vicinity of the secretary's secure office. Secretary Clinton, as with anyone, could use such non-SCIF spaces to check personal devices." Apparently, Clinton will use this arrangement for her entire four years as secretary of state. (Fox News, March 16, 2016)

Although top State Department officials are aware of NSA warning that her devices could be hacked, she takes her BlackBerry on her future overseas trips despite it still not being inspected and secured by department officials. (The Washington Post, March 27, 2016)

According to a June 2016 Wall Street Journal article, there are a series of Clinton emails in these two years regarding the US drone program in Pakistan. Starting roughly around June 2011, the State Department is given the right to approve or disapprove of the CIA's drone strikes in Pakistan as part of the US government's attempt to mollify Pakistan's concerns so they will continue their secret support of the program.

However, this creates a communication problem, because advanced warning of strikes varies from several days to as little as half an hour. According to the Journal, "Under strict US classification rules, US officials have been barred from discussing strikes publicly and even privately outside of secure communications systems."

Bryan Pagliano performs "technology services for the Clinton family for which he [is] compensated" by check or wire transfer in varying amounts at various times between 2009 and 2013. Most importantly, he manages her private email server as an outside job, including doing so during his hours for the State Department. However, exactly how much he gets paid is unknown. Other details such as who he directly reports to, who directly pays him, and how many hours a week he works on the task also remain unknown. It appears that Justin Cooper, an assistant to Bill Clinton who does not work in government, sometimes helps manage the server as well. But Cooper's role is even more unclear. (US Department of State, May 25, 2016)

CONCLUSION: Hillary was reckless in her criminal disregard for rules pertaining to classified information should have been prosecuted.

## Conclusion of the rap sheet

We have now proven that the Democratic party does for donors, not people, acknowledges privately they work for oligarchs and only oligarchs, does not believe in democratic elections, is run for and by rich White people for rich White people with very occasional token minorities in public positions, or not, has a massive propaganda arm in the mainstream media, failed in foreign and domestic party and in free fall in terms of winning elections, never mind passing meaningful elections. Also, they are guilty of crimes, killing innocent people, stealing money and rigging elections.

Richard Rorty's 1998 *Achieving Our Country* is going around the internet for its apparent prediction of something like Trump 18 years ago. He also predicted Obama's rhetorical optimism with Bernie Sanders's economic populism as a winning combination for the left. James Baldwin, novelist and activist, said the goal of the left should be and always is, "Achieving our Country." Sounds like FDR and Martin Luther King.

One day, it will be an accepted fact by almost everyone that the Democratic party circa 2016 was a criminal organization, that Barack Obama was a bad president, broke international and domestic law on war, ruined Africa, did nothing for Black America, sold out to CitiBank, and that Bernie Sanders would have beaten Donald Trump, that Bernie was the legitimate winner of the 2016 Democratic primary if not for Obama being a wet blanket and a failed leader with no vision, surrounded by sycophants in a bubble of memos ("let's play legalistic fun smartiepants with state murder!") and delusions ("focus group Republican women!"), and handed the imperial presidency to Trump because Obama is an arrogant fool. Why not get ahead of the curve, dear reader, and accept the truth now that I have presented it to you as clearly as I can?

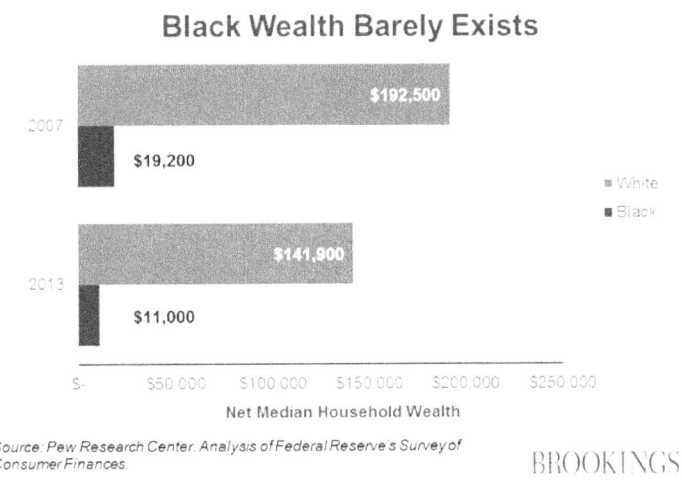

## Black Wealth Barely Exists

2007: White $192,500 / Black $19,200

2013: White $141,900 / Black $11,000

Net Median Household Wealth

Source: Pew Research Center. Analysis of Federal Reserve's Survey of Consumer Finances.

BROOKINGS

## The DNC spent vast sums from 2009 through 2016, a time of historic losses for the party

In a February 28, 2017 interview on The Real News ("Nina Turner: DNC Chooses Not to Be the Party of Everyday People"), Former Ohio State Senator Turner pointed out that "there are members on the DNC, voting members on the DNC, who are lobbyists. Someone who works actually works for Goldman Sachs, is a voting member on the DNC."

Nomiki Konst, writing for The Young Turks on Medium in the article "Are Multi-Million Dollar Consulting Contracts Worth the Future of the Democratic Party?" added:

"The Democrats have raised more money than ever and lost more seats than ever (1,000+ seats nationwide since 2009)... Former Chair Candidate, NH State Chairman Ray Buckley broke the news during the Phoenix DNC forum that as an executive member he had never seen the budget—and that most leaders at the DNC, as well as all of the members, had no idea where the record amount of money raised was being spent... Several DNC members have privately disclosed that they received calls on behalf of Tom Perez from Jennifer O'Malley Dillon, a partner of Precision Strategies.... They had an elaborate convention, beautifully crafted marketing, what was praised as the most sophisticated data operation to date and teams of veteran campaign strategists working in what was supposed to be the easiest Presidential race in recent history. But around 9:45pm ET on Nov 8, it was clear that the house of cards was on the verge of collapse. And that by the next day, the DNC would have to not just answer how they lost the Presidency and so many other races, but: Where did all that money go?"

Jennifer O'Malley Dillon is a typical insider, Democratic villain. Dillon—whose firm received almost $1.2 million in 2016—had a seat as a co-chair of the DNC's rules committee. If you have a consultant getting paid by the DNC also voting on the rules as to how consultants get paid, well, that's a crappy organization that is likely to screw up and leave Trump as president, is it not? A DNC member stated, "When a firm with a large contract with the DNC co-chairs the new rules committee and makes calls on behalf of a DNC candidate, you can't help but wonder whether Perez's interests lie with the DNC members or if he's cut a deal to keep the contract with Precision."

Today, it is openly acknowledged by many members that the DNC and the Clinton campaign were running an operation together. One firm, GMMB earned $236.3 million from HRC campaign and $5.3 from the DNC in 2016. Joel Benenson, a pollster and strategist who frequents cable news, collected $4.1m from Hillary for America while simultaneously earning $3.3 million from the DNC. Perkins Coie law firm collected $3.8 million from the DNC, $481,979 from the Convention fund and $1.8 million from HFA in 2016.

A simple glimpse of FEC filings, former Chair, Debbie Wasserman Schultz and some of her senior staffers remained on payroll with the DNC until December, well past she resigned on July 25, 2016.

What does this all mean? The DNC, which lacks an open budget, has been allocating dozens multi-million dollar contracts without accountability from its members and leadership. The money, of course, did not go into state parties and organizing, and the majority of members I've interviewed expresses resentment and frustration.

Under Obama, the DNC raised more money than any political organization in history and lost 1034 seats, leaving the party weaker than at any time since 1920.

**OBAMA FAILED AS PARTY BOSS.**

Wikileaks published emails from Lynn Rothschild, George Soros, and Eric Schmidt in the 2016 DNC and Podesta publications. Read their memos and correspondence.

**THE DEMOCRATIC PARTY IS NOT FOR WORKING FAMILIES.**

Hillary Clinton said she had public and private positions at a paid speech at Goldman Sachs.

**MOTTO OF THE DEMOCRATIC PARTY: "PUBLIC AND PRIVATE POSITIONS."**

More inequality than at any time in American history. War without end. Criminal injustice system. Fake elections. Propaganda media.

**TRUMP IS THE CANCER. WE'VE BEEN SMOKING THIS SYSTEM FOR TOO LONG.**

**BUTCHER, FAKER, HE'S THE BANKER'S MAN.**

The New York Times' Amy Chozik is the Judith Miller of 2016. MSNBC intentionally gave Trump free airtime on the request of Hillary's campaign. CNN rigged the debates against Bernie.

**TWO PEOPLE ARGUING ON TV DOESN'T MEAN IT'S NOT PROPAGANDA.**

Clinton/Obama created Isis, destabilized Africa and made war crimes routine.

# On Issues

This book began with an introduction. We then went through the rap sheet of Democratic crimes (barely mentioning the homebrew server ("your damn emails!") and Benghazi, leaving those to the Republicans to mess up). Now we will run through a series of specific issues and controversies with my thoughts, for what they're worth.

## On Bernie or Bust

Some say, going back to 2000, that the left behind Ralph Nader gave Bush the margin he needed to win. The Nader 2000 argument is nicely debunked in Truthdig "Don't Fall for It: The Nader Myth and Your 2016 Vote" (August 2, 2016) by Kevin Zeese and Margaret Flowers. But more to the point: Al Gore supported the invasion of Iraq. Would it have even mattered much if Gore had been president on 9/11? They both call shots from the same oligarch-imperialist playbook.

Now 2016. When I first encountered the idea of "Bernie or Bust" in a pro-Bernie Facebook group I did not take the sentiment behind it too seriously or maybe I just could not bring myself to take the phrase as something I would let come out of my own mouth. Where I encountered the term, mixed in a feed with cats in wine glasses and classified ads selling pygmy goats, influenced how I understood the sentiment or movement. You don't expect to find something with some political significance that might be a bit of history buried in your distracting, mind-numbing feed.

People post a lot of nonsense in Facebook groups, from silly memes to extreme sentiments that you probably should not take too literally. I have found many valuable links, ideas and phrases in Facebook groups and Reddit subreddits but the idea that something I might find in one of these places might actually have some long term historic interest, or be a real movement, did not really seem possible. I liked the sentiment, but I didn't think it was a big deal. I'm down with Bernie or Bust, that's me, but no, it's not a real "movement." Just some people mouthing off on Facebook.

Now that Trump is president, I think it's time to take the "movement" or vibe or idea or whatever it is behind "Bernie or Bust" a little more seriously. Maybe you do find something important improbably mixed into your Facebook feed.

On or about July 25, 2016, Bernie or Bust ballooned and the dividing lines on the left, or in the Democratic party, hardened and they remain hardened. The Intercept published, "Tim Kaine, Possible Hillary Clinton Pick for Vice President, Goes to Bat for Banks" on July 20. Disunity on the left continues now into 2017. There has been a dramatic failure of leadership in the Democratic party that millions of Blue Dogs pretend not to see. Woe! Upon! The! Nations! Nothing has changed from July 25, 2016.

Rachel Maddow, millionaire talking head for a biased pro-Hillary corporation implicated in fake news by Wikileaks, famously tweeted that "In Florida, if Jill Stein's voters and half of Gary Johnson's voters had voted for Hillary, Trump would have lost the state." She noted the same dynamic in Pennsylvania, with half of Gary Johnson's voters jumping to Hillary. In Michigan and Wisconsin, only Jill Stein's voters and not Gary Johnson's voters would have been necessary to flip the states to Hillary.

Maddow's attempt to blame Hillary's loss in 2016 on the Green party is quite silly. As the independent video series Let the Madness Begin said in a video, "Who were the other half of Gary Johnson's voters supposed to vote for if there were no third parties?

Obviously, Trump." It is quite a stretch to think Libertarians would vote for Hillary, or any Democrat. The catch phrase for Libertarians is that they are "Republicans with a joint." The Libertarian candidates have in fact been former Republican office holders: Bob Barr in 2008, Gary Johnson in 2016 and 2012.

Green Party voters could only have conceivably made the difference in Wisconsin and Michigan, but if Clinton had won those two states she still would have lost the election to Trump. But Hillary lost the electoral college 232 to 306 and needed three of the swing states to flip to win. Ohio and Florida were not all that close. Pennsylvania would be the most likely candidate for a third state, along with Michigan and Wisconsin.

Those three, Pennsylvania, Michigan and Wisconsin, had all been in the Democratic column for the previous four elections. Politico ran an article on December 14, 2016, "How Clinton lost Michigan — and blew the election. Across battlegrounds, Democrats blame HQ's stubborn commitment to a one-size-fits-all strategy." Union leaders across the midwest could not get Hillary's campaign to put resources where they were needed. On December 20, 2016, The Daily Beast ran a story called, "Team Bernie: Hillary 'F*cking Ignored' Us in Swing States. Hindsight is 20/20, but members of Bernie Sanders's team in critical swing states say they knew Hillary Clinton was going to lose well before Election Day— and their warnings were ignored." In this article, Bernie Sanders supporters in Wisconsin and Michigan found the same arrogance and cluelessness in the HRC campaign the union people found in the Politico story. Bernie Sanders himself spent the last week of the campaign in Michigan, whereas Hillary never visited Wisconsin even once during the general election campaign (see "Bernie Sanders calls on Kalamazoo supporters to vote for Hillary Clinton" mLive November 2, 2016).

"It was after 9 p.m. when Hillary Clinton stepped off her campaign plane into the pouring rain in Westchester. She had just finished a packed Thursday in North Carolina — a stadium-sized rally with Michelle Obama, a stop by a voting site in Greensboro, and a brief speech at a historically black college. And in just 12 hours, she would find herself heading back to this same airport to fly to Iowa. But instead of staying out on the road in one of those critical battleground states, she'd chosen to return here, to this tony enclave about an hour north of New York City" reported Politico on November 1, 2016. Many people in the campaign were quite horrified with the wasted time and expense of Hillary insisting on returning home most nights.

The relentless blaming of progressives for Trump's victory, blaming those of us who are determined to see government work for the 99%, is not only counterproductive, it's also not true. After turning the Democratic party into her private mafia, ignoring working families for her entire career, making money from banks and countries providing US arms to terrorists such as Qatar and Saudi Arabia, cheating through the primary, after helping Trump with the Pied Piper strategy, then failing to address the exposure of the cheating as a crisis on July 25, then ignoring pleas from people on the ground screaming about the dangers in Pennsylvania, Michigan and Wisconsin, Hillary Clinton thought that sleeping in a fancy hotel was too much of a burden and flew back to New York every night. But somehow, it's my fault she lost because I voted for Jill Stein in New York.

While turnout was not exceptional in 2016, who turned out mattered. Trump does seem to have energized his base better than Clinton. CNN reported on November 9, 2016, "Exit polls: Clinton fails to energize African-Americans, Latinos and the young." Key points, "Only 65% of Latinos supported her, while 29% cast their votes for Trump. In 2012, Obama won 71% of the Hispanic vote, while Romney secured 27%. Clinton also failed to capture as many young voters, who flocked to her rival Bernie Sanders in the primary and to Obama four years ago."

On November 11, the Washington Post reported, "Trump got more votes from people of color than Romney did. Here's the data." Twelve percent of Black men, or about one in eight, seemed to have been willing to admit to pollsters that they voted for Trump. At least two out five Hispanic men voted for Trump.

With Obama leaving office, the leadership of the Democratic party is almost entirely White and from the East and West coasts. The senate Republicans are more diverse than the Democrats in the senate both in terms of elected officials and top staffers.

Turnout was part of the story in 2016, as it always is, and Trump did better with turnout than Clinton although she spent three times as much money as he did, but Trump did not mobilize a massive number of first time or infrequent voters. Note the chart below of the turnout of registered voters in the six key battleground states. Only Ohio had higher turnout in 2016 than either 2008 and/ or 2012.

| State | 2016 | 2012 | 2008 |
|-------|------|------|------|
| Pennsylvania | 70.7% | 76.6% | 68.7% |
| Michigan | 64.2% | 63.7% | 67.1% |
| Wisconsin | 69.6% | 70.0% | 70.8% |
| Florida | 74.5% | 71.2% | 74.8% |
| Ohio | 70.4% | 70.0% | 69.0% |

If you look at the charts of the swing states below, at the end of this chapter, you will see that the Libertarians experienced a 300% to 400% increase from previous years, including an increase from 2012 when the same candidate was running, Gary Johnson. Also, write-ins jumped by about 200-300%, as did votes for the Green party, but these two categories remained less than half of the Libertarian vote. If anything, the impact of third party voters and write-ins was to make the election more in reach for Hillary.

About 250,000 people voted for third parties or wrote-in a candidate in Ohio in 2016. These people knew they lived in a swing state. They were inundated with advertising. They knew that either Trump or Clinton were most likely to win. And yet, they didn't fall in line with either of them. It's not a trivial amount of people: about the total population of Toledo Ohio, the state's fourth largest city. You got to see that people are pretty alienated.

I think we should register their protest. I heard you, even if the New York Times and the Democrats and Republicans might want to pretend you 250,000 people don't exist.

Why would so many more people vote Libertarian in 2016 when they had the same standard bearer, Johnson, available in 2012? Obviously the driving force was dissatisfaction with Trump. A non-insane Republican would have captured most of those Libertarian votes. What the increase in Johnson's total shows is that the Pied Piper strategy worked and a mainline Republican would have wiped the floor with a weak Democratic candidate, Hillary Clinton. Bernie Sanders would likely have appealed to many of these anti-establishment libertarians, increasing yet more his already wide margin of victory in a hypothetical match up with Trump, as we see in every single Trump versus Bernie poll from April through October 2016.

In the state-by-state charts below, also note that Pat Buchanan ran in 2000, with a political bent quite like Trump's and not particularly similar to Barr or Johnson of the libertarian party. I have included Buchanan totals in brackets in the column with write-ins. Also, in 2004 Ralph Nader ran as an independent, not on the Green Party line. Nader tended to win three times as many votes as the Green party candidate in 2004 and I have included his totals in the charts for 2004 instead of the official Green candidate to show the size of the disaffected left. Like Johnson on the Libertarian line, Jill Stein ran in 2012 as well, so the increase in Green votes is almost entirely due to disgust with the major party candidates, not any change in Jill Stein's popularity.

I included the write-ins here because online many people threatened to write in Bernie Sanders on pro-Bernie Facebook pages. Clearly, there was a dramatic increase in write-ins in 2016. When you add together the Libertarian, Green and write-in votes, all forms of dissent against the two main party choices, you see dramatic increases across the board.

Maddow was delusional to suggest Libertarian voters should have switched to Clinton, as she would have probably been most voter's third or fourth choice. Indeed, it is likely that most Green party voters would have been more likely to vote for Trump than Clinton if no third party option were available. Many people who voted for Stein hated Clinton more than Trump, although most despised both of them. Again, this was clearly the case on pro-Green party Facebook pages. For the vast majority of third party and write-in voters, staying home or voting for Trump would have been more popular choices than voting for Clinton. I read these Facebook groups regularly during the election and there is no doubt that Clinton was and is deeply hated and reviled, with the feeling of revulsion equal to or greater than any liberal disgust with Trump.

The "Bernie or Bust" contingent would consist of those who wrote in Bernie, those who stayed at home, and those who voted for Stein, as well as some fraction of people who voted for Bernie in the primary but were so mad at the Democratic party that they voted for Trump in the general election. Some 13 million voted for Bernie Sanders in the primary while 16 or 17 million registered voters were Bernie supporters (including those voters unable to vote for Bernie due to arbitrary closed primaries). Some of the most ardent supporters could not vote in the primary because they did not take the functional equivalent of a Democratic party loyalty oaths months before the primary in their particular state. Ineligible independents are from 30-40% of the voter population in New York, Pennsylvania, California, and other states. Thus, the total Bernie contingent is perhaps 16 million. Adding up all the kinds of disaffected Bernie supporters, as listed above, from write-ins to Trump voters, we would ask, how many of them did in fact refuse to vote for Clinton? Let's try to come up with an estimate.

In April 2016, FiveThirtyEight published an article called, "About A Third Of Bernie Sanders' Supporters Still Aren't Backing Hillary Clinton." But the primary wasn't over then. A minority of Gen-Y Sanders supporters plan to vote for Clinton in the fall, and nearly one-in-five will support Trump instead, according to an Economist/YouGov poll from June 2016. On October 10, 2016, Forbes wrote, "This is especially true among Bernie Sanders' supporters. Recent evidence suggests, despite Sander's efforts to garner support for his former rival, more than 55% view Clinton negatively. Although it may not matter, given Trump's spate of gaffes tainting his standing with voters, should worry Clinton." Should worry, but didn't.

Other polls showed 90% of Bernie's 13 million primary voters (not considering the 3 or 4 million disenfranchised Bernie supporters) supported Clinton, more than Clinton supporters backed Obama in 2008. On July 25, 2016 the Washington Post published "90 percent of unwavering Sanders supporters plan to vote for Clinton in November." Please note the date: at the same time as the Bernie Sanders delegates were revolting at the DNC convention, mainstream media reported this 90% figure. CNBC, Vox, etc. repeated the claim. The same Hillary Clinton supporters who said they would make up for the Bernie or Bust contingent with Republican women such as Rendell, repeated this 90% figure like it was gospel.

However, the original source was a single poll by Pew Research, results published on their website on July 25 under "On most issues, Sanders primary supporters further from GOP voters than Clinton backers." The results were published around the time of the convention in July but were based on surveys conducted in April to early June. This 90% figure was from before the DNC leaks published on Wikileaks. This early, pre-DNC leak, pre-Podesta leak, poll belongs with the meme pumped up by genius Chuck Schumer that Hillary would attract Republican women: in the garbage.

If we recall from earlier in this book, July 25 was an eventful time. Establishment Democrats latched onto the Pew Study but I suspect it was not relevant, as a dramatic event happened between the time the data was collected and when the study was used as an argument not to treat July 25 as a crisis: the DNC Wikileak release. Then came the divisive convention. If the "Bernie or Bust" contingent was one-third in April or 90% in June, what was the figure in November, when it really mattered?

Considering states with closed primaries, if you only poll the 13 million who were able to cast a ballot, you might miss an additional four or five million ardent supporters, particularly in New

York and California. About 40 to 50% percent of the delegates at the convention representing those 13 million voters walked out. It seems conservative to think that those delegates represent as many as 20% of the Bernie supporters, both primary voters and disenfranchised voters.

If we say that the convention and the DNC leaks alienated half as many voters as delegates who walked out of the Philadelphia convention, then we add in another third who were barred from voting due to closed primaries, we get the total Bernie or Bust contingent somewhere between two and five million people alienated from the Democratic party. Many of these people are among the most politically active people in the country, people who make donations, volunteer, and actively promote candidates in many forums. Of the some two to five million Bernie or Bust people, about 1.5 million voted for Stein or wrote in Bernie, some few hundred thousand stayed home or left their ballots blank, and a few hundred thousand voted for Trump. Two seems like a low estimate, but possible, and five seems quite high. You can see how I came up with the range and draw your own conclusion as to the numbers, but a range of a few million seems entirely reasonable.

Our hostility to Clinton certainly had a negative effect on turnout, but probably nowhere near as negative an effect as Clinton's Goldman Sachs speeches or any of the other problems with her candidacy. And the "Bernie or Bust" contingent is not as large as the alienated right-leaning voters who went for Gary Johnson at about three times the rate as left-leaning voters chose Jill Stein. Hillary Clinton was lucky that write-in and third party options were available, as she was the second choice for almost none of these voters, including Green voters. Trump would have won more comfortably without third party voters.

However, turning about three million progressives from enthusiastic and energetic supporters into enemies that hate you is probably not a good move. And, as far as I'm concerned, the hostility to the Democratic party is far from over. Better to let the Republican corporatists have it than let the Democratic corporatists run around calling themselves "progressives" that care about "working families."

Third party voting helped Clinton more than hurt her and a non-nuts Republican would have gotten most of the third party voting and would have beaten Clinton more solidly; if Bernie or Bust tanked her candidacy, it did so only due to a lack of enthusiasm and general hostility, not third party and write-in voting; you can as easily "blame" minorities for sinking Clinton as Bernie or Bust progressives (although obviously many progressives are also minorities and these are not mutually exclusive groups). One in eight Black men admitted to voting for Trump in exit polls, along with 40% of Hispanic men.

So, please, rank and file Democrats: you guys gave us Trump more than we few who resisted did. Clinton should have been yanked off the ticket before July 25. Obama failed to get her out of there. We told you. You stuck with a loser. You should have joined us in calling for her to go when you still could have. She was not a good candidate. She helped Trump. Wake up and smell the coffee: your leadership sucks. The Democrats gave us Trump. They put him on the ballot with the Pied Piper strategy. Then they put up the weakest possible Democratic candidate.

Ohio

| Year | Democrat | Republican | Green | Libertarian | Write-in |
|------|----------|------------|-------|-------------|----------|
| 2000 | 2,186,190 (46.46%) | 2,351,209 (49.97%) | 117,857 (2.50%) | 13,475 (.29%) | 10 (0%) [26,724] |
| 2004 | 2,739,952 (48.71%) | 2,858,727 (50.81%) | NA | NA | 142 |
| 2008 | 2,940,044 (51.38%) | 2,677,820 (46.80%) | 42,337 (0.74%) | 19,917 (0.35%) | 13,698 (0.24%) |
| 2012 | 2,827,709 (50.67%) | 2,661,437 (47.69%) | 18,573 (.33%) | 49,493 (0.89%) | 10,078 (0.18%) |
| 2016 | 2,394,164 (43.56%) | 2,841,005 (51.69%) | 46,271 (0.84%) | 174,498 (3.15%) | 40,771 (0.74%) |

Florida

| Year | Democrat | Republican | Green | Libertarian | Write-in |
|------|----------|------------|-------|-------------|----------|
| 2000 | 2,912,790 (48.84%) | 2,912,253 (48.85%) | 97,488 (1.63%) | 16,415 (0.28%) | 40 (0%) [17,484] |
| 2004 | 2,739,952 (48.71%) | 2,858,727 (50.81%) | 32,971 (0.43%) | 11,996 (0.16%) | 0 |
| 2008 | 2,940,044 (51.38%) | 2,677,820 (46.80%) | 28,128 (0.33%) | 17,220 (0.20%) | 20,801 (0.25%) |
| 2012 | 2,827,709 (50.67%) | 2,661,437 (47.69%) | 8,947 (0.11%) | 44,726 (0.53%) | 18,002 (0.21%) |
| 2016 | 4,504,975 (47.41%) | 4,617,886 (48.60%) | 64,399 (0.68%) | 207,043 (2.18%) | 81,632 (0.86%) |

Michigan

| Year | Democrat | Republican | Green | Libertarian | Write-in |
|------|----------|------------|-------|-------------|----------|
| 2000 | 2,170,418 (51.28%) | 1,953,139 (46.15%) | 84,165 (1.99%) | 16,711 (0.39%) | 2,061 (0.05%) |
| 2004 | 2,479,183 (51.23%) | 2,313,746 (47.81%) | 24,035 (0.50%) | 10,552 (0.22%) | NA |
| 2008 | 2,872,579 (57.33%) | 2,048,639 (40.89%) | 33,085 (0.66%) | 23,716 (0.47%) | 8,840 (0.18%) |
| 2012 | 2,564,569 (54.21%) | 2,115,256 (44.71%) | 21,897 (0.46%) | 7,797 (0.16%) | 14,332 (0.30%) |
| 2016 | 2,268,839 (47.27%) | 2,279,543 (47.50%) | 51,463 (1.07%) | 172,136 (3.57%) | 25,025 (0.52%) |

Pennsylvania

| Year | Democrat | Republican | Green | Libertarian | Write-in |
|------|----------|------------|-------|-------------|----------|
| 2000 | 2,485,967 (50.6%) | 2,281,127 (46.4%) | | | |
| 2004 | 2,938,095 (50.92%) | 2,793,847 (48.42%) | | | |
| 2008 | 3,276,363 (54.47%) | 2,655,885 (44.15%) | 42,977 (0.71%) | 19,912 (0.33%) | 14,291 (0.24%) |
| 2012 | 2,990,274 (51.97%) | 2,680,434 (46.59%) | 21,341 (0.37%) | 49,991 (0.87%) | 13,097 (0.23%) |
| 2016 | 2,926,441 (47.85%) | 2,970,733 (48.58%) | 49,941 (0.81%) | 146,715 (2.38%) | 47,305 (0.77%) |

Wisconsin

| Year | Democrat | Republican | Libertarian | Green | Write-in |
|------|----------|------------|-------------|-------|----------|
| 2000 | 1,242,987 (47.83%) | 1,237,279 (47.61%) | 6,640 (0.26%) | 94,070 (3.62%) | 1,896 (0.07%) |
| 2004 | 1,489,504 (49.70%) | 1,478,120 (49.32%) | 6,464 (0.22%) | 16,390 (0.55%) | 2,117 (0.07%) |
| 2008 | 1,677,211 (56.22%) | 1,262,393 (42.31%) | 8,858 (0.30%) | 17,605 (0.59%) | 6,521 (0.22%) |
| 2012 | 1,620,985 (52.83%) | 1,407,966 (45.89%) | 20,439 (0.67%) | 7,665 (0.25%) | 5,170 (0.17%) |
| 2016 | 1,382,536 (46.45%) | 1,405,284 (47.22%) | 106,674 (3.58%) | 31,072 (1.04%) | 22,812 (0.77%) |

About 130 million voted for president in the general election in November. About 70 million would have voted but aren't registered and/or won't show up on election day. This year about 45 million people voted in the presidential primary.

Getting people who don't vote is a Catch 22 situation. Many don't believe in any candidate, or that anything in politics matters. This is not surprising given that almost all politicians are pretending to do politics and almost all the debates we've had for at least 30 years have been fake shams. Neither major party is serious about giving people a hand up and the non-voters know it.

Let's say Bernie Sanders and his supporters were different. His agenda would have made the lives of many of those 70 million non-voters better quickly. Minimum wage, Medicare for all, free college, better infrastructure, break up the banks, law enforcement reform, no more war and fair trade deals: if the program was passed and signed, you'd feel the difference in a year or two and you'd know who changed the situation.

In order for Bernie to win, though, he'd need more of those people not only to show up in the general election but in the primary. It's kind of a tall order to get someone who doesn't even vote in the general election to sign up for a party 6 months before the election and figure out which party is legit, or has a single legit candidate, as you'd have to do in New York.

It would be a sea change in American politics if those 70 million showed up. But they will only show up when they see that they need to show up to get what they need.

The Democratic Party is making a monumental mistake in not insisting on Bernie's agenda at all levels and ignoring distractions that try to get the party to focus on anything other than, first and foremost, as goal one, making life better for the people. If you get the people on your side, you can then work on foreign affairs or climate change or gun control or whatever you want to do with your "political capital." First, give us health care, higher wages, education and a functioning infrastructure in the broadest sense (transport, parks, communications, etc.).

If Trump gives the people Medicare for all, he'll use the popularity and leverage to get his son-in-law elected after him or something as stupid as that. Bernie's Democratic party, if it existed, if that party gave the people what they need, would use the leverage to do something about global warming. Millions of votes are up for grabs. Whoever gives us Medicare, higher wages, and free college will have power for a generation.

People need stuff. The government can give it to them. Whoever takes the money out of the pockets of the oligarchs and gives the people stuff they need, will be a hero. It's simple. We want health care, decent infrastructure, education, and an economy that is growing down here where we live, not in the mortgage derivative, private jet, Kauai estate place where they live with inflated prices on useless stuff.

Instead of holding firm to the path and killing off the Republicans, the Democrats are meeting the Republican's white supremacy with identity politics. In the long run, that will work to a degree to get Democrats elected in big elections, but not to make any real change in policy.

The Democrats could consign the Republicans to the dustbin of history by steadfastly and consistently standing for giving the people a better life before and after elections. It is well within the power of the government to fix the main problems we face. The Democrats have decided not to try or to insist that the problems be fixed but to take corporate cash for favors and play identity politics and win that way.

The only real politics in this country is on the left. The right could make a real argument -- about freeing capital and high growth or something, a legitimate conservative politics could in theory exist somewhere -- but here in America the right is not making any coherent argument at all. The centrist corporate Democrats don't stand for anything at all either.

## On trade

While the many in-denial corporate Hillbot Democrats would paint the Trump victory as an example of white response to a Black president, blaming the voters and calling people racists, including one out of eight black men and two out of four Latinos, anti-globalism is a far bigger factor in whatever popularity Trump obtained. Both Trump and Sanders opposed the Trans Pacific Partnership, TPP and railed against NAFTA and other trade deals.

Trump appears to be an old fashioned protectionist. In February 2017, he jaw-boned Europe and Japan about buying American cars. He immediately withdrew from TPP upon taking office.

The disturbing aspect of this simplistic protectionism is that history shows that simply keeping out foreign products is extremely risky. Juan Peron's Argentina import substitution was a terrible policy that helped change Argentina from a First World, prosperous economy into a Third World country. In the crisis following the Japanese military's unauthorized actions in Manchuria in 1931, trade sanctions against Japan by the United States isolated the anti-military faction within Japan, helping to consolidate military control.

Listening to Bernie Sanders, you might think his opposition to these same trade deals is protectionist. No. As Keith Ellison in particular has made clear over the years, speaking for the progressive opposition to trade deals generally, the problem with these trade deals is not that countries trade with each other but that the deals are designed exclusively to enhance the interests of larger corporations over workers and consumers in all countries. We are not against trade because we are against workers in China or Vietnam or Mexico. Workers in America should demand that trade rules be a vehicle for raising all boats in a rising tide, not a race to the bottom requiring all workers to compete to work for less.

One of the worst parts of the now dead TPP deal was the Investor State Dispute Settlement (ISDS) provisions. Public Citizen says "formally prioritize corporate rights over the right of governments to regulate and the sovereign right of nations to govern their own affairs." As Communications Workers of America President Chris Shelton warned, ISDS provisions represent "a corporate dream but a nightmare for those of us on Main Street."

For Obama and the Clintons, free trade has nothing to do with worker's rights and the environment. For the left, we would be happy to sign trade deals that improve working conditions in China or Mexico, that bring the workers in other countries up to the standards we have here, not drive our workers down to the standards they have there.

In a working people dominated World Trade Organization, the only multilateral institutional framework for US trade with China, countries who suppress workers' rights to unionize, who do not allow for a free press to report on workplace safety, who pollute the environment, who do not have a system of unemployment insurance, retirement, and workman's compensation in place, cannot trade with other nations at the preferred rate.

Trump is an old fashioned and dangerous protectionist who, if he succeeds in building a tariff wall around America, could doom us to become a Third World country, unable to produce quality products the world wants to buy. As international trade becomes less important, individual nations and their doctrines of nationalism increase, raising the specter of international conflict.

The Ellison version of trade is different. We want world trade, but only with nations that are actively improving conditions for workers and protecting the environment. It's not about America first, it's about the workers and people of the world first.

## On the Deep State

The Deep State: The Fall of the Constitution and the Rise of a Shadow Government by Mike Lofgren defines the Deep State as a confluence of interests—military contractors, Wall Street firms, tech companies, and spy agencies—that manage to steer government policy without conspiring or having any cloak and danger meetings or secret handshakes or anything cloak and dagger. Rather, the Deep State is a system that evolved, as interest groups figured out how to work around each other's priorities to create a seamless web of corruption, incompetence and inefficiency.

Lofgren's book was published just before Podesta's emails were released on Wikileaks. Podesta seemed to be a node in the Deep State, a convergence point for oligarchs from different sectors, with direct contact with tech billionaires—Eric Schmidt, Jeff Bezos and Mark Zuckerberg—more from Wall Street—George Soros, and Lloyd Blankfein—from the media— Lynn Forester de Rothschild, Haim Saban, Maggie Haberman, John Harris, Donna Brazile, Jake Tapper, Dan Merica and a thousand others.

With these publications by Wikileaks, the idea that there is no collaboration or coordination by the Deep State should perhaps be amended. While there is no secret cabal that meets to set world government policy, there are operators such as Podesta who channel real interests through the fake election process. There is a semi-controlled process, a negotiation between sectors of the Deep State. Podesta's job was to be a point of contact between these special interests and elected officials such as Obama and the Clintons.

Originally applied to countries such as Turkey during the period when the military clearly had the power to overrule and remove elected governments when the leaders of the military disliked the decisions of elected officials, or for the former Soviet countries where a cabal of insider oligarchs clearly had more authority than the elected government, application of the term "Deep State" to the United States is entirely appropriate.

Broadly, the Deep State might be seen as all those unelected forces— from lobbyists, to generals, to the CIA, to the media, to some high ranking bureaucrats. More narrowly, the term might only apply to the spies and spooks of the CIA and NSA. The constitution authorizes various forms of official power, such as congress's power to approve the budget. However, as a thought experiment, what would happen if the congress authorized a budget with no money for the CIA? Would the employees, contractors and ex-officials of the agency simply go into quiet retirement?

The evidence of out of control spying on Americans and others without clear lines of authority— with the president as commander and chief and congress as having oversight and budgetary control— is so clear and overwhelming that to deny that the CIA and the NSA, and all the other spy agencies, pose a threat to democracy, to the extent we have any democracy left, seems to border on delusional and insane. And yet, the New Yorker published "There is no Deep State" on March 20, 2017 and as of mid-April 2017, Google rigged up its algorithm to make this the top response to searches for the term "Deep State." So, if you doubt there is a powerful Deep State, all you have to do is 1) listen to Chuck Schumer; and 2) Google the term "Deep State." The results should leave you with zero doubt that you live in a oligarchic system with widespread propaganda filling up all channels of information.

The news keeps interfering with me writing this chapter. Obviously, you can be against Trump and think he is a danger to Democracy and also be against the Deep State flexing its muscles and doing in an elected leader. I say "obviously" but the Blue Dogs and MSM seems to be unable to understand the obvious, such as unelected spooks should not be able to tank a president or lie openly to congress.

Wikileaks keeps pointing out the hypocrisy of those willing to let the Deep State flex its muscles: a leaked CIA memo calling for ethnic warfare in Syria on Twitter, a plan to interfere in the French elections, and all from the recent past, in a long tradition of anti-democratic practices. If undermining democracies and interfering in elections is wrong, why did the CIA do it hundreds of times, as recently as in France in 2012, or in Russia every time there is an election.

The underlying assumptions behind the Russia kerfuffle are 1) that Russian actions played a significant role in the 2016 election and that 2) Russia poses a significant threat to the American people. Both assumptions are wrong. The enemies of the American people are almost exclusively American. Russia did not make us go to war in Vietnam or Iraq or waste 700 billion year on the military.

The Russian government had no impact on the 2016 election. Wikileaks did not get the Podesta and DNCLeaks from Russia, as both Julian Assange and Craig Murray have stated clearly and explicitly. Russia did something to sway the election but the available evidence does indicate what that something was because... it's not a something. Craig Murray says a human being put a thumb drive in his hands in Washington DC and that non-Russian human had no connection to Russia.

We don't have to invent secret conspiracies. The connections of the Obama administration to CitiBank are clear. Michael Froman's team at CitiGroup vetted Obama cabinet and, not surprisingly, received a half trillion dollars in "liquidity" funding to assure that the current system continues. That is scandal far beyond any hypothetical Russian meddling in our election. Obama and Clinton knew that Qatar and Saudi Arabia are funding Isis and continued to sell them arms. That is a scandal beyond any Russian nonsense. Both of these scandals emerge from single emails released by Wikileaks. Then, we see hundreds of email showing FEC violations, collaboration between the MSM and the HRC-DNC campaign, cheating in elections, but none of this obviously true material leads to anyone losing a job, let alone going to jail, let alone changing directions.

The top 100 CEOs make 789 times more a year than the average worker. Life expectancy is declining for huge parts of the population. Black households on average lost the little wealth they had accumulated. War continues unabated. Slavery becomes the norm in Libya. We have, as Jimmy Carter said, a system of unrestricted bribery in American politics. We have spent an average of almost 700 billion dollars a year on the military for decades. 22% of all American children live in poverty. We have a rust belt, urban ghettos and rural poverty, meaning about a third of the entire country neglected. Russia didn't have anything to do with any of that. A combination of domestic forces--the military industrial complex, the propaganda media, and the oligarchs buying elections--is the enemy of the people.

If a populist, progressive president who won with a landslide forcefully and publicly said, "I want to do away with the CIA and NSA" and was shot, that would be a cleaner scenario than a President who is not ideologically opposed to undermining constitutional rights and the balance of power, he just doesn't want his own power challenged. If the Deep State were to work FOR him, that would be fine with Trump... It's not a clear situation with Trump and the spooks, and it seems to be rapidly changing. Nevertheless, there are clearly no good guys in this fight.

Can we imagine an America without a CIA or NSA? Wouldn't the bad guys kill us all or something? Don't we have real foreign enemies? Do you mean every politician is lying to us that we need to have these agencies?

If important people in your society, dressed in the robes of authority, say that something is true and necessary, and if the state spends money and other resources on this necessary and true project, and everyone you know agrees that the project is necessary and true, the project may still not be necessary or it may even be detrimental and the underlying facts justifying the project may be entirely false.

The CIA is entirely opposed to the interests of the people of the United States. The agency has never gotten any important information right, never stood for human rights, and never conducted any operation that made the citizens of the US safer.

If every single one of your elected officials disagrees with my assessment, including both Democrats and Republicans, I am still right and they are all still wrong.

Here is an example so that you might come to believe that little old me just might be right, even in the face of the overwhelming power structure telling you the opposite: in medieval England during the Black Death in the 14th century, the church declared national days of prayer and fasting to beg God's forgiveness. In 1832, as Asiatic Cholera outbreak gripped New York, U.S. Senator Henry Clay asked for a Joint Resolution of Congress to request that President Jackson set: "A Day of Public Humiliation, Prayer and Fasting to be observed by the people of the United States with religious solemnity."

For more than 400 years, powerful, respectable people thought that if everyone prayed all at once, God would certainly hear the appeal and end an epidemic. They did not know that there were tiny creatures called bacteria, and indeed the idea of microscopic life is pretty wild. You can't blame them for trying something. Their constituents wanted an end to the crisis and the leaders responded.

Nevertheless, communal prayer never had any effect on any epidemic. Now, if someone had proposed germ theory, that would have been a better place to look for answers. It wouldn't matter who proposed germ theory or how many senior and serious people said germ theory was wrong, communal pray still would not work.

The germ theory was proposed by Girolamo Fracastoro in 1546, and expanded upon by Marcus von Plenciz in 1762. A transitional period began in the late 1850s as the work of Louis Pasteur and Robert Koch provided convincing evidence; by 1880, miasma theory was struggling to compete with the germ theory of disease. Eventually, a "golden era" of bacteriology ensued, in which the theory quickly led to the identification of the actual organisms that cause many diseases. Viruses were discovered in the 1890s.

Boiling water before drinking, getting rid of fleas, regular hand washing with soap, burying fecal matter deep below the surface and away from wells would have worked to avoid most epidemics in history. You didn't need antibiotics or modern technology. You just needed new ideas, or in fact to accept an idea first proposed in 1546. Yet, there we were in 1832, still praying.

Do you think humanity stopped making mistakes in 1832? Do you not think that many of the truisms no one challenges today are not wrong? In the early 1900s a campaign against hookworm in the Southern United States focused on getting people to avoid contact with fecal matter. A public health campaign like that, one of the first and most effective in history, is different, you might say, than making changes in the political structure or economics. I disagree. In public health, as in public administration and government, breaking free of accepted truisms and imagining something different is absolutely necessary.

We tried communal prayer to cure epidemics for at least 500 years. Few people would have believed that the United States could be a multi-racial democracy in 1860. There were no constitutional republics in the world when the United States set up our system of government in the 1780s. We have to think outside the box.

We do not need spy agencies. We do not need a massive military. We can have a new kinds of participatory democracy. Racism could end. We can generate all of our electricity from renewable energy. We should think about the poorest of the world and bring them into the community of global humanity. We could see an exoplanet. We should have more open, public space, more free time. We don't have to consume, and be consumers, and be mere spectators. There is no good reason to pay for schools with local property taxes. You should be able to take a train from LA to San Francisco. You shouldn't have to fill up your bathtub in a rural area before a storm in case the lines go down. There is no good reason for one person to have a billion dollars. The King of Saudi Arabia steals the oil under the sand as certainly as the British did before him. There is no good reason to let elected officials be the only ones running the official part of the government and there is even less reason to let unelected spooks rule over the elected officials.

Weapons of mass destruction, Gulf of Tonkin, etc. the same dynamic can apply in politics and economics. It seems obvious to us that if the government issues more currency the value of existing currency may well drop, or inflation. Nero and other emperors debased the currency in order to supply a demand for more coins. Debasing the currency means that instead of a coin having its own intrinsic value, coins represent value. In the 1930s, even FDR thought that he should worry about the national debt in a time of depression and deflation instead of increasing government spending based on borrowing to restart the economy.

Since World War II, the United States has spent billions and trillions (and we do not know how much) on spies. Ostentatiously, the reason is to keep the people safe from foreign enemies. The fact that one enemy disappeared, the Soviet Union, and that there was a gap of twelve years until another credible enemy appeared, Al Qaeda, seems not to have affected the belief that we need well-financed spying agencies.

While it may be true that the United States has powerful

foreign enemies other than criminal terrorist organizations that are spying on the government and industry of America, it is also true that over the course of their existence the spy agencies like the NSA and the CIA have done far more harm to the interests of the American people and people around the world than good. We'd be better off without them.

They are often wrong. We went to war in Vietnam based on a stupid theory: the Vietnamese were never the puppets of anyone. In 1969, our representatives were meeting with Soviet agents to discuss the Soviet-Sino split, which threatened to degenerate into war, and as part of a bargain by which the Americans would not object to a Soviet strike against China, the Americans requested the Soviets call off the North Vietnamese. What the Americans did not know was that the Soviets absolutely lacked the ability to enforce a cease fire the Vietnames did not want.

We went to war in Iraq with a false justification: weapons of mass destruction. The agency failed to call the fall of the Soviet Union before 1989. A more stark endictment of this whole "spy agency" gambit could not be imagined. A worse record is imposssssssible, with a number of extra s-es. I'm sure SOMEONE in the agencies got something right. But the right information never gets to the right person at the right time. Also, the enemy changes but the structure, budget and mission never do.

Maybe the whole thing is a con and a fraud. The spooks like getting paid, having toys, and playing mastermind with other people's countries (and then our own). They don't actually do anything useful, or whatever small good they do is so insignificant compared to the useless and bad stuff they do it's not worth considering. The CIA is no better at achieving its mission that was communal prayer at stopping epidemics.

What? Our great CIA and NSA? Useless and self interested? Are you saying the bishop who called this national day of prayer and fasting is wrong? Who are you? Do you have a TITLE? Now we have the claim that Russia hacked the US election. 17 agencies assure us Russia meddled in our 2016 election. Yet back in 2002, Colin Powell said that 16 agencies supported the idea that Iraq was developing weapons of mass destruction. I guess we grew one new agency? What are these 17 agencies called? How much in aggregate do we spend on the magic 17? What good things have they ever done for the people of the United States? Would it make more sense for a country to have one security-intelligence or a whole bunch of them competing with each other? Serious questions ignored while silly nonsense is the talk of Washington.

We know we don't have a democracy on the "voting" level of government. Do we also have a network of fiends under that level? Is the network of security agencies a Deep State? Could a democratically elected government eliminate the CIA and NSA and dramatically reform the FBI if this theoretical government wanted to make serious changes to these agencies?

These questions about why we do so much spying seem like serious questions to me. What, if any, role Russia had in hacking John Podesta's and the DNC's email seem like trivial and silly questions. Any threat posed by Russia, Iran or Syria (on one hand), or by Isis, Saudi Arabia, and Qatar (on the other), or by China, pale in comparison to the threat posed to Americans by the NSA, the CIA and, frequently, the FBI.

If we don't engage in foreign military adventures, we won't need local intelligence to conduct military actions. If terrorists are planning criminal actions, they should be tracked by law enforcement using whatever spying techniques are necessary.

Otherwise, we'd better off not having spooks corrupting our government and interfering in democracies abroad.

On January 3, 2017, The Hill ran an article called, "Schumer: Trump 'really dumb' for attacking intelligence agencies." In short, Schumer, who obviously cannot imagine that any issue might be worth risking your life for, thinks that the Deep State might well kill Trump, or someone close to him, or bring him down with leaks or other subterfuge.

If you're a politician and there is a network of powerful unelected spooks who think they have the right, and certainly have the ability, to murder the president of the United States, shouldn't you bravely call for ending all funding for these agencies and tracking their employees in the future to guarantee they don't continue to represent an ever present danger to American democracy?

They might kill you? Okay, you should say, go ahead and kill me. If you give in to fear and are easy to terrorize, you lose. If you really feel no fear, they can't intimidate you. Martin Luther King, John Brown, Eugene Debs, Medgar Evers, Abraham Lincoln, Ella Baker, innocent Haymarket martyrs Adolph Fischer, George Engel, Albert Parsons and August Spies, Rosa Parks, freedom riders martyrs Andrew Goodman, Michael Schwerner and James Chaney, and many others went to jail or were murdered, sometimes by the state. They weren't afraid, like Schumer, and they didn't think standing up to the powerful was stupid.

The CIA has clearly undone democracy in Chile. The CIA admits to dealing "with coup-plotters, false propagandists and assassins." The CIA has undone democracy in Guatemala. The CIA has overthrown and killed elected leaders in Iran and the Congo.

**No More Presidents**　　　　　　Follow

Liberals be like "We will not normalize Trun
but fail to see how in normalizing
capitalism/imperialism they've already
normalized Trump.

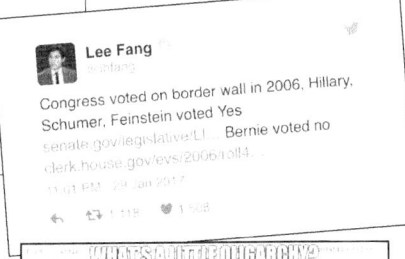

**Lee Fang**

Congress voted on border wall in 2006, Hillary,
Schumer, Feinstein voted Yes
senate.gov/legislative/L...　Bernie voted no
clerk.house.gov/evs/2006/roll4...

1. The Democratic Party is on the...
Congress, the presidency, and most state
governments.

2. The Party's Washington establishment – big
funders, major lobbyists, retired members of congress
who have become bundlers and lobbyists – are one
big reason for the Party's demise.

3. The life of the Party – its enthusiasm, passion,
youth, principles, and ideals – came to the fore in
Bernie Sanders's campaign. Stop trying to deny that.

4. The Democratic Party must change from being a
giant fundraising machine to a movement uniting the
poor, working class, and middle class -- who haven't
had a raise in 30 years, and who feel angry and
powerless -- to take back our economy and
democracy from the oligarchs who now run both.

5. Squabbling over any of this is nuts. Democrats have
to be tough, have backbone, and fight like hell against
Trump and the regressive forces that are about to
destroy everything Democrats have built since the
New Deal.

**Robert Reich**

The Hillary Clinton vs. Bernie Sanders contest
divide the Democratic Party -- in

## Intelligence Budget Data

On February 9, 2016, the Administration submitted its Fiscal Year 2017 budget request,
including a request of $53.5 billion for the National Intelligence Program (NIP). The
Department of Defense requested $16.8 billion for the Military Intelligence Program
(MIP) in FY 2017.

| FISCAL YEAR | NIP BUDGET | MIP BUDGET | TOTAL |
|---|---|---|---|
| 2016 | 53.0 billion | 17.7 billion | 70.7 billion |
| 2015 | 50.3 billion | 16.5 billion | 66.8 billion |

Meanwhile, the NSA gathered up everyone's email and then lied to congress about it. If the Deep State can lie to congress, who is really in charge? Not congress for sure.

Until World War II, we didn't have permanent spy agencies. On the CIA's kid's page (see cia.gov/kids-page) (get them while they're young), in addition to non sequitur clip art of kids that will not be working for the CIA, the fact that we did not have a permanent spy agency from 1776 to 1941 is obvious and beyond dispute.

We would be safer as a people without the CIA and the NSA. They have done nothing but harm to us as a people, nothing but harm to our democracy, and they are always wrong. They are wrong again about Russia influencing the 2016 election.

## On immigration

Trump is making a lot of noise about deporting twelve million people. I don't think it will happen. After pounding his chest and acting like a drunk gorilla, the situation in terms of illegal immigration will be more or less the same in 2020 as it was in 2016.

Deporting 12 million people would require hundreds of thousands of agents, take up time in the courts, and would be resisted by many local governments, including some of the jurisdictions with the most undocumented workers, such as California. To some, "kick them out" might sound good, but the friction it would take, the lives upended, would touch millions of people beyond the deported in such a way, that achieving a goal based on his anti-immigrant rhetoric would be worse for Trump politically than backsliding and giving up on a thorough deportation policy. His symbolic deportation campaign will be much like what we saw under Obama: close to 400,000 deported every year with a significant fraction of that number moving in every year and no substantial change in the overall demographic picture.

At that point, we can stop talking about deporting people who are now members of our communities. Maybe after Trump's theatrics go nowhere, everyone will deal with the fact that we have about 12 million people living here who need to be legalized.

If you have a law that is widely disobeyed, you get to a point where the law cannot be enforced and the law needs to bend to reality. We have had many tax amnesties to collect back taxes. We have legalized marijuana in much of the country.

Undocumented immigrants hurt working conditions for everyone. They often work off the books, creating a shadow economy. They often cannot complain about mistreatment at work. They work for lower wages and fewer benefits. Legal immigrants, however, do not bring down work standards generally. Immigrants want to be paid the same as native born workers and expect the same rights. Undocumented immigrants are afraid to call the police to report crimes, avoid taxes not because they want to cheat the state but because they fear being caught for their undocumented status. Since they aren't going anywhere, we need to legalize them as a society.

Hypothetically, if your only concern in terms of immigration policy were the economy, letting in any and all immigrants with a high degree of education and capital to invest in America, with no limit, would make sense. People who bring skills and capital into the country only create more jobs and economic growth. Likewise, agricultural guest workers who come without their families, work doing jobs Americans don't want to do, and in fact are not healthy enough to do on a long term basis, has no negative impact on the economy.

However, of course, the economy is not the only concern. How big should the population of the United States be? Most immigrants fall somewhere in between the extremes as outlined above. How many should the country let in per year? How should they be selected?

As a country, we are morally obligated to take in some people not because they will help our economy but because they need a place to live. Is it right to let refugees from Central America stay in the US when other refugees from somewhere further away, say in a refugee camp in Central Africa, have a more serious human rights claim to entry?

Also, once people establish lives in the community, it is very painful and heart breaking to make them leave. Even if by some intellectual argument you convince me that my neighbor should not be allowed to stay in America because he "jumped the line" or because someone else needed to immigrate to America more than he did or because he or she didn't have the right education and skills before he or she came, I don't want them to go.

There are good intellectual arguments against illegal immigration. I have pointed out that the presence of undocumented immigrants can bring down working conditions for all workers. Legal immigrants have to be "sponsored" to come in, take language and citizenship classes. So there's kind of a fairness issue here, too, for those who went the legal immigration route. That's why undocumented immigrants should have to pay fines, do community service and jump through the kinds of hoops legal immigrants had to follow. They broke rules and laws. After a fair hearing, some undocumented immigrants should be deported.

But to just seemingly randomly rip people out of their families and lives, to wreak havoc with 12 million deportations, too many to be done with proper habeas corpus rights, is just too disruptive and cruel to be justified by an intellectual argument. Here I am thinking of specific neighbors. They have two kids, own a beautiful house. The husband renovated the house himself. He runs a business. Their older son is going to an elite college. Yet they came here without immigration papers and no obvious "skills" or capital. It's not an intellectual argument; they have to stay here as part of our community and valuable members of the American body politic. They have done nothing wrong. They are good for the neighborhood, this is their home, and if they were to be deported because of an abstract argument, it would be morally indefensible.

Another man I know came here as a refugee, learned English, his third language, went to college, worked his way up in a business, learned Spanish, his fourth language, and is now engaged. He had a Green Card but mailed in some paperwork, which was lost. When he got someone on the phone, the officer asked him if he mailed it certified mail, and he had to admit he had not. Well, too bad, then. After working and studying here legally for years, he's suddenly an illegal immigrant. I'm sure many of us know stories like this. How is ripping him out of his life, stopping him from being able to improve himself even as he supports and invests in his home country, going to help anyone? Foreign aid, from government to government, or through non-governmental organizations, is prone to corruption and bureaucratic waste. Letting people work and send money home seems like a relatively efficient form of development aid.

No one is an illegal person, as many have pointed out. Almost everyone breaks some kind of law. Some cheat on their taxes; breaking a law doesn't make you an unperson. Undocumented workers broke some aspect of immigration law, or some sort of bureaucratic snafu happened to render their status undocumented. I know an undocumented worker who simply missed a filing deadline because a paper went missing and he lost his Green Card.

The government could do this: declare a period of time, say a year, in which anyone who has lived in the United States for a given period of time, say three years, must apply for amnesty. In the application intake, they will be assessed on how they got here. Overstaying a visa is not as bad as using coyotes or smugglers to cross the border illegally. How long have they been here? How much did they pay in taxes? Have they been convicted of a crime?

After going over their history, they will be offered an amnesty deal: pay a fine of maybe $5000 to maybe as much as $25,000 and/or do community service, maybe pay back taxes if necessary, with a year to pay and complete their service. When they have completed their deal, they get Green Cards. Then if the nation decides to crack down on new illegal immigration, along with guest worker provisions, set asides for refugees, and programs to attract skilled workers, the immigration authorities will only have to focus on a few hundred thousand people, not several million.

It's perfectly legitimate to control the number of immigrants and have a process that picks some people over others, a selection and vetting process, going forward. It is not okay to storm into communities and rip members of the community out of their houses and make them disappear with no due process.

In the current environment such a program seems politically far-fetched. But after Trump fails to achieve anything and no one's life is improved by a crackdown on illegal immigration, the tide may change.

# On Trump

**O**f course Trump's conflicts of interest are cause for impeachment. But so were Obama's war crimes. Unless you throw Obama under the bus, you cannot legitimately call for Trump to be impeached. The Russian role in the 2016 election is not significant. Trump is popular with the Republican rank and file, so he will not be impeached.

Obama should be arrested and tried for war crimes, as his actions in seven countries cannot be legal acts of war under international or domestic law. Cheney and Bush should be tried for torture and aggressive war. When they are tried, Trump should also be impeached.

Be consistent in opposing unconstitutional lawlessness. Neither the Democrats nor the Republicans are consistent. Cut the crap and charge Obama (and hopefully convict and then pardon him afterwards, not to be vindictive, but to establish the rules) so you can then impeach Trump. Once again, Democrats think they are so special that they are more important than the law or the future, the planet or the human race. Obama is too precious to face the music, even if in doing so, the Democrats would have the credibility to curtail the war powers of Trump.

If you love Obama, you love lawless American imperialism and oligarchic control of government, because that is what his administration represents. Stop loving Obama and the Democrats to present a plausible charge against Trump for conflicts of interests.

# On leadership

If Abraham Lincoln had gotten rid of George B. McClellan earlier, the American Civil War would have been shorter. McClellon, who on paper looked like the perfect general, was so much worse than Ulysses S. Grant and William Tecumseh Sherman, who had completely horrible resumes as of 1860.

In "The Utter Uselessness of Job Interviews" by Gray Matter in the April 8, 2017 New York Times, you can get a sense of how little evidence backs up most of the ways we pick people for positions in society. People think they can identify a good leader by listening to them but they do no better than guessing. When people vote, as when they conduct interviews, much of what we do is tell ourselves a story and then fit the evidence into the story we already believe. Our reluctance to change the main narrative mean we are not good at picking leaders or exceptional people.

Lloyd Clark in his book *Blitzkrieg* argues that the Germans succeeded in France in the 1940 invasion largely due to policies pertaining to leadership. The German army allowed even lower ranking officers to modify instructions and plans on the go. Thus, while the Germans were adapting as quickly as the circumstances on the ground changed, the French were using slow communications to check every move with the headquarters. This book suggests that you can have structures that allow people to be leaders and excel and take the group forward or you can have structures that repress good ideas and teach people to mindlessly follow orders, to assume that higher ranking people know more than lower ranking people, and end up occupied by the enemy, or otherwise completely beaten.

Bernie is an unlikely leader too. Our whole model of leadership is false. Resumes don't matter. On paper, Obama looked good too. But he failed.

Reading biographies, I noticed that in civil wars, when the rules break down, often people who should not have been given command of anything get command and sometimes prove to be brilliant. Great leaders just pop up. You never would have guessed these people could be so great. Even their families seem surprised. And these great generals didn't ask to lead. They never would have been given positions of power if not for the complete crisis.

Late in life, regarding his time in a San Francisco experiencing a frenzy of real estate speculation, William Tecumseh Sherman recalled: "I can handle a hundred thousand men in battle, and take the City of the Sun, but am afraid to manage a lot in the swamp of San Francisco." On paper... Grant wasn't on paper, he was drunk.

Oliver Cromwell would have been a quiet country squire if not for the English civil war in the 1640s and ended up being the greatest cavalry leader in Europe. Toussaint Louverture was a semi-literate wagon driver in Haiti when the revolt started and went on to be one of history's greatest generals. Maybe what these examples suggest is that the way we pick people for leadership positions is not really rational. Maybe you can't really know who should be doing what unless you let them try. In all the cases above, the leaders were doing other things until fairly late in life when all of a sudden they were thrust into a new role, and excelled.

This theory of leadership may put into question the whole model of representative government. If the electoral process tend to lead to egomaniacs coming out on top, people with little conscience, ruthless people, then maybe we should pick leaders in another way. We let juries decide life and death decisions. This collaboration of equals with no ambition can be productive units and leadership can emerge from these randomly selected groups.

Why do we elect representatives? Why can't at least some of them be chosen at random? Instead of creating these cults of personality around egomaniacs, why can't we let the hidden talents of a retired nurse in Cleveland rise to the top and lead us in some way? Great leaders like Cromwell, Toussaint, Sherman and Grant are out there. We can't get a worse crop of losers than we currently have. It would be better to draw straws or have a lottery. Literally, I would rather have the president randomly selected then have to choose between Trump and Clinton. Something like a jury to have a say over policy, or to police the other branches of government, would be a great addition to our creaky constitutional order.

If we had participatory democracy, if we put people into positions of some authority randomly, if we had counsels and other groups of unelected citizens with real power, some of the people would emerge as leaders of these groups, people who never would have run for office, but are natural leaders. We could not do worse than what we have. We trust the average person to sit on a jury, but not to make a government budget. Why? Since we do not have a perfect way to find leadership, we should mix some randomness into the system and see if we can't increase and diversify the pool of potential leaders.

Random selection worked for ancient Athens. We should also draw lots for our representatives. If you want to be in congress, let's say, you'd submit your name online to a database. Then, say, in addition to the 435 elected representatives we also allow 200 or so unelected citizens chosen at random to vote in the House of Representatives for a two year term. Those 200 people would not have relationships with lobbyists. Some of them would be dumb, some would be lazy, but many would be engaged, intelligent citizens. I doubt that the randomly selected people would as a group be more corrupt, intransient, and self-interested than the elected officials.

# On Vermont

**W**hile we're on the topic of representation, consider, if you will, the state of Vermont, where Bernie Sanders comes from. The House of Representatives of the state has 150 members, or about one representative for about every 4000 people. My mother could walk over to her representative's house and talk to her about any matter of state government. The legislators are in no way "bigwigs" or people who feel they are entitled to perks or feel they are somehow appointed by the gods to rule over others. They are ordinary folks.

The New York State assembly also has 150 members, or one per every 130,000 people. Unlike their counterparts in Vermont, the New York politicians get staff, a state car, budgets, member items and a high salary. If you drive along the border between the two states the towns on the New York side tend to have more serious problems with poison water, as in Hoosick Falls, depopulation, failing schools, crime than do the comparable towns on the Vermont side. Not all the Vermont towns are thriving and prosperous and there are real problems in Vermont, but in general the state approached a functioning democracy and whole communities are not allowed to simply fall off the map, too bad, without some intervention from the state to help re-start the economy with some development project, such as an agricultural college, or some tourist infrastructure.

Bernie comes out of this Vermont political culture. Bernie grew up in Brooklyn but in terms of political style, he's pure Vermont. No bigwigs allowed.

The organization Thirty-Thousand (.org) points out that the same dynamic operates at the federal level. Federalist Papers 55 and 56 explicitly promised, without qualification, that there would be one Representative for every thirty-thousand inhabitants. Only a bill in 1929 capped the number at 435. As Missouri Representative Ralph Lozier pointed out at the time, "There is absolutely no reason, philosophy, or common sense in arbitrarily fixing the membership of the House at 435 or at any other number." The organization would allow as many as 6,000 representatives in the House, with members meeting in various location around the country. We should be able to consider such a well reasoned proposal.

## On the minimum wage

If you only look at the hourly wage, salaries for the lower earners are not vastly higher in Northern Europe (Germany, Netherlands, the Nordic countries, representing a population about 40% of the US) than in the United States. However, when you factor in benefits, including healthcare, childcare, possible college, and pension, the lowest wage across a wide swath of Northern Europe is about double what low earners get in the US.

Since 2009, the federal minimum wage is $7.25 an hour. The Congressional Budget Office estimated in February 2014 that raising the minimum wage would reduce the number of persons below the poverty income threshold by 900,000 under the $10.10 option versus 300,000 under the $9.00 option. About 3% of workers in the US earn the minimum.

In Canada each province sets a minimum wage and the overall average wage is not substantially higher than the US wage, when the exchange rate is factored into the equation. As many minimum wage workers in America are eligible for government healthcare, as are all workers in Canada, the difference in benefits for American and Canadian workers, on top of their wages, is not entirely clear. Japan's minimum is also exactly the same as the rate in the US. The Australian minimum is about $11.50 in US dollars as of the start of 2017.

In Denmark, wages are negotiated between unions and employer associations; the average minimum wage for all private and public sector collective bargaining agreements was approximately DKK 110 ($18 US) per hour, exclusive of pension benefits. Switzerland and Norway also have systems that do not depend on a simple hourly minimum and very few workers earn less than $15 per hour if adjusted for the exchange rate. An average worker at McDonalds in countries like Denmark, Norway, Switzerland and other high wage countries ranges from $16 to $24 per hour, plus healthcare and pension on top of the wage. For Germany, the national minimum is about 10.56 US dollars as of 2016, although many areas are higher, and the minimum is higher in many professions. Of course all workers get health care, child care, family leave and pension benefits as well, with benefits averaging 40% of the value of the wage itself.

If Bernie's proposal to raise the minimum to $15 were instituted, the United States would have one of the highest minimum wages in the world. If you factor in benefits, however, the wage would be comparable to Nordic countries, Germany and Australia.

In the past, doomsday stories about companies going broke or unemployment skyrocketing due to a minimum wage increase have been proven to be false. If we preclude the option of competing to be a low wage country, will have no choice but to become a high wage, high education economy.

# On taxes

**N**orthern European tax rates are about the same as overall tax rates in the United States. Simply comparing income tax levels is deceptive. Property taxes, for example, are orders of magnitude higher in the US than in Germany. Meanwhile, gas taxes are as much as four times higher in Germany.

The property tax is one dumb tax. Taxing people's real estate holdings is a wealth tax, but only on one kind of wealth. A middle class family with a house worth $300,000, but with a $200,000 mortgage, pays a wealth tax on as much as 300% of their net worth. Meanwhile a billionaire with a 50 million dollar estate pays a wealth tax on 5% of his wealth.

Real estate taxes are expensive to collect. You have to assess all the property regularly. Real estate taxes are easy to corrupt, as the assessments can and often are fraudulent and unfair, or preceived to be unfair. In my county, I uncovered evidence that the Hook Boat club was listed as a state park to avoid taxes, costing the taxpayer millions over several years, a clear case of fraud, and yet nothing happened to ameliorate the problem, which continues. Also, a state study showed that my county could save one million dollars a year in the cost of assessments by having a single office for the county instead of 17 offices in each town but, of course, no action followed to actually make this change.

Real estate taxes to pay for local schools put a higher burden on poor communities and is one of the prime ways that racism is written into the law in many urban areas. Property taxes work against creating balanced communities, with evenly distributed numbers of young single people, retired couples, families with children, poorer and richer inhabitants. A healthy community is a mixed community--old, young, married, single, richer, poorer-- but if you have to pay $20,000 a year in taxes to own a house, it's only a good deal if you have two school aged children and a high income. Quickly, you get a cycle of tax increase, leading to more wealth and age segregation, followed by higher taxes. As people retire in high tax areas, they leave, meaning a higher percentage of residents are using the schools, driving taxes up yet higher.

The speculation tax Bernie proposes, on stock sales, would bring in a vast amount of money and likely improve the operation of financial markets. Capital gains should obviously be taxed at the same rate as earned wages.

Inheritance: why should vast fortunes be passed on from generation to generation? We have to put a stop to that by taxing inheritance such that no one is born and lives their life as a billionaire. No one should be able to inherit $200 million dollars (more like a billion in today's money) like Donald Trump got from poppy Trump. You see what happens to them when you throw money at morons? They think they're smart. These dynasties are dangerous to democracy.

Teddy Roosevelt said, "There can be no effective control of corporations while their political activity remains.. In every wise struggle for human betterment one of the main objects, and often the only object, has been to achieve in large measure equality of opportunity. In the struggle for this great end, nations rise from barbarism to civilization, and through it people press forward from one stage of enlightenment to the next. One of the chief factors in progress is the destruction of special privilege. The essence of any struggle for healthy liberty has always been, and must always be, to take from some one man or class of men the right to enjoy power, or wealth, or position, or immunity, which has not been earned by service to his or their fellows.

Ben Franklin said, ""All Property, indeed, except the Savage's temporary Cabin, his Bow, his Matchcoat, and other little Acquisitions, absolutely necessary for his Subsistence, seems to me to be the Creature of public Convention. Hence the Public has the Right of Regulating Descents, and all other Conveyances of Property, and even of limiting the Quantity and the Uses of it." Similar quotes about the dangers of inherited wealth from almost all the founding fathers are available.

Bill Gates recently proposed a tax on robots. Look up the video. The room for reform in the tax structure is almost infinite, as is the money hoarded by a group of less than 10,000 people. This small group of misers and theives control more than 50% of the wealth of the nation and that must change.

## On narratives

**N**arratives will battle it out about 2016 and the election of Donald Trump as they have over every issue in history. Only when those with personal interest in a particular version of the story are long dead will the truth be the most important factor in which narrative wins.

Since the mainstream media and the Republican and Democratic leadership are complicit in Trump's victory and his ability to co-opt an intact imperial presidency, the truth, that the DNC/HRC/MSM complex with an RNC assist in their earlier pandering to racism gave us Trump, will not be the consensus until 30 or more years from the scene of the crime, 2016. You won't get the news about the truth until about 2046 due to the powerful covering up their crimes, as they always do.

Too many powerful people are still invested in the dominance of false narratives. Once they retire, their narrative will lose its institutional backing and fall apart, as it is not based on the truth. That process will take decades.

Get ahead of the curve and see the truth now. The Pied Piper memo. The "congrats" email. The Doug Band memo. Michael Froman. The New York Times collaboration with HRC/DNC. The Goldman Sachs speeches. The truth is right there if you want to see it.

Here, below, is the DNC narrative, what Obama or John Podesta or Bill Clinton might say (or what they would tell others to say) if they had to try to explain how Trump won. As they control so much media and have so many powerful politicians in their camp, they don't actually want to have too much discussion as to how Trump won, and certainly don't offer a single coherent reason, but I think I have an idea of what they believe.

There is now a narrative floating around that includes these elements: 1) White reaction to a Black president, Barack Obama; 2) sexism against Trump's opponent Hillary Clinton; 3) media promotion of Trump to increase ratings early in his campaign; 4) decline of manufacturing in the midwest and economic unease in that region; 5) Russian interference through "hacking"; 6) FBI interference via the Comey letter to congress in October 2016 before the election; 7) third party voters; 8) leftists who are more concerned with ideological purity than winning; 9) Hillary was an acceptable candidate; 9) Americans are a right of center people and left wing politics is still a fringe movement and not worth taking too seriously; 10) fake news; 11) the Wikileaks releases of DNC and Podesta emails do not reveal anything profound about American politics we didn't already know; 12) the release of those emails was illegal and hurt Hillary's campaign; 13) Obama was a great president; 14) Bill Clinton and Obama have more charisma than Hillary; 15) Bernie Sanders hurt Hillary; 16) the 2016 DNC convention in Philadelphia went well; 17) for some strange reason people hate Hillary; 18) the economy is good in 2016; 19) Obama saved us from a depression; 20) Obama made peace with Iran and Cuba and kept us safe from terrorists.

When you line up all the arguments made by mainline Democrats, you can, I think, see that they have no case. It's not that there is no validity to any of this. The Democrats would have us believe both that the 2016 Wikileaks publications are boring and only show us that politicians act politically and, in contraction, that the same publications show that Russia helped Trump somehow cheat his way into the White House.

The central narrative of the Democratic party as above is flawed in a number of ways: 1) it's not true; 2) it doesn't make any sense; 3) even if it were true and made sense, it has no baring on the lives of Americans and is therefore irrelevant.

Russia stole an election by publishing boring emails that are not false or doctored but actually true? To put a guy in power who then bombs their base in Syria? Aslo, who cares? Does any of this fix the water in Flint?

Ardent Trump supporters liked his sexist statements and denigration of Mexicans at the start of his campaign. Many people were outraged that a Black man, Obama, became president. But how many really came out to vote that would not have voted for any Republican? And if racism is key to understanding Trump's win, why did more Black and Hispanic voters support Trump than previous Republicans? Did trade have no role? Declining life expectancy? Declining wealth? Cheating in elections? Pied Piper strategy to fumble the White House to Trump?

There is something in America we call the "Rust Belt" and people there are disaffected. There is a legitimate argument that the left as epitomized by Bernie Sanders is not popular with many voters in the current political environment. It's not a great argument, but it exists with some empirical evidence. I also think that the complete blackout on the real agenda that would end oligarchic government in the corporate media means we don't know what an informed populace would want. Despite the massive propaganda in the US corporate media, we know coherent, non-Trump-con, anti-oligarchic sentiment is alive and well and growing. But none of these Blue Dog Democratic stories as outlined above actually fit with the available empirical evidence as to why the 2016 election was different and/or the same as elections in 2000-2014.

I have laid out evidence here in the front part of the book. Racism and sexism do not seem to explain the voting patterns in 2016. The economy was not good in 2016. Obamacare was not popular. Disaffected Bernie Sanders supporters were not a trivial group. Trump was not wildly popular and lost more votes to third parties than did Hillary. Minorities preferred Trump to past Republicans. The corporate media is the main purveyor of fake news. Wikileaks released very profound information in 2016.

In general, it's not that every item on my list of 20 DNC talking points is false (some are entirely false while others are off base and irrelevant) it's that they don't offer a good fit the available evidence. The DNC does not offer a coherent story, but a grab bag of unrelated items. What does Russia have to do with the FBI? How do Green Party voters relate to the charisma of Obama? It's just a lot of sand -- throw it in our eyes and hope we don't see that they are grabbing at any straw they can find.

Some of the 20 items I came up with in my list are not incorrect so much as irrelevant. Others of the stories the Blue Dogs tell are completely absurd and laughable. Nevertheless, millions of people believe that Russia played a significant part in the election of Trump, for example, and supposedly credible news outlets, such as the New York Times, wrote many stories about the influence of Russia between November 2016 and January 2017.

The Berniecrat story is more coherent. Politics in America, Democrat versus Republican, excludes from consideration most of the important debate by design. Oligarchs control both parties and allow a narrow debate to offer the illusion of choice. This manipulated system includes the media. Because the oligarchs control all the branches of government and the media, the outcomes are good for them and bad for regular working people. Thus, people in 2016 are worse off than in 2000, and in 2000 were worse off than in 1980.

Into this environment, a guy, Bernie Sanders, threw up his fist and said, "Revolution." He was on his way to win the Democratic Primary. This was intolerable to the elite. Even if Bernie himself is fake, which I do not believe, as I believe he is one of the greatest figures in American history, politicians are not supposed to get outside of the narrow debate that the oligarchs allow. He put up his fist and said "revolution" then got 13 million votes. Even if he wasn't serious, even if he sells out now, just putting up a fist and getting somewhere without getting killed makes Bernie a hero. They cheated him and accidently handed power over to an illiterate, White supremacist, egomaniac, con man. But he's still a hero.

Let's say I'm right about 2016 and the New York Times, almost every member of congress, every journalist on TV, the Washington Post, etc. are wrong. How can that be? Who am I to question these institutions?

Well, I may not have a title or be an institution but my browser does successfully resolve when I type the following URL into the search area: Wikileaks.org. And that's all I need to challenge 17 intelligence agencies, both parties, all the media, Barack Obama.

By typing "wikileaks.org" into my computer, I can prove my narrative while their narrative isn't even internally consistent, let alone provable. So it doesn't matter how many titles they have, how many billions of dollars. I'm winning the argument. The Pied Piper memo. The "congrats" email. The Doug Band memo. Michael Froman. The New York Times collaboration with HRC/DNC. The Goldman Sachs speeches.

Don't believe the hype. America is not a democracy. The truth is right there if you want to see it. And then… obviously… once you see it… I mean it's totally clear. We don't live in a democracy. We're being cheated and robbed. War, war, war, death, money that should go to Flint, we can see it all in Podesta's email, how they do us. So… therefore, obviously, the American people should overthrow their government and media and revolt.

Neither party is worth a warm bucket of spit, and Trump is a walking piece of crap. The Supreme Court is full of hacks, the media lies, the military only hurts us and anti-American hatred abroad is justified, our spy agencies are evil, the rich are hoarding the money we need to build a decent society, innocent people have been convicted of crimes they did not commit and then executed, nothing works right, other countries are better governed than we are and the world is warming and the sea is going to rise and we're not doing anything about it. It's all completely obvious and true, uncomfortable, but true.

If you don't want to read hundreds of pages meant to prove my narrative, you can do what I did with the 1980 October Surprise story: just think about it from a distance. Hillary Clinton outspent Trump many times over. Most media outlets endorsed Hillary, by orders of magnitude. Something happened on the ground that the elites missed and didn't like. There is some kind of elite-voter disconnect going on. That much has got to be clear. When you accept that precept, many items on the list above simply fall away.

History is a battle of narratives. There will be a battle of the narratives over what happened in 2016 and how Trump came to be president. There will be books battling over which narrative is more accurate and the writers of these books will have political perspectives.

The battle of the narratives requires books. We have blog posts and Facebook feeds and Reddit threads and all kinds of information available but a book is something people can point to: in Howard Zinn's *People's History of the United States*, for example, we can get the narrative that the reason the United States never developed a worker's party, nothing like the Labor Party in the United Kingdom or the Social Democrats in Germany, was that there was more state-sponsored elite violence against workers in the United States and the divisions between immigrants, native born Whites, and Black workers prevented the solidification of a worker's movement, as in all other industrialized nations.

You could make that argument without a book. But since the book exists, I don't have to go through all the details of why this narrative about workers in the United States is the truth, I can just say "Zinn."

If you already believe the Zinn narrative, you don't need the Zinn book. If you are opposed to the Zinn narrative, you won't read the book. In general, there is no progress and no one listens to the other side and no one has an open mind. But somehow, narratives do change and arguments made in detail in books do matter, even if no one really reads them. Let's consider a couple of narratives to get a sense of how they work.

From the first commemoration on October 12, 1866 in New York City to the proclamation of the day as a national holiday in 1937, Italian identity was the driving force behind the idea of Columbus day. Now, Columbus Day is challenged by an Indigenous People Day movement, not looking at Columbus as the proud symbol of Italy, a country which did not exist and had never existed in 1492, to the start of a genocide of American Indians. The story changed.

William A. Dunning at Columbia University in the first years of the 20th century trained a team of historians that vilified "carpetbaggers and scalawags" as the bad guys in Reconstruction. Republicans in Congress were too radical, pushed too hard for Black civil rights. People like Adelbert Ames, originally of Maine, were smeared as corrupt. There is no evidence he ever profited in any way from his tenure as Governor of Mississippi, elected almost entirely by Black voters. That Dunning narrative is still out there, under threat, whispered more than printed in textbooks, but it hasn't died. If Reconstruction failed because of Black incompetence and radical Republican extremism, that would let the White people in general and the supreme court of United States v. Cruikshank off the hook, wouldn't it?

Or integration: in 1954 the supreme court in Brown v. Education ruled against segregation. This was the beginning of the end of Jim Crow laws. The Civil Rights movement, lead by Martin Luther King Jr., got rid of legalized racism and all we have now, according to a still popular narrative, is discrimination. Other narratives would counter that school segregation rates today, 2016, are almost as high as they were in 1954 and that school district boundaries are laws too, that there is still a structure of racism in the law but that we entered a new phase of American racism around the time of the Civil Rights movement.

You can see battles between "left" and "right" in the cases of Columbus, Civil Rights and Reconstruction. These are not the only kinds of narrative battles. Who killed John F. Kennedy? Was there a conspiracy? That one doesn't break down ideologically as clearly as do the battles over Columbus, Civil Rights and Reconstruction.

If Native Americans and liberals who want to support the cause of Native Americans want to take over Columbus Day, the opposition will not be as vociferous as it would have been 50 years ago. Italian Americans don't really need Columbus anymore. Now, conservatives would oppose any effort to change Columbus Day into Native American Day almost reflexively, but it's not a vital or critical battle for anyone.

Here's another one dear to my heart: October Surprise, 1980 version. I read two books entitled *October Surprise* back in the day, one of which may have been by Gary Sick. The idea was that the Reagan-Bush camp made a deal with the revolutionary government in Iran to keep the American hostages in captivity until after the election. If Carter had managed to free the hostages prior to the November 1980 election, he might have defeated Reagan. By preventing Carter from making a deal, the Reagan-Bush team committed treason.

The key pieces of evidence include an offer made by the Carter administration to give Iran US made spare parts that was not accepted by the Iranians, a book written by an Iranian official making the same claim as in the October Surprise narrative, a deal, the subsequent discovery of the Iran-Contra scandal under Reagan, and some missing days from the schedule of then vice presidential candidate George Bush. I have always thought that you don't need a lot of cloak and danger evidence to conclude that a treasonous deal was struck: why else did the Iranians in fact not release the hostages before the election when they had maximum leverage and Carter was clearly ready to deal?

We now know with a great deal of certainty that Nixon's campaign sabotaged the peace negotiations of the Johnson administration in 1968 with secret offers. Nixon was locked in a tight presidential race with Democratic nominee, Vice President Hubert Humphrey, and President Johnson was making progress in Vietnam peace negotiations. Johnson encountered surprising resistance from U.S. allies in South Vietnam. President Nguyen van Thieu was suddenly laying down obstacles to a possible settlement in the Paris peace talks. Nixon offered Thieu incentives to scuttle the deal.

So, Presidents do cheat their way into the White House. It's certainly possible that Reagan did too. If he did, would it matter now in 2016? Apparently, as the 1980 October Surprise is a forbidden topic of discussion. Yet, Trump is now accused of being a Russian puppet. If Trump's people met with Putin's people, that would not compare in magnitude to what Reagan or Nixon likely did by working with foreign powers in their own days.

Iran had the hostages. South Vietnam could sabotage the

peace talks. All Russia had were some emails, if they even had that much. What exactly could or did Russia do? They don't seem to have the power to influence the election, other than the Wikileaks hacks, which most likely did not come from Russia.

No one is particularly invested in defending Nixon today, as Nixon is not a critical figure to anyone's politics now in 2016. Reagan and Bush are more critical to the Republican party, at least up until the election of Trump. Until recently, Reagan was untouchable in the Republican party, much as Democrats would like Obama to be beyond reproach.

As a narrative recedes into time, turning into mere history, the truth is more able to emerge. Nixon and treason: that's no big deal. Yes, sure, we were mean to the Indians way back then. No, we shouldn't have let the Confederates take the South back in the 1870s and put in Jim Crow laws. Or, if you disagree and think the Confederates were right, it's not really a battle you need to fight hard.

Right now, people are invested in various narratives about why Donald Trump won the 2016 presidential election and what that result means. I'm writing starting on the day after Trump was inaugurated, so it's very recent history. Trump supporters will have a narrative. Republicans who were and still are uncomfortable with Trump will have another. Democratic loyalists have one. I belong to the only political faction for working people, Bernie Sanders supporter crowd that has yet a fourth version, another narrative.

At this point, the narrative that dominates will dominate due to that story's ability to co-opt powerful voices. The best narrative is not going to win for now; the most powerful narrative is likely to dominate for some time. Columbus was just as much a harbinger of Native American genocide in 1880 as he was in 2010 but in 1880 Italians didn't want to hear about dead Indians and the Italian vote was up for grabs. Reagan likely was elected due to treason in 1980 but the narrative of a "new day in America" was still at the heart of Republican politics in 2012 so a re-evaluation of October Surprise was likely to meet some stiff resistance. Black people were lynched, massacred and deprived of their right to vote in Reconstruction but while Woodrow Wilson was president, the Southern White vote mattered a whole lot more and Black people and progressives not a whole hell of a lot.

History is full of the most powerful narrative silencing the less powerful narratives, the truth be damned. Indeed, the world's largest religion, Christianity, emerged from exactly such a process. All the Gnostics, Marcionites and Ebionites who had a different idea about Jesus, well, they got killed, banished and threatened into silence.

Did you know there were Christians who thought Jesus was just a man, then a spark of the divine entered his body when he was baptized by John the Baptist, then that spark left his body when he was on the cross? That story is consistent with the Gospel of Mark, but not the other three gospels. So why does the Nicene Creed insist he was the "begotten" son? Because at the time, some people thought Jesus was the adopted son of God.

How do you settle an argument like that? Well, historically, you crack the skulls open of the people who disagree with you and burn their books. That has worked out well in the past, but these days the powerful seem to be working on new, more subtle techniques.

I feel like I'm a political gnostic. We are few. We don't have the ear of the powerful. If we don't bury some of our books in a jar, as the gnostics did do, we will be forgotten by history. Look up "Nag Hammadi." That's kind of the impetus behind this book.

Often, that's how these narrative battles play out: the strongest win. That can't happen in science, as objective reality really exists, but history is just gone, evaporates, leaving nothing but evidence to interpret forever. You can destroy or ignore evidence and change history, at least until it doesn't much matter anymore.

But not always.

I am offering a narrative in this book to get one out there from my pro-worker point of view in order for other Berniecrats to have something to point to and say--there, that one. I expect to be ignored. Mainstream Democrats don't really need a book: they have CNN, MSNBC and the New York Times to tell their narrative. Trump is in the White House, so his team can get their story out without too much trouble. Any Republicans who have some reservations about Trump seem to be quiet at the moment.

The narrative here is primarily directed against the mainline Democratic narrative and is not particularly concerned with Trump supporters and how they understand the victory of Trump. The pro-Trump story can be pretty short and clear, as I understand it.

The story of concern here is how he came to be president. That story shouldn't depend on what happens when he is president. As I write this, we don't know what the Trump presidency will mean. Will Trump veer right, find that right wing policies are unpopular, then swing left, like Arnold Schwarzenegger as governor of California? Will foreign policy change dramatically? Will racism and sexism get worse? Will Trump be a tyrant? Will Trump push through some left wing policies? Will he implode? We just don't know.

# On electoral reform

For us who want government in the hands of the ninety-nine percent, Democrats howling about how unfair the electoral college is, is the height of hypocrisy. The Democratic party has a system of "superdelegates." In 2016, Obama could have used this system to insist that all superdelegates switch to Bernie after July 25, as the DNC leaks on Wikileaks showed that the primary process was flawed. Of course he didn't. So if there were any value to the superdelegate system, it would have been to stop a train wreck we all saw on July 25, 2016. Most of us super Berners saw the writing on the wall at the Democratic convention. You had the majority of the Bernie delegates, representing 13 million people, booed Bernie Sanders himself when he told them to get along, then they walked out. Those of us who followed the convention through live feeds know that the Philadelphia convention was a gift to Trump. Those who saw it on television thought it went perfectly.

Google, CNN and other media outlets refused to take the superdelegates out of their delegate totals until the primary was almost over. This sleight of hand gave the casual viewer the idea that there was no way Bernie could win the nomination. Now, with the Podesta Wikileaks, we know that all the media outlets that insisted on keeping this fake news delegate total prominently displayed were collaborating behind the scenes with the HRC campaign.

If you have superdelegates in your primary, you can't complain about the electoral college. Primaries are not private functions of a private organization called a political party. All taxpayers fund primary elections, even those who are not allowed to vote. Election law applies to primaries.

Democrats complain about voter ID laws and other methods to suppress the vote. Yet, in 2016, the most energetic voter suppression operation was run by the DNC/HRC against Bernie Sanders voters. Again, I really don't want to hear John Lewis complain about the voting rights act and Republicans undermining the right to vote unless he says something about New York State's closed primary system.

In New York, in 2016, you had to declare your party affiliation six months before the primary if you wanted to vote. Who knew that was the rule and who knew Bernie and Hillary would be candidates battling it out in New York six months before the election? Why should a publicly funded election, which is what a primary is, only be open to people who are willing to take a loyalty oath to a party without knowing which candidates that party is likely to field? On top of the system, there were massive purges of voters, bringing in the Justice Department and costing election officials their jobs. And the CNN exit poll showing Bernie close, only two percent behind, mysteriously disappeared.

New York State's closed primary is the worst example of undemocratic voter suppression in America and it was entirely designed and supported by Democrats. If we had proportional representation or ranked voting, the primary would not matter as much, but with this winner-take-all system, the primaries cannot be this rigged if you want to call your system democratic.

We don't have a proportional system. Primaries matter. In New York, voters had to declare their party six months prior to the primary. Why six months? Why do I have to essentially swear allegiance to a party before I even know who the candidates of that party will be? Maybe a Ron Paul type of Republican might be ahead in the Republican primary and a Hillary type of Democrat would have wrapped up the Democratic nomination. Then I might want to vote Republican. Or maybe Green. How can New York tell me I have to swear allegiance to a party with no obligation to follow its own platform? How do I know what I'm swearing to support?

If Democrats were interested in changing the structure of government to make it more democratic, they should first stop using devious tricks to exclude voters they don't like. They should clean their own house.

Maine's ranked voting system, approved in 2016, is new. Until this historic change, all elections for state, local and federal office have been winner take all. As a thought experiment: let's say that 49% of the voters in every state wants to break up the big banks. We would hold senate elections and the banks would get 100 seats and the anti-bank contingent would get no seats. Obviously such an extreme distribution of voters never happens, but the general pattern of this thought experiment is valid. Minorities (ideological, ethnic, etc.) only get representation if they happen to group together to form a local majority in some district or geographic area. Without residential patterns of segregation, minorities would get zero votes in congress.

In a parliamentary democracy, you don't need a primary because all minorities get seats in the legislature. If the United States were a parliamentary democracy, Hillary and Bernie would not be in the same party, nor Jeb Bush, Rand Paul and Donald Trump. If we were in Spain or Germany, we would hold an election and the mainstream Republicans would have gotten about a quarter of the votes, the Trump Republicans would have gotten another quarter or so, the DNC Hillary party would have gotten a quarter, and Bernie's party would have gotten about a quarter. If we held a national election and apportioned seats, the Bernie's party could well have been the single largest party in parliament in 2016. Then, the parties would meet and make a collation. We might have a coalition of the left, with Hillary and Bernie striking a deal, or a coalition of the right, with Trump and Marco Rubio or John Kasich striking a deal.

Since we don't have such a system, we have to have primaries. The coalition has to be built before the general election. Coalition building is why John Kennedy chose Lyndon Johnson as his running mate in 1960, why Ronald Reagan chose George Bush Sr., or why Donald Trump chose Mike Pence. Unfortunately, Hillary Clinton was too arrogant to do that normal coalition building and compromising, and Obama was too wimpy and clueless to insist she build a coalition, so Trump won.

Next, the Electoral College is indeed stupid. That Hillary got almost three million more votes but lost is pretty ridiculous. Here is a way I think might fix it and that might appeal to Republicans as well: The swing states have clout every four years but otherwise they don't have much in common. Florida, Nevada, New Hampshire and Ohio are obviously very different. Some swing states, like Florida, are large. Others, like New Hampshire, are small. Geographically dispersed, with some concentration in the Midwest, their economies are not similar.

It's hard to see why it's good to be a swing state. Many of them are in that "Rust Belt" we hear about. (That a major region of your country is rusty should be a cause for alarm and emergency measures, but real action by the US government only seems to be for big banks that gambled with the economy (TARP) and foreign countries with dictators who thumb their noses at oil companies (Gaddafi).) Are people in Ohio better off for being in a swing state versus those in Indiana and Illinois who are not?

It's not really the swing states who systematically benefit from the electoral college but the small states. Small states have a real self interest in not changing the system, as they get more electoral votes per inhabitant than do those in big states.

Simply, why doesn't congress pass a law (or a constitutional amendment) that all states must apportion their electoral votes for president proportionally by state? The federal government would defund any state that did not change how they apportion electors, so there would be no issue of state sovereignty, if a constitutional amendment does pan out.

I don't see why anyone wouldn't prefer proportional allocation to the currently system, except maybe some of the swing states. Even the swing states might like a break from being swing states.

A small state like Nebraska would get three votes, as now. However, one might go to the Democrat and two to the Republican, for example. Small, red states would have more clout in the presidential election than they do now. This system would not change the rural bias to national elections but it would make voters in every state relevant to the outcome of a presidential election and end this swing state stuff without a constitutional amendment. So, Republicans would get votes in New York and California. That should outweigh the loss of an occasional elector in Alaska.

Election by popular vote could be messy. What if we had to do a recount? Of 140 million ballots? Wow. Impossible. If we continue to vote by state, we might only have to do recounts in a few states in the case of a close election.

My kind of proposal might work. Democrats were howling about the electoral college, then moved on to complain about Russia. Somehow, it would be nice to smooth out the edges of the electoral college system so as not to have a president who lost the popular vote by that much.

The same logic applies to congress. There is no rule in the constitution that states must apportion their seats by geographic district. If New York, for example, wanted to apportion its 24 seats by state-wide vote, or some of them in regional or statewide elections, the state could do that. Such a system would offer a chance for proportional representation and third and fourth parties to get seats in the US House of Representatives, so of course the two party hegemony doesn't want such a thing to happen.

Noodling around with some ideas, a few tweaks, you could make America closer to being democratic. We'd need to think about media and information. Voting, money in politics. But it all could be done. It can't be done by professional politicians from two entrenched self-interested parties.

Sun Yat-sen, one of the most important figures in Chinese history, looked at the American system of government as a possible model for China, and he liked the idea of three branches of government: judicial, executive and legislative, and he said, "Where is the fourth branch to keep the other three honest?" It's a great point. An anti-corruption branch of government to remove people from the other three, an additional check, seems like a great idea. Sun Yat-sen did not get to implement that terrific idea in China but it is still a great idea.

Sun Yat-sen's idea is not an historical footnote, or it shouldn't be. He proposed a structure for China with four branches and we should seriously consider why he thought this would be better and copy his idea.

Ideas will follow here in this book which should be worth considering no matter who won in 2016. But the context would be wildly different, no doubt, had Bernie won. We shouldn't be afraid to kick around a few "pie in the sky" ideas like creating a fourth branch of government to check corruption in the other three branches. Changes are in order.

## On healthcare

The United States spends vastly more per person on healthcare than any other nation. About 78% of workers get their healthcare through their employers, or more than half the total population (including retirees and children and others who don't work). No other nation has this system to provide healthcare, depending so much on private insurance through employers.

This system not only costs too much, it leaves many people without insurance and reduces labor mobility, as workers have to think about health care when making job decisions, and is a pain in the ass for the employers.

Our life expectancy is not particularly impressive, so we're not getting that much life out of the system. Other countries, such as Canada, have more than two years on average with far less expense. As big as the United States is, we spend additional trillions to lose 640 million years of human life every year. You can't say this situation makes sense.

Bernie's Medicare-for-All plan would cost $1.38 trillion a year, but would save most of us thousands of dollars every year on healthcare costs. Gerald Friedman, an economist from U-Mass.

Amherst, estimates a family earning $50,000 a year would save nearly $6,000 each year.

Furthermore, a single-payer plan for universal healthcare would save us $6 trillion over the next 10 years. Friedman estimated that Sanders' Medicare-for-All plan would save $6 trillion over the next 10 years compared with the current system, in large part by eliminating what the Sanders campaign described as "expensive and wasteful private health insurance."You can't look at this chart and not see there are savings to be had.

| Country | Healthcare per capita | Life expectancy |
|---------|-----------------------|-----------------|
| USA | $9451 | 79.68 |
| UK | $4003 | 80.54 |
| Germany | $5267 | 80.57 |
| Chile | $1728 | 78.61 |
| Israel | $2533 | 82.27 |
| Canada | $4608 | 81.76 |

# On education

The US is about fifth in per capita spending on education but scores routinely less than 30th in international rankings on education. The evidence that American education rarely serves the function of allowing those with less advantage find opportunities their parents could not access is particularly disturbing. Inherited wealth, residential segregation, a system of a private and elite education system all combine to make the US more stratified and to allow less class mobility than comparable societies in Asia, Canada and Europe.

We elected a semi-literate president. Celebrities seem to think we should listen to their expert opinions because they are professional actors. There is a type of talking head on television or radio, considered some kind of public role model, who in fact do not seem to understand anything about history or basic science. There may be a systemic and cultural aspect to America's disdain for education.

The politics of public education in America rotates on three axes: advantaged versus disadvantaged, choice versus district schools, and race. By throwing all the issues into one basket incoherently, we might not see what is going on.

Many people send their kids to the neighborhood school and think it's fine. The kids get a good enough education to achieve their goals locally. The buses are new and sports are well-funded. The parents aren't really complaining. Some grumble about the property taxes. Some would like a few more classes of one kind or another, or have some other relatively minor beef with the overall structure, but are fundamentally satisfied. For the sake of argument, this group might represent about half the population of parents. However, more money is spent educating this same group of students than in almost any other country on a per capita basis and yet their test scores are about average or below when compared to the world. So, if half the people are more or less satisfied, even if maybe they shouldn't be, it's not going to be easy to change the system fundamentally.

Some of the other half include those in really bad schools. In America, much of our population is dispensible. Some elites, like Trump and his billionaire friends, seem to think they are rich and powerful by divine right, even when they are evidently not the best and the brightest in any activity that matters. Some who fell into a track leading to riches or were born rich don't see how anyone worth a damn didn't also get rich. Other elites are not that rich themselves but casually refer to an area as "butt fuck Mississippi," off-handily speak of behavior as "ghetto," use the term "white trash" as it was meant to be used, and call a whole series of states part of the "rust belt" without realizing in a single sentence they just condemned millions of people to sub-human status. When you use these terms, and we hear them all the time, our society just tossed a bunch of people in the garbage. We are a brutal society if we do that. No wonder life expectancy is declining for large segments of society: they've been cheated out of a good life. Education and life expectancy, more than purchasing power, indicate a good life, if a statistic can ever convey such a concept even vaguely, and in both cases, America is going the wrong way.

In America, you might ask where the dangerous, usually Black or Latino neighborhood is in the city you're visiting. You can assume there is a population of people who have been segregated by development, redlining, and racism to a neighborhood with bad schools, poor infrastructure and transportation and high crime. That's just the way it is, sort of like the weather. You don't really have to think too hard to explain it.

Somewhere someone will say, "You know, we're all born equal citizens of this country and it's not really right to cheat some children out of an education… or send them to prison after forcing them to accept a plea bargain." Don't all the children deserve a chance? Ah, well, you see… what are you going to say? Is "tough luck" good enough?

This American Life published a podcast called "562: The

Problem We All Live With" on July 31, 2015 on segregation in St. Louis, mostly from 2013 to 2015. Short version: desegregation works to improve black educational outcomes but white people fight it tooth and claw.

After discussing the legal history of segregation and desegregation in the St. Louis metropolitan area, the episode becomes shocking: hearing white parents saying outrageous racist things to thunderous applause. These parents were facing an increase in one year in their district as black students moved in from a neighboring district that had been de-accredited. The heartwarming parts were school staff and students in one school making sure the new black arrivals felt welcome.

A key message from this episode are: overwhelming evidence that integration works and nothing else works, at least in situations like Missouri. Because better teachers, infrastructure, etc. goes to white schools and always will, separate will never be equal. Black students who are bused to white schools do better academically and there is no evidence of any drop off for white students. The white parents talked about violence, as inner city black kids moved in. But there was no increase in violence.

Ironically, the NAACP team that was working up to the challenge to separate but equal in the supreme court, leading up to Brown v. Board of Education in 1954, first took on the state of Missouri in Gaines v. Canada (1938). The facts of that case show how determined the state of Missouri has been for more than 100 years to avoid integrating its schools.

The state of Missouri jumped through many hoops to kill integration in the 1980s even as evidence emerged that it was working. Then the kicker, the summer that the black families got the letters saying they could not go to the white schools any more is the same summer Michael Brown was shot by police, August 2014. In the same month, parents learned they could not send their kids to good schools and that a teenager had been shot by the police, his body left for hours where it lay.

Here I'm talking about racial segregation. But we also have millions of White students condemned to bad schools, with richer White students segregating themselves as well. A school district boundary is an arbitrary line drawn on a map. God didn't make the line: we did. We could unmake it, but some of us don't want to.

If you refuse to integrate the schools, if you refuse to provide a quality education to everyone, then you either admit that you are basically not interested in equal opportunity and that America is only for the few or you come up with another story. Thus, school choice, and charter schools.

Charter schools are politically popular because they offer the possibility of achievement or the appearance of achievement without integration. If the problem is public education itself and not discrimination against minorities and concentration of wealth in certain areas, then you don't need to radically change the economics of how we pay for education. Even if charter schools occassionally do score better in some areas on some tests, and even if competition is a good thing for improving education, the fundamental problems of segregation and inequality are more significant than the issues charter schools and school choice programs can address. School choice is not an alternative to a fair society that values everyone, gives everyone a chance regardless of race, gender and class and values education generally.

The PISA test, comparing math, science and reading

performance between countries, routinely finds the US in the middle, about average, but on the low end of the 35 richest countries, coming in at 31 or 30, maybe 29, in a given year. The achievement gap between rich and poor students is the leading cause of poor American performance, even if our top students in math are still not as good as the top students in Asia.

We have much smaller class sizes than the top countries, such as South Korea. That's one area where some charter schools might just be onto something: small class size is very expensive and does not seem to help much. Large classes, followed by meetings with an individual advisor, might be more cost effective for some grades.

The United States has far fewer "resilient students" than most European and Asian countries, meaning students from poorer backgrounds with parents with less education who nevertheless excel. Rather than being the land of opportunity, the United States is one of the more stratified countries in which education serves the purpose of re-creating the social class structure from generation to generation.

Some people can "make a few phone calls" and-- presto-- their son is in a prestigious college. Politicians who promote charter schools for poor and minorities students make those calls regularly. Somehow, Donald Trump graduated from Wharton School of the University of Pennsylvania, a prestigious Ivy League school, in 1968 with a bachelor's degree in economics even though he can barely read and claims he has in fact never read any book from cover to cover, including the ones he "wrote."

That's the American system: illiterates get Ivy League degrees while 40-50% of the students have no idea how bad their education is until it's too late and they will never get a second chance. We rank fifth in spending per capita but 31st in objective assessment results. Something is wrong there, for sure.

# On freedom of information

The ninth amendment to the constitution - ever heard of the ninth amendment? Here is what it says: "The enumeration in the Constitution, of certain rights, shall not be construed to deny or disparage others retained by the people."

Reading the history of the amendment and even just the plain language, what this amendment says, as Madison and Hamilton made clear, is that the list of rights in the first eight amendments is not the whole list of rights. All the ninth amendment says is there are rights out there that are not in the Bill of Rights.

Makes sense. In the 1780s, the founders were wise enough to see that in the future the people would need more rights, new rights, that they could not imagine at the time. People have tried to apply this provision to various areas of law, including abortion, but the ninth amendment is not the basis of any real rights that anyone can enumerate. In other words, the courts have never used the ninth amendment to expand our rights beyond those listed in the Bill of Rights and has been dormant since the beginning of the republic.

Abortion would have been a bad place to use the ninth amendment for the first time and it's good that the court based Roe v. Wade on the established right to privacy. Abortion is an issue between citizens, a controversy.

I have a better choice for the first real use of this amendment, number nine, that has been sitting there unused by courts since

1789: information. The term "right to information" is in the New York State FOIL (Freedom of Information Law) and in the Federal FOIA (Freedom of Information Act). Every state has some kind of freedom of information law. These laws have been in place for 40 years without anyone making any effort to reverse course on the "right" to information.

All of this means that there is consensus in the population'— left and right, rural and urban, state and federal—everywhere, everyone agrees that the public has a right to information about what the government is doing. If the law exists in every state and at the federal level, why do we need the ninth amendment to make this an inalienable right? Is some state looking to reverse their FOIL system and deny information? Well, yes, at the edges.

Were the right to information to be identified as a fundamental right, not something granted by a particular law that could, in theory, be revoked by the legislatures of various states, we would have the following benefits: 1) the ninth amendment would finally get used and in a way that is not a partisan controversy but in a way all parties can agree is in fact a true right; 2) exemptions, such as in New York the legislature exempted THEMSELVES from the law, could be challenged, as there is no good reason for it; 3) the weak enforcement regimes in most FOIL systems could be strengthened gradually through court decisions not based on the sometimes squirrely language of these laws, but as a fundamental right.

Everywhere governments SAY "right to information" but they don't really mean a "right" like freedom of speech. They have admitted that it is a right, but then try to get some information and see what happens.

If the ninth amendment cannot kick in when all the states, all

50, the federal government, and 40 years all agree that information is a right, when can it kick in? Never? We the people are due a new right. Information is perfect. In 1789, no one could have imagined photocopy machines, let alone the internet. They did include rules for POSTING information, as in nailing a notice to a post, but we can do better now.

The way to make this happen, making the ninth amendment a real right, would be to FOIL request documents EXCLUDED under New York FOIL (or another state) lose an Article 78 lawsuit propounding this argument (ninth amendment), lose the appeal to the higher state court, then appeal to the federal court, lose in the first round, and, eight years later, have an outside chance for consideration by the higher level in the federal courts and maybe the supreme court.

From James Madison: "It has been objected also against a Bill of Rights, that, by enumerating particular exceptions to the grant of power, it would disparage those rights which were not placed in that enumeration; and it might follow by implication, that those rights which were not singled out, were intended to be assigned into the hands of the General Government, and were consequently insecure. This is one of the most plausible arguments I have ever heard against the admission of a bill of rights into this system; but, I conceive, that it may be guarded against."

From Wikipedia: Professor Laurence Tribe shares the view that this amendment does not confer substantive rights: "It is a common error, but an error nonetheless, to talk of 'ninth amendment rights.' The ninth amendment is not a source of rights as such; it is simply a rule about how to read the Constitution."

Conversely, in 2000, Harvard historian Bernard Bailyn gave a speech at the White House on the subject of the Ninth Amendment. He said that the Ninth Amendment refers to "a universe of rights, possessed by the people — latent rights, still to be evoked and enacted into law....a reservoir of other, unenumerated rights that the people retain, which in time may be enacted into law." Similarly, journalist Brian Doherty has argued that the Ninth Amendment "specifically roots the Constitution in a natural rights tradition that says we are born with more rights than any constitution could ever list or specify."

We do have rights beyond the list in the constitution and by precedent in all 50 states, information is one of those basic rights that cannot be taken away by the government.

## On free college

Sanders' College for All plan, costing about 75 billion a year, could be paid for by first, increasing the top income tax rate to 50%, from the current 39.6%, bringing in more than $100 billion. Alternatively, a 10% cut in the military budget would cover the cost of free tuition at state colleges for all Americans. Further, we could impose a 0.5% fee on stock trades, 0.1% fee on bonds and a 0.005% fee on derivatives. This would raise up to $300 billion a year, according to a 2012 University of Massachusetts Amherst report. A speculation tax might reduce volatility in the market. It's not an investment tax. There is no downside to this proposal for the general welfare of the people.

The federal government would pay $2 in matching funds for every dollar states spend on making tuition free at public colleges and universities. Also, it would cut student loan interest rates to about 2% for undergraduates, and allow those with student debt to refinance at low rates. This would cost about 75 billion per year.

Investing in education is a better bet than investing in military adventures. I say we do it.

The speculation tax and marginal rate increase gave us 400 billion, paid for college, and we still have 325 billion left. Now, we could cut defense spending by 400 billion, add in an inheritance tax, cut out all Panama papers-style tax evasion and we'd have enough money to rebuild water supplies, upgrade the electrical grid, offer free Wifi to the entire country, build high-speed rail, improve regional transportation, transition to all renewable electricity, build a space telescope that can see exoplanets, Medicare for all, with a small payroll tax increase, and still give every man, woman and child $3000 cash. The economy would grow, working people could build some wealth, life expectancy would increase, poverty would decline, air and water quality would improve, the threat of climate change would decrease and nothing bad at all would happen.

We're facing rising seas, endless wars and Donald Trump is the president and yet we're supposed to be scared little bunnies that if the oligarchs can't buy private jets and 700 acre retreats on Kauai, the economy will somehow collapse. If the invasion of Iraq and the election of Donald Trump didn't cause the apocalypse, we can stop quaking in our boots and redistribute the wealth.

# On criminal justice reform

Black Lives Matter activists sometimes get cornered into saying they aren't against police, that we need police. We have also seen actual increases in crime as police engage in something of a work slow down when they do not like the actions of elected officials, bending too far in the direction of curtailing some of the powers of the police.

Obviously, we should be able to have effective policing without undue violence and prejudice. To be backed into either the "stop police violence!" or "support our police!" argument is almost unavoidable.

When debate gets twisted into these kind of poles, you get partisan deadlock. Instead of backing everyone into a corner, we should start the discussion with "How could we design a system of criminal justice that is as inexpensive, fair, and effective at stopping crime as possible?" The answers would be so far different than the system we currently have that it's possible that a significant number of prosecutors, judges, police officers, and prison officials would lose their jobs and status. Maybe that's the reason we can't have a reasonable discussion about this issue: the system is broken but so many people are invested in maintaining the machine as is that even the idea of a rational discussion that might potentially lead to policy change cannot be tolerated. Meanwhile, people who see their loved-ones ground up by a cruel and unfair system are not likely to be patient. So, is reasonable discussion possible? Only in the abstract, if these discussions have no bearing on actual policy is there any discussion of real fundamental reform.

Let's start from the beginning and imagine a reasonable system. The criminal justice system exists to stop crime. What do you think a crime is? What is your prototype of a crime? Someone snatching a purse and running down the street? If the first thing you think of when you hear "crime" is a purse snatcher, then you will imagine a young, male cop chasing the mugger down the street.

Technology like facial recognition, gait recognition, digital tracking, satellite imagery of entire city to "reverse" the flow of events around a crime and see where people went and came from, algorithms to apply police presence efficiently: machines may make many street crimes more rare, or could. Meanwhile, we have become aware of how many diverse situations the police find themselves in, such as cases of mental illness and domestic violence between people who know each other well. And what about white collar crime?

The police wear uniforms and are generally young men. That is a testosterone-rich environment with militaristic overtones. Societies put many young men in conformist situations with weapons available when they want aggressive behavior. So, you will get aggressive behavior. If they think their job is to get the bad guys, and then a particular prototype of bad guys is in their heads, then groupthink will overwhelm some training they did a year ago somewhere else.

Shouldn't the prototypical cop be an ex-nurse, 62 years old, female, who can assess the mental state of an individual and help someone experiencing a psychotic episode to relax? Should the prototypical cop be someone sitting in front of a computer, looking at a spreadsheet to check if the county office is playing games with foreclosed houses and selling the good ones to themselves?

Should a cop responding to a domestic abuse call know that in similar cases (based on the age, profile, situation, degree of alcohol consumption, etc.) that the perpetrator has a 20% chance of killing or otherwise hurting someone other than his domestic partner based on poor impulse control? Information can be collected and disseminated immediately to the police, prosecutors, and judges to inform their decisions. If these law enforcement officials ignore or counter the evidence in a particular case, they should have to state the reason for contravening the empirical evidence. The reasons should then be subject to scientific analysis and should be publicly accessible.

And knowing that, what would we as a society do? We can't arrest someone in advance and prison is likely to increase the probability that this person will explode violently in the future.

What if we mandate that a person with a history of domestic abuse who shows poor impulse control attend weekly talk therapy counseling to discuss anger and be provided with an app on his phone? He should also push the button on the app whenever he worries his anger is getting the better of him, and his caseworker, or someone, will come to him within 10 minutes and take him out for a walk, or to get coffee, or just give him a pat on the back and try to get him to calm down? Would that work to avoid impulsive violence?

And when the defendant is before the judge ready to be sentenced, shouldn't the judge have to tailor the sentence to what we know works? If in 95% of similar cases, defendants who get counseling, job training, tracking devices, and other help manage to avoid further encounters with the law, but the judge ignores the evidence and gives the defendant 20 years of hard time… then is that okay? Or, if we know that an individual falls into a category that is very likely to reoffend and is very dangerous, that person should be denied parole. The parole board needs high quality data to make that important decision.

In the Terminator, the robot cop is a merciless killer. But so far, no android robotic cops have actually killed anyone. This may be due to the fact that no robot cops exist. Probably, yes, that's the reason, although drones and robots are on the beat.

If they did exist, we probably shouldn't trust the complex matter of criminal justice to machines. But it's hard to beat human beings when it comes to idiocy and cruelty. I'm not sure we should trust ourselves either.

Like everything else in life, criminal justice could be handled by human-machine hybrids. We all depend on our phones for information. As every area of life is "disrupted" by technology, criminal justice languishes in the 19th century.

How we do criminal justice makes absolutely no sense if you take history out of the equation. The only way to explain why you get 15 years for breaking and entering in one parish in Louisiana and two years probation for the exact same offense in a county in Nebraska is to refer to history. You wouldn't tolerate this kind of explanation for other areas of life: sorry, you can't call your credit card company on Sunday in Oklahoma.

If outside forces and technology could run free on criminal justice and upend and re-create it, things could be different. "Take the inefficiency and unfairness out of law enforcement" is not a harder task than "get 50% of your electricity from solar power" or "make sure 4 million people can get to work by 9 AM" or "find a way to get everyone on the internet." We could do these things fairly easily. If we don't do them, it's because someone is stopping us or we don't really want to achieve these goals.

"Criminal justice reform" is a catch phrase you hear at election time, mostly by Democrats but increasingly by Republicans too. Many of us have heard that the US has more prisoners than any other country, at about five times the international rate of imprisonment. We also have all seen videos of police shooting black men and sometimes someone else. For all our tough sentencing, our murder rate is four times higher than Western Europe.

You look at the videos, hear a few key statistics, and you know you need "reform." But then you hear the proposed reforms, and you wonder if it's enough and if it will work, if the politicians are serious. Here is what Hillary Clinton said at the debate with Donald Trump on September 26, 2016:

> So I have, ever since the first day of my campaign, called for criminal justice reform. I've laid out a platform that I think would begin to remedy some of the problems we have in the criminal justice system. But we also have to recognize, in addition to the challenges that we face with policing, there are so many good, brave police officers who equally want reform. So we have to bring communities together in order to begin working on that as a mutual goal. And we've got to get guns out of the hands of people who should not have them. The gun epidemic is the leading cause of death of young African-American men, more than the next nine causes put together. So we have to do two things, as I said. We have to restore trust. We have to work with the police. We have to make sure they respect the communities and the communities respect them. And we have to tackle the plague of gun violence, which is a big contributor to a lot of the problems that we're seeing today.

She is talking about "good cops" and "bad cops" and whatever reform she might propose, the police, or some of the police, would have to agree to the reforms. It doesn't sound like Hillary really wants to do anything systematic or even propose any change that would actually get at the root of the problem. The "some cops are good" trap is irrelevant. To say that human nature is subject to natural forces and can be analyzed, that a system works according to a pattern, has nothing to do with whether or not individuals are "good" or "bad." To think that a person is wrongfully convicted or that a cop shoots someone unnecessarily because they are "bad" is simplistic and beside the point.

Training is often the first thing that comes to mind as a "reform." For example, in the shooting of Keith Lamont in South Carolina in 2016 his wife was right there saying he had a traumatic brain disorder. You would think "training" would suggest that the officers ask his wife to intervene and talk to her husband while they backed away and tried to de-escalate the situation.

I'm not sure you can "train" your way out of this problem. Body cams have resulted in a 95% decrease in civilian complaints, so that is one great technology, seems so far. Tracking every department for the number of police reporting their colleagues, how closely the department and even individuals adhere to best practices based on empirical evidence would be another way to mix human judgement with technology.

Meanwhile, in the same debate I referred to above, Donald Trump called for a return to the stop and frisk policy, as practiced in New York in the nineties and early 2000s. You might be surprised to hear that I agree with him.

I think any man in a suit, particularly white men, over the age of 35, particularly those found in high crime areas such as Wall Street, midtown Manhattan, or any comparable area of another city, the entire capital areas of state and federal government, or entering a known establishment of vice, such as a courthouse, bank, town hall, police headquarters, or any premises associated with either the Democratic of Republican party, should be immediately stopped, his tax returns should be checked, he should be questioned about what boards or other organizations he may be associated with, etc. Suspect such individuals of price fixing, red lining, insider trading, tax evasion, pension fraud, HR practices that violate equal protection laws, bribery, extortion, filing false financial instruments, embezzlement, obstruction of justice, etc.

Anyone making over $200,000 annually should be put on a criminal watch list. White men in hoodies are less suspect and should not be frisked as frequently until information emerges that the gangs have changed their dress style and abandoned their "power tie" colors, identifying them as members of criminal gangs. Women in suits in these high crime areas should be subjected to searches as well, although less frequently. Anyone working as an elected official, even including less suspect black men, or prosecutor, police officer, lawyer, banker, insurance company executive, will also be put on the watch list and forbidden from being able to donate to political campaigns, borrow money, or otherwise continue to undermine the basis of social order.

Does that paragraph seem funny to you? In New York over 780,000 people were stopped and frisked, almost all young minority men. That the policy basically criminalized an entire group is simply offensive to the conscience and intolerable. Stop and frisk is an abomination, and as ridiculous as setting up a checkpoint outside of Goldman Sachs. Well, no. A checkpoint to search bankers might actually produce billions for the treasury.

Should we cure schizophrenia by having two politicians, one Democratic and one Republican, say short sound bites and then let everyone vote on what will be most effective? How about we pass laws for minimum sentences that sweep up many more people than necessary and have these laws applied randomly based on where people are arrested?

So, training and mild reforms are not going to work. Profiling is out. Locking up so many people isn't working and is offensive to the claims that this is a land of the free. So, what then?

How about we start over. Let's pretend we didn't have a

criminal justice system and we were building a new one from scratch right now in 2017. Would the new system look anything like what we have?

If I look at guy and say, "He's a bad dude," as the officer in the helicopter said in the case of the shooting of Terence Crutcher in Tulsa, that's bias. You might know who are not the "bad dudes" by applying statistics. A guy involved in one domestic violence outburst five years ago or something, isolated socially, expressing hateful ideas, might be the bad dude who walks into some locale relating to his bias and murders people. A good algorithm based on good data might be able to see this guy. A cop in a helicopter cannot.

It may be that perpetrators of domestic violence are a high risk to the community in general even if the victim in a given incident refuses to testify or press charges against her (or perhaps his) partner. Such people are more likely to also go nuts one day and shoot someone in a road rage incident. But maybe, if you narrow the data, a given case doesn't fit the profile of a continuing danger to the community. What does the research say about imprisoning people guilty of domestic violence? Does it ever help reduce the frequency of such violence? What programs do work?

The data isn't perfect in figuring out what the best response might be. But "professional judgment" of the people in the system is worse. Here I am thinking of sentencing. Right now, sentencing is chaotic and random.

One person in one place is arrested with a weapon and gets a long sentence. Another person has the same weapon, criminal history, and there is no crime at all. Drug possession might get a long sentence and a violent crime a short sentence. It depends on where you are arrested, who you happen to run into in the course of your process through the system, and, of course, who you are, your race being a huge factor.

Many of us know the criminal justice system is racist. But "race" is not written into any law. So how does racism creep into the system? Through people. People have racist ideas. The law gives people discretion to act according to their ideas. So the law allows racism to get into the system.

People have to enforce the law, not computers or algorithms, but data should be right next to the people at every step. When legislators get ready to put in a mandatory sentence, the research on what the sentence actually means and whether it makes sense should be right next to them. When judges hand down sentences, they should have detailed and accurate data to guide those decisions. When cops are hired, we should know what is likely to be the outcome of those hiring decisions.

"Criminal justice" in America means cops, prisons, district attorneys, judges. All of those need reforms. Why are district attorneys and local county judges usually elected?

I live in Columbia County New York. The voters are 95% white. If there is systematic bias against black defendants, and there is, the voters are not going to punish the perpetrators, the DA, for example, but laud him and re-elect him. And they do.

We have seven police departments in this county of 60,000 people. The state police have two stations, the county sheriff has a couple of spots, and the city of Hudson, the towns of Greenport, Claverack and Chatham have police, along with the village of Philmont in the town of Claverack. If there is a crime wave in Philmont, the cops in Hudson can't come help. If there is a crime involving the internet, as many do, the state police are the only ones with the institutional back up to handle the case, so the cops in the local area just sit there doing nothing while state police in another county deal with the internet aspects of the case.

Also, street crime almost doesn't exist here. Yet there are many cops making over $100,000 a year. When a crime does occur, they have to make a big deal out of it to justify their existence, often ruining the lives of young minorities in the process.

As many of us have known, the application of data to law enforcement has been a key to the reduction in crime in New York City over the past 25 years. You'd think that kind of efficiency might be copied elsewhere. Guess again.

Radiolab did an excellent piece on using data in criminal sentencing called Forget About Blame. There are many studies showing that professionals, like judges, think they have impeccable judgement when they actually tend to impose harsher sentences on people who are ugly as opposed to those considered good looking.

I should be able to log into a federally funded website and look up a police department. Let's take a fairly big one as an example. If there are 5,000 cops in the department, how many made complaints against fellow officers in the past five years? I can just look it up on the website. If better not be zero. It defies belief that over five years, not one of the 5,000 officers did anything wrong and not one of their colleagues noticed.

I should be able to look up a given judge or look at all of them in a given area at once. If the research says that non-violent drug crimes should not lead to prison terms but a given judge is ignoring the research, I can see that there may be a problem with that judge. Maybe not. But he should be flagged.

What does crime look like? A white guy in a suit? What is

a "bad dude"? Someone likely to go ballistic and shoot up the joint? Where is he now? How do we find him? What hurts society more? Tanking huge financial institutions? Stealing millions from the government? Or breaking a car window? The bomber Ahmad Khan Rahami may have been inspired by Isis but he was involved in domestic violence beforehand. Any other way to spot him in advance?

If you find someone who is making bad decisions at the age of 18, should you break him apart and turn him into a lifelong criminal? Punish him harshly? Is he already hopeless? Is that what the research says? What about at 14, was he already punished in school then? Punishment might be good for business, if you are in the business of locking people up. But maybe we should have other businesses.

Criminal justice reform, the phrase, is showing up all over as a sound bite. The term is gaining traction. That's a start, maybe.

Racism explains a lot in America. We as a people are not caring about black kids already in school. Harsher punishments. Breaking people apart and using them as fodder for a system, with white guys in suits strutting around feeling proud that they are on the side of "justice." I can see the guy. I know him. I know how he ruined a kid's life without thinking twice as he would never have done to the son of his crony, who is worse.

America has a lot to answer for. So many black people in prison is an absolute disgrace and if we cared, we'd "reform" this sucker right out the window. Slavery, then Jim Crow, then this, and every time more patience. Racism is the stuff of American history, the glue, the theme, the whole story.

Exaggeration? Another police shooting in some city. The poor black neighborhood in that city erupts in protest, which is met by force, which morphs into a riot.

Nevermind the shooting, why is there always a poor, black neighborhood? Why do we tolerate the existence of poor black neighborhoods? Weren't we supposed to fix that too, and not wait for the shooting? How did that happen that there is a poor black neighborhood in every city? We could fix that if we wanted to.

# On democracy

T he victory of Trump leads to statements all over the place about the failure of Democracy. Consider, for example, "The Case Against Democracy" by Caleb Crain in the New Yorker. This article, among other things, reviews a book that says, essentially, smart people, presumably like the people who read and write for the New Yorker, should be allowed to have more say in who gets elected than the dummies who voted for Trump. The author of the personal essay in the magazine, Crain, isn't clear that he disagrees with the sentiment in the book he considers, *Against Democracy* by Jason Brennan.

In addition to writing for the New Yorker, Caleb wrote a great book on friendship in the 18th and 19th centuries which changed how I saw the past, maintains a fascinating blog called Steamboats are Ruining Everything, plus wrote a lovely novel set in the 1990s in Prague. He's a great writer.

In response to his "smarties vote twice article" I said to Caleb, "The Domino theory was total bullshit. The Vietnamese were never the puppets of the Chinese or Russians. If you failed to note this in your article in the New Yorker in 1970, your article would now be an example of an apology for a failed war. In parallel fashion, the United States is not a thriving democracy in 2016. The will of the people and the results of the government are completely unrelated. If you fail to note that we are not as democratic as we should be, then you cannot conclude that the problem with the 2016 election was too much democracy."

To me, the failure of American democracy is as obvious as was the injustice and illegality of the Vietnam war (or Iraq war, or Syrian war, or Libyan war, etc.). The point about democracy was critical, as Caleb presupposed that Trump's rise proved democracy wasn't working well. But maybe the problem is the opposite: there is no democracy. I would think spending some time to think about whether or not we live in a democracy is a better use of New Yorker space than considerations of whether or not smarties should get to vote twice and dummies only once, but then again, I sometimes have no choice but to shop at Walmart. Angels voted for Trump. I know one. He made a mistake, I think, but I understand why he did it. He is still a great man: a middle aged White guy, a farmer who never went to college, shops at Walmart and voted for Trump and I respect him more than almost anyone else I know.

Caleb defriended me for this comment about his article and didn't respond. I don't mind a good argument. If I post a link to an article I wrote and you want to say it's crap, go ahead. Maybe it is crap. Let's hash it out. But no. That was not the move in 2016. Apparently this is where we are as a people today: I post what I think, and you're supposed to agree with me and applaud me for my views or I defriend you and end the discussion.

I could cite more examples of this anti-democratic response to the rise of Trump than the one I mention here from the New Yorker. The thing about the Crain review is that I found it on Caleb's Facebook feed. All his liberal friends wrote in to say, "Great article!" At no point did anyone, not Caleb or his friend, many of whom are also my friends, notice that letting some people vote more than others is a TERRIBLE idea and the liberal arrogance behind the idea is one reason why Trump is president.

You know that Jonathan Swift, with his modest proposal to eat the babies of Ireland, is a great writer. I loved the prose styling and think his suggestions deserve to be aired in a wide format, not that I agree with eating the babies the poor keep making and dumping on us, but maybe we should consider some aspects of the proposal...

And you never noticed it was satire? Or that eating people is bad? That's how I saw this review. Shouldn't we all realize that letting some people vote twice is a very bad idea? Brennan's wasn't writing satire? He actually thinks some people are better than others? No one noticed what a terrible idea that is?

## On rule of law

If it was wrong for Bush to violate the United Nations Convention on Torture, as a treaty approved by the senate and signed by the president has the force of US domestic law in America, then it is wrong for Obama to engage in acts of war without congressional approval, as Obama did in seven countries while president, routinely. Forget party and the fog of the corporate media to create isolated pockets of competing Democrats and Republicans: no. What about the law? Our government is clearly acting above the law. Bush passed the TARP bailout and Obama administered it. There was no issue at all in transitioning from Republican to Democratic rule. They both agreed: bailout the banks and let the homeowners fall.

Wikileaks blew a hole in their comfortable fake game.

Wikileaks blew open the Bush administration, then the Democratic party. Your duty is to wake up and stop being a Democrat or a Republican. They are working together to screw the American people. All of the significant enemies of the American people are American and none of them are foreign. We spent 30 trillion dollars on defense since the end of the Cold War and we're more defenseless and terrified than ever.

The right rises and falls almost exclusively on disgust with elite liberals. Racism is bad, but do you think the kids of these high minded liberals go to integrated schools? All the shit the right dumps on the liberals is true. Yes, the conservatives are just as bad or worse. In fact, they are pretty much the same. Even if you are affluent, you are still going to be cheated by this con game.

This idea, that Trump's victory proves or suggests that "democracy doesn't work" is exactly backwards. Trump was not elected in the context of a functioning democracy. The idea that the United States meets none of the internationally accepted standards of a true democracy.

1) One person, one vote: not in the US. Clinton won the popular vote over Trump in the general election and superdelegates and closed primaries are an affront to democracy in the first round of the election when Bernie in fact had more support than Clinton. Some states get more representation per capita than others.

2) Free press: not in America. Both ruling parties and the media are owned by the same corporations and exclude any discussion or news that might reveal the co-mingling of their ownership.

3) Elections free of fraud: not here. Criminal fraud was rampant in the 2016 Democratic primary but no action was taken to

fix the problem. Exit polling was cancelled when fraud was revealed in 2016 and the media covered the crime up.

4) Equal access to the ballot and right to campaign: nope. Big money politics means that those that challenge the system of corporate oligarchic government are denied the chance to reach the voters. If you protest, as at the Dakota Access Pipeline, you can go to jail. People were thrown off the voting rolls by party officials in the Democratic primary and denied the right to vote when they refused to take a loyalty oath.

5) The judiciary is not free of oligarchic control. A convoluted system of rules and procedures make justice expensive and judges cannot and do not challenge the rule of billionaires or their dominance of the political system.

6) The Deep State means that civilian control of the government over the military is an open question. If elected civilians cannot control the budget or operations of the NSA, CIA or FBI, then we do not have clear lines of civilian control.

7) If Bush can ignore ratified treaties and international law, if Obama can ignore the war powers provisions of the constitution, if Trump can ignore the emoluments clause, if the CIA can spy on congress, if the NSA can lie to congress, if the Supreme Court includes illegitimate justices such as Gorsuch... then there is no rule of law for the powerful.

8) If innocent people have been and will be executed in the future, if the police can shoot people for no reason in the street, if a journalist is being illegally detained in an embassy in London... there is no rule of law for the powerless.

For all these reasons and more, the United States, while not a totalitarian state, is not a democracy. All of the mainstream narratives about what went wrong in 2016 are exactly backwards.

We do not have enough free flow of information. The alternative news sources, most clearly Wikileaks, do a better job than the legacy media if you want accuracy and truth. We do not have too many choices as voters but far too few. We are not too free to make decisions but too restricted.

We need more democracy, not less: more freedom of information, more democratic free media, more voting, more participation. We live in a fake, pseudo democracy full of propaganda and election manipulation and fraud. Gerrymandering, the electoral college… yes, those contribute to the money in politics complex of fraud. We are chained to the past, the tyranny of the dead in the straightjacket of an ancient constitution that never bends, an ossified process. We are manipulated and bribed by oligarchs who cheat to capture the government and turn it into an instrument of repression. What is the name for the system we live in? Pseudo democracy.

The election of Trump ought to give us a chance to rethink how we organize ourselves politically. Those of us who are or were Democrats can now organize themselves coherently for the first time, or at least since FDR died. We could have a good, open discussion and consider multiple points of view. To make this process work best, Democrats should stop shouting "Russia!" and "Trump is Hitler!" It's hard to think with that kind of racket on CNN and in the New York Times.

Democracy is still our best bet. The ancients and the founding fathers were not wrong to worry about the mob following a demagogue. James Madison in Federalist Paper 10 wrote, "a society consisting of a small number of citizens, who assemble and administer the government in person, can admit of no cure for the mischiefs of faction…. By a faction, I understand a number of citizens, whether amounting to a majority or a minority of the whole, who are united and actuated by some common impulse of passion, or of interest, adverse to the rights of other citizens, or to the permanent and aggregate interests of the community." To check these factions, Madison proposed a strong federal judiciary. Unfortunately now, you need like a million dollars to get anywhere in federal court.

The ideas behind the US constitution, of setting competing interests against each other, is still a good solution to the potential for chaos in the unrestrained behavior of a mob. We now have more information and experience to check the passionate mob with something other than entrenched, self interested elites. Algorithms, big data, instant, open publication of documents: we have tools we can't use if we are strapped to the letter of the ancient constitution instead of being inspired by the ideology behind the entire government edifice: a confluence of competing interests checking one another.

In Plato's Republic, we find the model of the philosopher king, an idea that continued to appeal for centuries. Plato himself went to Syracuse to see if he could make the idea work. Voltaire spent time in the Frederick's court in Prussia more than 2000 years later also working on cultivating a philosopher king. Both Plato and Voltaire went home disappointed. Plato did say that democracy had a kind of beauty to it, with competing and, in his opinion, stupid factions battling it out. He just didn't trust the people. Aesthetically, there was some value in democracy, seen from afar. Up close, no, he didn't like it and outlined a totalitarian state. Stalin was something of a philosopher king, as he thought he had scientific proof of where we would be in the future in the form of Marxist laws. Plato has an anecdote in which people are on a boat with one experienced navigator aboard. They hold an election as to what to do without considering the expertise of the navigator and crash and burn. You see? We should listen to the experts! You see how badly we went wrong in 2016!

Well, no. The problem is that Obama is not a navigator. He is more like one of the passengers on the boat, the most charismatic one, who gets everyone to follow him right into a reef. A climate scientist is like the navigator. The problem is not that the people in the democracy heard the expert, considered what she had to say, and then voted badly, it's that they never got to hear her at all. The elite the people want to chuck out of power are not the experts but the oligarchs who absolutely refuse to listen to the navigator in the parable. Soros, Bezos, Trump, Clinton: the oligarchs are the ones drowning out the voice of reason, not the people. Wealth does not make you an expert, even if Hillary Clinton in secret told an audience paying her to speak that it does.

## On Germany

Here is a test of when American has become a progressive nation: when German residents in the US don't have to make dentist appointments in Germany when they go back. Of the many Germans living in America I have known, almost all go to the dentist in Germany, even if they've been living in America for decades. Some still keep their doctors in Germany. Why? Those services are just better and cheaper in Germany. Yes, both better and cheaper. Another test: can kids get on their bikes and go for a ride? Leave the house, bike somewhere safety, and come home? In Germany, this is normal.

What most of us mean by socialism is not the USSR in 1982 or Venezuela in 2015. We want compassionate, affluent, free societies like they have in Northern Europe. Germany is a large country of about 80 million people, plus the Nordic countries, Netherlands, and some more in the area and you have a population approaching about half of the United States.

We might in fact mean a bit more, a more democratic society than currently exists. The closest existing model is northern Europe, as the ideal of a true social and political democracy does not exist.

The test of the success of an administration has to be on the "feel it" in your own life basis. Democrats have been citing statistics about how many millions of people got some benefit while they were in office due to some act they passed, but except for Obamacare, most of the time, whatever it is they claim to have done cannot be detected by opening the door and looking around.

On the "feel it" basis I can tell you about my relatives and friends in Germany: no one worries about what will happen if they get sick, if they will lose their job or how they will pay for care. No one worries about how to pay for college for themselves or their kids.

My in-laws paid about $100 a year in property tax on a big, beautiful house. If you compare overall tax rates, the United States and Germany are about the same, and both have more and less regressive aspects to their taxation system. Whether you pay more or less in each country in overall taxes (including every local, state and national tax) would depend heavily on how you make your money, and where in each country you live.

What we can say without a doubt is that Americans do not pay a lot less than Germans. They may pay more. But Americans get back FAR less in services.

In Germany, they never painted their houses with lead paint. Why? The painter's union nixed it. In America, we never had a painter's union. So we have lead paint in all our old buildings. The lead paint issue was before congress shortly after the Red Scare of 1919. Guess what? A red scare in 1919 can produce lead poisoning in 2016. Crazy how that works, right?

For one thing, Germany today doesn't really have corrupt politicians. Markus Feldenkirchen presented a contrarian view in Der Spiegel in October 2015. Feldenkirchen says no, we really also do have scandals like Italy, Spain and the US. What can he come up with in the way of scandal?

"In 2011, Karl-Theodor zu Guttenberg resigned from his post as defense minister when it emerged he had plagiarized parts of his PhD thesis."

He has a PhD thesis? And he got to be in the government? That never happens in the US. And I am supposed to be scandalized by the fact that he didn't write the whole thing? That's a scandal? What else you got, Germany, because over here in New York State you're looking pretty damn clean.

"The University for Hannover is currently investigating whether Ursula von der Leyen, hotly tipped as Merkel's potential successor—should give up her doctor title." Another plagiarizer? Academic? Set to run the country? Shame!

"The president of Germany got a slight discount on his lease of an Audi." See Der Spiegel February 06, 2012 keywords Christian Wulff. He got almost 100 euros off a month! Horror!

Okay, here's a bigger one from the Feldenkirchen piece: "Volkswagen, the archetype of German companies and the epitome of reliability, so brazenly manipulated the emissions data of its automobiles that it has single-handedly transformed "Made in Germany" from a seal of quality to a warning." Well, yes, but that's not the government. Doesn't count. Sorry. Anything else?

"There is plenty of evidence to suggest the 2006 World Cup

in Germany only came about because of fraud and bribery." Okay that's bad… but it was also not within the confines of "German" government. So Germans are perfectly willing to be corrupt when they work at the EU or for Volkswagen or FIFA. But somehow these same people are not particularly corrupt when they work for the government.

The chancellor, the most powerful politician, Angela Merkel, lives in the same apartment she lived in before she was elected. Her husband walks over to the grocery store to buy the same groceries he bought before she was elected.

The closest thing to a scandal for her comes up in the Podesta Wikileaks, as Hillary Clinton's son-in-law tried to fix arrangements at the time of the Greek crisis to make a killing on insider trading with Greek debt (and losing it all… can't even get insider trading right). So as long as Angela manages to stay away from Hillary, she's as clean as a whistle. (See Armstrong Economics July 5, 2016, keywords Marc Mezvinsky and Eaglevale Partners).

You see: it doesn't have to be like it is here. We don't have to tolerate the revolving door of corruption we see all the time in America. What passes for a scandal in Germany… it's a joke compared to what John Podesta and his crew did every single day.

I like a lot of things about Germany. Planning, urban and rural, is rational. You have a bike path around the city most of the time and there's plenty of green space. German cities are very livable. The playgrounds are beautiful. You see nice schools set in parks surrounded by bikes. Farmland is farmland. You go to the center of the city and there are stores and shops, you walk around and do your business. The parking lot is where the parking lot should be. You don't see ugly stuff, or inappropriate development. The economy is humming along, crisis after world crisis. People get the right education. The whole thing basically works.

Why? Because politics, out in the open, democratic politics, is where the real business of government actually occurs. In America, we do politics, but only as a show. The real business, both local, state and national, is done after the public is out of the way. What politicians say has nothing to do with what actually happens. It's all backroom deals.

You see that ugly stupid development? Well, that's because someone got paid off. You see that idiotic invasion of Libya? That's because a politician is angling for a better position in the next election. You mean, you didn't have an open, honest debate in congress before you committed to an invasion? No, we didn't. Could such a major decision happen in Germany without consulting the legislature? Never. And in the legislature, the public positions of the parties they represent will give you some clue as to what they will say and do about matters of state interest.

No one in Germany ever has to wonder what will happen if they get sick: they will go to the doctor and insurance will pay. No one ever has to wonder how they will pay for college: it's all free.

It would be nice not to live in the Third World. It would be nice to have sane development and energy policies. But to achieve first world status, we couldn't let Hillary Clinton make 153 million by "making speeches" to banks.

# On 1831

On January 1, 1831 William Lloyd Garrison started publishing his antislavery newspaper The Liberator in Boston. Eight months later, on August 21, Nat Turner led a group of slaves on a bloody rampage through Southampton County, Virginia. Turner and his band eventually killed at least 55 white men, women, and children before they were stopped by the Virginia militia. Turner initially escaped capture by hiding out, but he was caught on October 30, tired and then hanged on November 11.

Garrison wrote of the Turner rebellion, "What we have long predicted, at the peril of being stigmatized as an alarmist and declaimer, has commenced its fulfilment.... What was poetry-imagination-in January, is now bloody reality… 'The dead bodies of white and black lying just as they were slain, unburied'-the oppressor and the oppressed equal at last in death-what a spectacle!"

Southerners blamed Garrison and other northern abolitionists for the uprising because Garrison had predicted it would happen, while making it clear that he himself, Garrison, was in favor of non-violent action.

I don't mean to insult Turner's memory by comparing him to Trump, but there is something familiar in the dynamic of people being apparently so clueless they cannot tell the difference between a prediction and an endorsement. Democrats, when we predicted something like Trump if you continue on your pro-corporate, corrupt, cheating ways, we were not supporting Trump, just letting you know what to expect.

I wish I could predict an uprising. We are overdue for one.

# On 1919

In some lecture or article, I recall a reference to a book written in the 1970s in which the author first proposed "firefighter" and "police officer" and a whole slew of gender neutral terms. The lecturer read passages from this 1970s feminist book predicted that it would take generations to change language use, that to get people to say "he or she" would be nice but is not realistic... and then about 20 years later all of her suggestions for gender neutral terms are in wide circulation. It was miraculous.

I remember distinctly that the lecturer said that "freshman" was not in her list of terms that need to be fixed, and, so, we still say "freshman" instead of "fresh person:" an oversight, or maybe due to the etymology of the word "freshman" itself. One of the points of the lecture was that the proposals in the book were thought through carefully, a creative and well constructed list of new terms. The author proposed "chair" of a committee instead of "chairperson" and "firefighter" she thought would be a good term, more action, and more appealing than "fire person."

If these claims were right, then this author could claim to have as much individual influence on English language usage as any single modern person. So, I wanted to go back and find the lecture to make sure I was giving this credit to the right author from the 1970s. A 1975 book called Language and a Woman's Place could be the book, making Robin Lakoff this influential person. There are other possibilities (see Sciencedirect and search "Language and sex textbooks: A review" by Rita M. Hoffmann).

This story—a single book changing the way English speakers use language—would mean we as a people can decide to change the way we speak. It's not only something that happens to us, sort of by osmosis or some natural tendency of language: we can also choose to change. I like the metaphor.

If we can choose to change language, we can choose to change laws. We can choose to change economics. We create these structures—languages, constitutions, economic systems, markets—then act like some god ruled that we have to keep doing things as people in the past did them.

The tyranny of the dead is a form of oppression. Laws written on paper become as if written on stone. A dysfunctional systems keep on keeping on.

I live in a county with 42 amateur town judges because in 1808 or whenever it was, asking people to travel 20 miles to the county seat to have a hearing with a professional judge was a burden. I pay property taxes because in 1790 the only way to get a sense of who was richer and who was poorer was to count the number of chimneys and windows each person had.

We have at least two national security operations, the NSA and the CIA. Before World War II, we didn't have any permanent spy agencies. The Cold War is over. Did anyone ever think of maybe scaling down or eliminating excess institutional baggage that seems to serve no productive purpose (or only a top secret positive benefit) to the people?

Empirical evidence is available to predict which incarcerated people are likely to re-offend and who would benefit most from which types of education prior to release. We can know with some certainty that people need to maintain a network of friends and relatives while in prison in order to re-integrate upon release. We can know that eyewitness testimony is faulty, that defendants perceived as good looking receive lower sentences, to say nothing of race, and that what a person is accused of, or convicted of, is far less significant to how much time that person may serve in jail than where the offense was committed and who happened to get the case on their desk, and of course how much money the accused can scrounge up. I could go on in many fields of government and other institutions. Much of what we do, we do because it is what we do without any rational reason to keep doing it.

Edmund Burke, a conservative Englishman, supported the American Revolution but condemned the French Revolution. He was one of the first people to articulate a conservative political philosophy. Until Burke wrote his essay on the French Revolution before the terror killed as many as 30,000 people, conservatives didn't need an explicit philosophy. The church, social class, the monarchy don't need to be justified by a theory: they just are. Burke offered a theory basically saying that tradition is valuable, necessary. There are no human rights, per se, but only rights based on history and tradition. Burke supported the American revolution because the colonists were demanding their rights as Englishmen. He opposed the French revolution because of the complete break with tradition, meaning that people in charge can change anything at all.

In her study of totalitarianism, Hannah Arendt said that the Holocaust and the rejection of refugees before the war proves there are no rights of man in the tradition of the French Revolution and that we only have rights as citizens of a particular, local tradition or nation. She was clearly right; Syrian refugees now have no rights because they lack the right passport. Leaving billions of people outside the community of those with rights may doom civilization.

High flying oligarchs often think they don't need the nation state, that they are above the petty rights of citizens. They are only correct as long as they in fact control the governments. Were a truly democratic government to take power in a major country, particularly the United States, we could imagine a future where no one is above the law.

A Jacobin might point out that if the tradition bound nations of Europe had not conspired with a sizable minority within France to attack the revolutionary government, creating civil and international war affecting large parts of the country, there might have been no terror. It was war and foreign-reactionary attack on what was, in fact, the most democratically elected government in European history, with a wide base of popular support and a program of reform so great that no one will ever be able to take it away (as indeed no one could: after the restoration of the old monarchy, almost all of the administrative reforms of the Revolution remained in place).

Even if Burke has a point in the abstract, or about France, excessive reform hardly seems like a realistic danger in America. We have the opposite problem.

Consider 1919 again. The Extraordinary International Socialist Congress at Basel, November 24-25, 1912 declared "the economic and political crisis created by the war to arouse the people and thereby to hasten the downfall of capitalist class rule." Two years after promising to remain loyal to class and resist a capitalist, nationalist war, all the socialist parties of Europe fell into line and supported their individual national war efforts. By necessity and as a reward, after the war, socialists and labor parties were incorporated into the political structure of European political systems.

Not so in the US. Eugene Debs, head of the US socialists, spent the war in prison for resisting the capitalist war. In 1919 and

1920 the US saw: 1) a peaceful, well organized Seattle General Strike of 1919 from February 6 to February 11 collapse in the face of a threat by the mayor to call in troops, and attacks on strikers in mainstream press; 2) an effort to organize the police force in Boston collapse when the Massachusetts governor, Calvin Coolidge, called in the National Guard, and attacks on the police in the mainstream press; 3) a steelworker's strike collapse under media criticism, and an attack that left 12 strikers dead; 4) the Tulsa race riot, shortly after 1919 in 1921 over 300 black people killed by a white mob with police standing by; 5) the forced deportation of immigrants if they were perceived as pro-labor in the Soviet Arc; 6) another racial attack in Chicago that left approximately 28 black residents dead; 7) the passage of the amendment prohibiting alcohol sales in the US. All of the stuff in that list happened in a little over a year.

Far more violence in the drive for a US labor movement than in any European country. On July 28, 1919, the New York Times wrote a story under the headline "REDS TRY TO STIR NEGROES TO REVOLT; Widespread Propaganda on Foot Urging Them to Join I.W.W. and 'Left Wing' Socialists. ATTACK COLORED LEADERS Publications Circulated Among Uneducated Classes in Southern States." While race riots are murdering Black Americans by the hundreds, as lynchings peak, the New York Times throws a little red oil on the flames: "Evidence is accumulating in the files of the Government to show that the negroes of this country are the object of a vicious and apparently well financed propaganda which is directed against the whole people, and which seeks, by newspaper, pamphlets and in other ways, to stir up discontent."

The New York Times was even worse with Judith Miller in 2003. In 2016, we had Amy Chozik trying to push Hillary into the White House by sabotaging Bernie Sanders, as she was instructed to do by Lynn Rothschild (yes, a real Rothschild). Guess what? The New York Times undermined the candidate that could be beat Trump. Lynching, the Iraq War, Trump: New York Times, fake news on behalf of the oligarchs for 100 years.

In short, while Europe was accepting labor into the structure of government, workers in America using the same basic tactics were being crushed by force, by divide and conquer with racism and anti-immigrant sentiment. The media and the government, local and national, conspired to repress the labor movement in the United States. There was repression in America before 1919 and in Europe. It's just by 1919 it became clear that the ruling class in Europe had to compromise in a way the ruling class in America was unwilling to do and did not have to do.

Bernie's stump speech: do 1919 over. I am drawing a direct line between 1919 and 2016. If we had managed to get a labor movement incorporated into the political structure of America in 1919 like the Europeans, we would have national healthcare now, like they do. We would have tuition free college like they do. We would have a decent minimum wage like northern Europeans. Bernie wouldn't have had a stump speech.

Bernie's stump speech is basically calling for us to re-do 1919 and not break up the Seattle strike but compromise with the workers, to not stir up racism and Klan membership in the Midwest but to bring black people into unions with white workers, to not demonize immigrants as radicals and deny basic civil rights to people who have committed no crime, to not distract the populace in smaller towns with nonsensical campaigns blaming alcohol for a society that is not humane to the workers who build the economy.

The DNC/CNN types think we're going to forget the rigging

of the 2016 primary? Seattle and Tulsa in 1919 remain open wounds, let alone the 2016 primary. As a nation, deep down there somewhere, we never got a labor movement and race is still there to be used to stir us up anytime the oligarchs get nervous. 1919 is not ancient history, a different America. It's the same dynamics are still in play politically, of race and class and control of government.

We, the human community, make up words over time. The words refer to things in the universe that are real but the words are just conventions we made up to refer to reality. A cat is a real animal. The word "cat" could just as easily be "gato" or whatever. If we want to, we can change language. Mira, es muy facil. Ahora hemos cambiado de idioma sin problema.

Just because we invented it and it doesn't really exist in the world outside of our collective minds doesn't mean language isn't powerful. The Greek gods could do things like shoot individuals with lightning bolts from the sky, and Barack Obama can do the same thing. Shiva could destroy worlds, and so can we, as Robert Oppenheimer pointed out. How did we get to be more powerful than our own ancient gods? By sharing information over time and space.

Money is something we humans made up too. Why do some Americans have more money than others? "Because bankers rig democracy to ensure they control and manage the institution of money," says economist Richard Wolff in an interview with Actvism.

The Native Americans on the East Coast used wampum. The Lydians invented coins a few thousand years ago. Bank notes turned into paper money. Now, the Federal Reserve can create money on a computer in the basement, increasing the money supply like this: 10,000,000. There, we just made ten million dollars that didn't exist before.

Value is real. My dog loves to chew sticks but if I show up with a piece of meat, he drops the stick and runs over to get the meat. The meat is vastly more valuable to him than the stick. Value is like the real cat in my language analogy. Money expresses something real in the world: value.

Some skills are more valuable than others for making more money. Some items are more valuable than others to certain people. From value and money we move to markets. Markets have been a great boon to human well being. Markets are also incredibly powerful institutions we invented and that only really exist in our own brains. The Language Revolution occurred probably 100,000 years ago or longer. The Industrial Revolution around 1800 led to a massive acceleration in the rate of increase in life expectancy, and population and markets were a part of that.

Money and words are some powerful stuff. We can control them through collective action expressed by democratic institutions and with social determination.

But some people have 50 billion dollars. "Top 10 richest people in the world" on June 28, 2016 in the Indian Express does not include the king of Saudi Arabia or Vladimir Putin, as we don't know how much money they have. About 800 million people on the planet get by with less than $2 a day, according to the World Bank ("Poverty and Shared Prosperity 2016"). What this says is that some people are billions of times more valuable than other people. Those in the middle might not think about it much, but most of us are closer on the bell curve of income to the 800 million than to the .1%.

The Wikipedia page called "Social and psychological value of money" in late 2016 said, "Money today is fiat money, a symbol of value created by the human imagination with no intrinsic value of its own. ... A coin or paper currency note has value because people accept it as a symbolic medium of exchange. The economic value of money as measured by its purchasing power is a subject of economic theory."

I love this Caitlin Johnstone quote about narratives: "Political power is held in place by narratives; the only reason anyone has any power is because everyone else agrees to pretend that that's where the power is. Government, money, and in fact all of human culture are made up of conceptual constructs invented by humans to serve humans. Whoever controls those conceptual constructs controls the world, so it makes sense that the powers that be are so desperate to maintain control of the narrative. Without that, they've got nothing."

Now, put the idea about money with the idea about narratives. Yes, some inequality is necessary. Yes, Mr. Burke, change can get out of hand in theory, although that has never happened in America. But even so, the degree of inequality and the arbitrariness of control, the establishment of a permanent oligarchy, is simply intolerable.

We tried to revolt in 1919 and they beat us. We tried again in 2016 and they beat us again. We're not well organized. We are up against an establishment.

# On 1932

In 1929 before the crash, the Republicans controlled the White House, the senate by 17 votes and the House of Representatives by 104 seats. In 1933, after FDR's election, the Democrats had the presidency, the senate by 23 seats, and the house by more than two to one, with a massive 126 vote advantage.

FDR made mistakes, got criticized from the left and right, and maybe his New Deal didn't really end the depression; the war did that. But no one doubted that he and his party under him were for the people, even if the New Dealers didn't always know exactly what to do. The people liked work relief, social security, electrification, etc. They knew who to thank and the Democrats held the presidency for 20 straight years, and 28 out of the next 36 years. Democrats maintained control of the senate until 1981, except for four years, so 44 out of the next 48 years. Democrats controlled the house until 1995 except for four years, so 58 out of the next 62 years.

After the US entered World War II, FDR proposed a 100 percent top tax rate. At a time of "grave national danger," Roosevelt told Congress in April 1942, "no American citizen ought to have a net income, after he has paid his taxes, of more than $25,000 a year." That would be about $350,000 in today's dollars. In early October, he issued an executive order that limited top corporate salaries to $25,000 after taxes. The move would "provide for greater equality in contributing to the war effort," Roosevelt declared. Infuriated conservatives saw red, literally. The "only logical stopping place for this movement," fumed Princeton economist Harley Lutz, would be "a completely communistic equalization of incomes."

Obama also had a crisis on his hands when he took office in 2009. Not the same, I know. But the way he handled it, we can be sure he was for the bankers. He bailed out the bankers, not the homeowners. He also put in a big new public policy, Obamacare. But he did it without pissing off the insurance companies. And unlike social security, Obamacare failed.

This is the problem with the Democratic Party. Today, the purpose of the national and state parties seems to be nothing more than to have high ranking staff people and elected officials get rich and feel powerful. They do policy only so much as they need to say something to get elected some of the time. If they don't win, that's not too bad, since they can scare people about the Republicans in fundraising letters.

If the party were actually a party, as in 1933, and if the party and the leaders acted in the interests of the people instinctively, if sometimes incorrectly, and the people knew that the party was for the people, the party could have another 62 year run of good luck. Instead, careerists are feathering their own damn nest and watching inequality blast through the roof like it ain't no big deal. That's what Republicans are supposed to do.

Losing to Trump won't make the careerist see the light. Nothing will ever make them see the light. They have all the light they need, win or lose. They can revolving-door themselves in and out of the corporate media while they're at it. As long as they don't step on the toes of the bankers, insurance companies, military contractors, oil companies, etc.

Any time between May into late July 2016, Barack Obama could have stopped Trump from becoming president by uttering three little words, "I endorse Bernie." The empirical evidence, even before the DNC leaks on Wikileaks, made Bernie the clear choice to assure victory in the November general election. Being the great orator, he would have kept talking after those little words, but three were all he needed to say. Hillary's weak polling against Trump could have alarmed him in May. Then came Wikileaks. Then the convention disaster, when the Democrats lost two to three million Bernie or Bust voters. At no point did he pull the plug on the terrible plan Hillary and Barack came up with in a backroom in 2008 or 2012.

This is an emergency. We'd better get Nancy Pelosi and Chuck Schumer in here quick to approve Trump's cabinet of monsters. Feel better now? Phew. I was worried the Democrats might sell out again.

This book exists to tell the story of 2016 from the 99% perspective. While the election is still fresh in our minds, this book seeks to crystalize the keep moments, ideas and facts common among some of us in that minority of Bernie Sander's supporters in the democratic primary who refused to follow his lead and did not support Hillary Clinton in the general election.

Those Berners who agree with the point of view in this book can use this volume as a handy reference. Instead of a writing out a long response to someone online, you can refer to particular chapters of this book, if those chapters express more or less what you were going to say. You can give this book as a present to your Hillbot friends in case there is a run on toilet paper (because that would be about the only condition under which they might actually open the book). You can give a copy to your Trump-loving friends too. Plead with them to read just a bit. Or better yet, read it to them out loud with a lot of bluster and emotion and see if that works.

The book includes an argument from history about the repression of workers and other movements in the United States which is the deep background of why so many of us are dissatisfied with corporate and elite domination. We are actually part of a long history. In here we discuss the role of propaganda. There is an argument that the United States is not a democracy.

We got all the arguments you need to keep you from having to argue with your friends and family who still think CNN does "news." Remember when Bernie threw up his fist and said, "Revolution!" at a democratic debate? He didn't think we'd take him seriously, did he? Whatever he thought, we should. In 2016 Bernie or Bust was a thing. I say we double down and make Revolution or Bust a double thing.

## On 1971

It's 1971, the year before Watergate became a national scandal. You meet someone at a party or some such setting. She says:

"You know, the president made a deal with the Viet Minh before the election in 1968 in order to prevent a peace deal that could let Johnson win re-election. That's high treason, and Nixon could be executed for that." You start to roll your eyes. But then… "George Will Confirms Nixon's Vietnam Treason," August 12, 2014, Common Dreams.

"And not only that, the FBI has a program to frame Black Panthers and other radicals for crimes they didn't commit, and also execute them and plant evidence to justify the extra-judicial murders, a straight up death squad. The only way anyone will ever find out about this is when some radicals break into the FBI office and then keep quiet about it for 40 years." What a nut, you're thinking.

Now… Google COINTELPRO. And then…. "Burglars in 1971 FBI office break-in come forward after 43 years… Documents exposed surveillance state under J Edgar Hoover" Guardian, January 7, 2014.

"And to top it off, this idea that we have to fight in Vietnam to keep the dominos from falling, basically that Vietnam is a Soviet puppet? It's total rubbish. The Russians and the Chinese have almost no influence over the Vietnamese communists and none of them are coordinating any kind of communist world take over with each other. In fact, they will all be at war with one another soon." Yeah, right.

"And the president is so paranoid and has such a small circle of followers that he is surrounded by actual criminals who would break into the offices of the other party to corrupt an election." Really? What a wild-eyed radical.

"US troops are committing war crimes in Vietnam and there is no reason for us to be there." Go on. You know that Martin Luther King, speaking up about the war, he shouldn't do that. His issue is race. What a communist.

Fast forward to 2016. Another wide-eyed radical steps up. "Hillary Clinton stole the primary from Bernie Sanders."

"The secretary of state was getting money directly from the Saudis and then worked to make sure they got billions in American weapons, which they then passed on to Isis. American allies and innocent civilians were routinely killed by our own weapons. We used this killing to justify attacks on Isis' main opponent Assad, if you can believe that."

"The electronic voting machines are not secure and are

routinely corrupted... The FBI investigation of Hillary Clinton was a whitewash and she's clearly guilty of multiple felonies."

"Hillary Clinton's campaign made up the primary schedule, pretty much picked the debate moderators and got the questions in advance."

"The campaign more or less co-wrote stories with all the major media outlets, like they were part of the same team."

"Hillary says she's sorry about the Iraq war, but then made the same 'mistake' in Libya. And her foreign policy team is working on doing more of the same in the next administration."

"Citibank picked Obama's cabinet then was the principal recipient of TARP bailout money."

"The government can read anyone's email or other correspondence any time they want with no warrant."

"A major journalist responsible for reporting all of the wrongdoing in the government is openly under threat to his life by the US government."

Those wide-eyed radicals: always basing their opinions on what they themselves see instead of listening to the conventional wisdom spouted by the people in suits, with titles and authority.

Meet 1859, John Brown on slavery. 1916, Eugene Debs on World War I. Hung from the neck until dead, shot, put in prison. Julian Assange is suck in an embassy in London. Telling the truth is dangerous in the land of the free.

# On socialism

Social Security in America is straight redistribution from the young to the old and disabled. Considering the vast amounts of money involved, the administrative costs and losses due to corruption are pretty small. These simple schemes that apply to everyone, or almost everyone, are the ideal form of socialism.

The market just can't take care of basic needs. Radiolab had a podcast on antibiotics, perhaps Staph Retreat of November 2, 2015, that noted that bacteria have been becoming resistant to antibiotics at a steady rate since these drugs were introduced. Part of the problem today, aside from the overuse of antibiotics, is that the cost of bringing a drug to market is too high, given that the drug is likely to stop working in 15 years. There is an economic problem here. Viagra is profitable. New antibiotics are not. So, if you get an infection that cannot be currently treated, too bad, you die.

Also, there are a number of rare diseases, affecting as few as 100 people a year. The profit margin isn't there. Or chagas, a tropical disease mostly affecting poor people in Brazil and Africa: millions of people die. Drug companies don't care. Since the market can't deal with these problems, "too bad, you die" is kind of a heartless answer. Here you need the government to step up and do something. Antibiotics are important but the market will not make sure we have a steady stream of new antibiotics.

I am suspicious of government in general and grants and programs with human intervention in general. However, controls can be put in place to avoid cheating, if expertise is needed. The government needs much more transparency and democracy. We need better government because we all need more intervention in our society.

# On Team Hillary

As in 1932, it was either fascism or a New Deal in 2016. Democrats stabbed FDR 2.0 in the back. So guess what? Option zero. Tough primary… trouble in the midwest… I know what we need to save our candidate: Tim Kaine. You know, he speaks a little Spanish.

Obama must have wanted Trump to be president. Otherwise, why would he have let the DNC and Hillary cheat Bernie and not compromise on a VP pick? He could have been a leader, a good general, and changed his plan. Maybe there was a deal in 2008 after the Obama-Clinton primary: Debbie Wasserman Schultz, Hillary's woman, would take over the DNC, Hillary would be secretary of state and then the Democratic nominee in 2016. Or maybe the deal was done in 2012 leading up to the January 28, 2013 60 Minutes sit down joint interview with Hillary and Obama right after Obama's second inaguration.

Either way, by July 2016 the plan resulting from a 2008 or 2012 deal was coming apart. Obama twiddled his thumbs. Generals don't stick to losing strategies: they change. Mr. Hope and Change went for blind hope over sure victory. Politico headline "Clinton: 'I am not a natural politician' of March 9, 2016 raises a question: then why are you doing this to us?

On January 17, 2017 The Inquisitr wrote that "The Clinton Foundation has shut down the Clinton Global Initiative in a move that political opponents have taken as confirmation that the organization is a slush fund." No one has come forward to explain why donations dried up immediately after Clinton lost if the fund was in fact actually a charity.

Why did about 15 people get into the Republican race but only five Democrats? Because Clinton used her money and foundation to buy everyone off and intimidate them. All the Democrats in Washington knew she was laundering money but said nothing. The April 1, 2016 Counterpunch story "How Hillary Clinton Bought the Loyalty of 33 State Democratic Parties" is a good source for the 2015 money laundering story.

This fiasco, President Trump, is all on team Hillary. No one else. It's not the voter's job to unify the party. The leaders have to try to do that. Hillary and Obama never tried to bring us pissed off opponents of the Deep State back in the party and we stayed away.

Democrats are in trouble. They will reform or go away. See you in four years for Trump's second inauguration, unless this rift is healed through real compromise. We want a party of working people and that ain't the Clinton/Obama/Podesta/Soros/Schumer/Pelosi Democrats.

Any Democrats out there who thinks FDR was a great president should remember that the communists were out there nipping at the left's heals. Doesn't matter if the communists should have taken over America in the Great Depression or not, agitation from the left helped move the country left, where we need to go again, further left this time than in the 30s. We need movements like they have in Spain, in Iceland and other places, calling for dramatic change from the left.If Democrat rank and file people are, in part, progressives in their hearts, they should encourage left wing agit ation, not resent it.

# On inequality and money

**M**ore deeply, beyond the tragedy of 2016, the entire narrative of the American political-economic order, covering both our system of government and economics, the system of capitalist liberal democracy that is not very democratic, is built on a lie. We should be able to imagine an America free of oligarchs and special interests, and money in politics, where the public sphere, the government, is actually a force influencing trade and the market and not the other way around.

Thomas Piketty, Anthony B. Atkinson and others, economists, have demonstrated elegantly, see the numerous articles in the New York Review of Books, that inequality in America is not the natural result of trade, globalization, technology, or any other force beyond our control, something that just happens by natural historical forces. Rather than accept high degrees of inequality as natural in the same way the division of labor is natural under industrial capitalism, unequal distribution is primarily the result of government policy. Absent the capture of the state by oligarchs, our distribution of wealth would be more like the period from 1940 to 1970. When the state oppressed the workers, as it did from the late 19th century to 1932, or in other ways from 1980 to today, inequality grows to dangerous and destructive levels.

There is nothing inevitable or natural about the current obscene level of inequality. There is no hidden hand of the market that says the United States has to have a "Rust Belt." Does Norway have a rust belt? Wasn't the East pretty rusty, antiquated and industrial when Germany unified in 1990? And the West grumbled about the tax they had to pay to rebuild the East. But they paid and now Germany has no Rust Belt.

It's not natural to have urban ghettos, a part of town where mostly Black people live and crime is high, schools are bad. Do you think that happened due to some natural consequence of economic exchange beyond the ability of the collective through government to change?

No, we can't make it rain in the desert (or not a big desert consistently over a long period of time). We can't drain the ocean. We can't visit planets in distant solar systems (not yet!). That's nature. We can't change a lot of it. Economic and political stuff: we can change a tremendous amount. Even the air you're breathing now Morpheus.

No one is talking about a utopia without inequality. In 1950, there were rich and poor people in America. There are rich and poor people in Japan and Norway today. But in these other times and places, the difference is not so pronounced as to corrupt the entire function of the society.

If I mention 1950, it doesn't mean I think Jim Crow was a good thing or that I don't know that the equality I cite was among White Men. I do not cite the year 1950 because I want to "make America great again" but to offer one example in American history along with other examples in other times and places of prosperous, growing economies in societies without massive concentration of wealth among a small group. Inequality was less pronounced in America from the end of World War II until about 1975. That doesn't mean America was in all ways better in that period, of course.

The market, private property and money are good at what they do and have been a boon to humanity. But inequality is not natural, normal or good for the economy. We can and should redistribute the wealth.

# On money and value

**V**alue is real. A dog knows a bone is better than a stick. The bone is worth more. Money is an explicit expression of value that is transportable and convertible. This invention is necessary because value would exist without currency, as in a monarchy or in the old Soviet system. Access to power is valuable (just check the Clinton's net worth) and will be traded. A king can confiscate lands and redistribute them at will. The party under communism can fire and replace quite well off and apparently "rich" bureaucrats at will. If there is no way to create a stable system of value outside of the value determined by raw power, as under communism or an absolute monarch, your entire society cannot breath, grow or develop and tyranny is everywhere.

As great as some level of inequality as a natural byproduct of markets has been for the greater good in many ways, let's consider the following as a thought experiment, not exactly a policy proposal: If we were somehow to take the money from all the billionaires and multimillionaires, say, everyone with more than 200 million in assets, maybe trying to cap the per person wealth at no more than about a billion, and then, at the same moment, send the money out to the regular people this action would be: 1) perfectly moral, democratic, fair and right and 2) would improve the economy, our quality of life and the environment.

As to morality: by "take" the money I mean through a wealth tax and an inheritance tax. Few doubt the right of the government to tax. Confiscation is another story. Confiscation can raise questions of property rights.

The people have a right to property, even now, despite supreme court decisions like Kelo v. City of New London that have allowed the state wide latitude to take property. However, in the same period when the court chipped away at property rights, we got new private rights to do the work property rights used to do before the Supreme Court gutted the right to property. At the time of the constitution, the phrase that a person has "a property in himself" that you find in the writing of the founding fathers suggests that our modern privacy rights are doing much of the work of ancient property right.

Property remains a right, if less fundamental than privacy in the modern world. Wealth never was or is a right. When I propose wholesale redistribution, there is no question of right involved.

There is no right to wealth. On the other hand, over regulation and arbitrary abuse of power by the government to target individual wealth can be bad for the economy. Whether something is bad or good for the economy does not make that matter one of fundamental rights.

Indeed, I do not think redistribution is bad for the economy but quite necessary and good. But even if it were bad, the government would have the authority to redistribute wealth by taking wealth, as long as they do not strip individuals of their property. Corporations are not persons and do not figure into the equation at all.

The state cannot be allowed to arbitrarily pick winners and losers. If the Koch brothers are to lose most of their fortunes, then Bill Gates and Warren Buffett must lose most of theirs. The state should be even handed. Even the whole class of the extremely wealthy: the point is not to punish or ruin them. Simply, money is a symbol of value. Value is real. The symbolic representation can become divorced from reality. When that happens, a correction is in order. The only entity capable of making this correction is the state.

Inherited wealth is corrosive. Massive accumulation of wealth is bad for the economy. It is a valid function of government to redistribute the wealth. So, with no question of rights involved and no threat to the economic foundation of general prosperity, we must redistribute the wealth.

## On redistribution

In 2016, I bought a foreclosed house and renovated it. When I'm not in it, I rent it on Airbnb. People in the city can rent a nice house for not too much money. They spend money at restaurants when they come up, sometimes take a train and rent a car. A property is back on the tax rolls. I paid workers and bought stuff in local stores. The neighborhood picked up a bit, one less eye-sore. Yes, big companies like AirBnb, Enterprise, and Home Depot make some money, but so do local shops, businesses and governments.

Rich people don't do investments like that. They can't, really. If too much money flows up, the neighborhood stays blighted, the house stays foreclosed, the work doesn't happen, the family in the city can't have as many nice vacations, and so on. If you ripped the money out of the hands of those that are hoarding it and spread it around, some people would party, buy coke and squander their money. Some would get back on their feet. Some would start new and better careers. Some would invest in very real needs and opportunities right where they live.

In 2009, CitiBank got a low interest loan from the US government equal to $1,400 per man woman and child in the country. If instead the government had loaned the same amount of money to the people of the nation under the same terms, the economic benefit to the economy would likely have been much better. One could send out the checks to everyone with a social security number and the citizen could chose to accept the loan and cash the check or destroy the check and not take the loan.

If every man, woman and child with a social security number were to open up an envelope with $10,000 per person in it, they would pay off debt. Some of them would buy a foreclosed house and renovate it and rent it out. Others would go to college. Somebody would make a t-shirt company. The economy would explode with growth and there would be zero negative consequences to the economy broadly.

Many people live by having access to rich people (financial advisors, interior designers, etc.). These people would still have work and good lives. There would be just as many of them. Right now, all the money is concentrated in the hands of the rich and that drives up the prices of rich people assets: luxury houses, start up tech stocks, mortgage derivatives, Panama law firms, private jets, etc. Rich people cannot possibly "earn" vast amounts of money. Wealth accumulation is not a right and no one "deserves" 70 billion dollars. No one human is worth 70 billion more than another.

If in addition to handing out money the government also invested in infrastructure, including open space to recreate and exercise, the people would have jobs, live longer, be healthier. Obesity would decline. In addition to that, people could avail themselves of education at any time, as all these adjunct professors are put to work elevating the minds of their neighbors instead of regretting they spent five years studying art history. All kinds of new ideas would flow through society. Having ideas would be valued. Art history is not a waste of time and money, a distraction from the real work of day trading penny stocks, making complex mortgage derivatives, building pipelines and building apps to provide real time images of naked breasts.

Most of the super rich inherited their money and even those who deserve to be rich in some sense, who were first, who invested, who took a chance, who strived for great achievement, don't deserve to be THAT rich. Yes, you should invest or you should excel at your work or found a new company and get rich, up to a point. After a certain point, billions, it becomes immoral to hoard the money the rest of us need to have fulfilling, healthy lives.

The only reason we don't rise up and take their money and share it out is that we're trapped in their ideology. That's why they cheated Bernie Sanders and let Trump win. Fascism is a risk they are willing to take. Socialist liberation scares them. It doesn't matter who Bernie Sanders is: he stood on a stage and said "billionaires," and then, when someone from the crowd shouted "fuck them," he agreed. Then he put up his fist and said "revolution." The sacred earth goddess smiled and sent a little bird who landed on Bernie's podium on March 23, 2016, to tell the people to love the world and their fellows, to be free of oppression. Karl Marx got a lot wrong, but not everything. Workers of the world unite. We have nothing to lose but our chains.

You see what happened? We're busting our asses to get a hundred dollars to survive and not having time and not getting the education we need and polluting the earth and fighting wars and all we need to do to have a much better time of it is to forget this Republican versus Democrat nonsense, pretend debate, fake politics, and rise up and change the social economic system to make it decent, compassionate and humane. Trump was a better bet for them, them meaning the DNC/MSM/RNC/Deep State/ spooks/military industrial complex, than was Bernie.

Democrats like Pelosi and Schumer stood there in their safe seats and watched wealth concentrate in the hand of the 1%, watched war go on forever, and said and did nothing but criticize the Republicans for not supporting some idiotic program they proposed that wouldn't change anything fundamental.

# On denial

I don't see a flaw in the logic or any evidence to the contrary: the Pied Piper strategy of John Podesta was the key to Trump's victory in the Republican primary; Obama could have pulled the plug on Hillary after the DNC leaks/Tim Kaine fiasco but failed to do so; the weakness of Obama's elites-only recovery meant a populist had a good chance in 2016; the media and the oligarchs favored Hillary; all the arguments in favor of Hillary over Bernie were false ("vetted" "electable" etc.); the false arguments were relentlessly promoted in the MSM and there was a blackout on coverage of Bernie through the early part of the campaign; Bernie would have clearly won the general election; the DNC primary was stolen. The naked and unsuccessful attempt by the mainstream media to bury the Podesta Wikileaks only allowed the more salacious and scandalous, but relatively poorly sourced, allegations to fly around the internet and do more damage. The correct response to the DNC leaks of July 2016 was to call for Hillary to step aside. Therefore, Trump is the responsibility of the Democratic leadership. Evidence and logic lead to the conclusion that HRC/BHO/DNC/DWS and the Podesta brothers gave us Trump.

I moved to the Hudson Valley twelve years ago. The man who sold me my house, the previous owner, warned me about snowmobiles. Groups of guys speed through in the middle of the night and cause quite a ruckus. They come from far away and drink beer and cause all kinds of hell. That problem went away in the past few years. They all sold their snowmobiles.

There is a relic of a factory, the ice house, in my town. A book called The Ice  Horse by Thomas Locker gives you an idea of what the ice house did back before refrigeration: cut big blocks of ice out of the Hudson river for ice boxes in the city. The factory required a massive investment and was an ongoing business. Every year, farmer spent the winter cutting ice. Since I have lived here, there were only about six weeks total spread over three different years when you could have walked out on the Hudson with a horse.

See how real global climate change is? I can open my door and see it. Without global evidence, we could say these changes are local, or dispute my results in many other ways, but with the comprehensive evidence available from many other sources, the conclusion is obvious.

That the 2016 election of Trump is the fault of the systemic failure of American democracy, with a huge assist from Democratic party leadership, is as obvious as climate change. I can find empirical evidence in reliable sources that I access through the internet and by opening my door and looking around my own neighborhood: it's that clear. You either see evidence and let that evidence change your mind or you are an ideologue.

In 2015, I was a staunch Democrat. I donated $2000 to Obama in 2008. I volunteered for Obama. I also seem to have donated to other Democrats, when I look myself up at the FEC, but I honestly can't imagine that I really gave money to Kirsten Gillibrand's campaign, but apparently the FEC thinks I did.

In 2016, I changed. Obama was a sell out and cheated me. How do I know?  Wikileak ID 8190. Remember that one? Blue Dogs try to wave it away, CitiGroup vetting Obama's political appointees, that Michael Froman was on the transition team, etc.

No. That email deserves an investigation, a commission, to find out:
1) how many CitiGroup employees worked on the spreadsheet?;
2) what were the criteria for selection?; 3) during the administration
of the TARP money under Obama, how did the people named in
that spreadsheet effect Obama policy such that CitiGroup was the
biggest recipient of TARP money while homeowners in underwater
mortgages were not bailed out?

## On authority

Be alert to this meme from MSM propaganda outlets: people
are against elites so they don't appreciate expertise. This
dynamic of lack of respect explains the political climate. These
undereducated commoners think they are smarter than climate
scientists, for example. Then, by extension, these same people
vote badly based on no expertise.

This kind of deceptive claim is one way the MSM does their
fake news. To fully take this apart, we'd have to consider the
concept of "expertise." When a claim of authority is a good reason
to accept a conclusion and when such a claim is not a good reason
has been the subject of philosophical concerns for hundreds of
years. More recently, research often shows that the "professional
judgement" of many professionals is no better at predicting disease,
or psychological problems, or legal outcomes, or other matters,
than is a wild guess. In short, while expertise certainly exists and
deference to real knowledge is good, the range of inappropriate
appropriations of authority is vast, common and a real problem, and
likely worse among Democrats who are surprised Trump won.

I will offer the best possible way to think about climate change
politically in one short paragraph. Without Googling anything at all,
as good a way to approach the issue politically as you'll probably

find (more or less) to prove that I don't need a weatherman to know which way the wind blows:

> *There are a variety of models in the peer reviewed literature for what climate change will mean in the future. Models for sea level rise, for example, vary widely in how high and how fast we can expect the sea to rise, depending on a huge number of factors. These predictions include horrible possibilities but there can be no one precise estimate. Human society currently depends on the systems that produce greenhouse gases, particularly carbon. We live by burning fossil fuels. However, moving away from fossil fuels, as difficult and initially expensive as that will be, appears now to have no significant adverse consequences over the current system of energy production. In other words, there is no long term apparent risk to the environment or the economy from moving to renewable energy if we can figure out the short term impediments in the transitional phase. Given the potential for a crisis, and the lack of a clear danger in changing to a new system, there is absolutely no reason not to make the reduction of carbon emissions and other greenhouse gases among the primary goals of the government.*

See? You don't bow down to authority, or overestimate what we know, but apply logic and critical evaluation of expertise. You don't want to see me do the same thing to the 2016 election? Because humans, like the climate, do exist in the real world and are understandable.

> *Before the Democratic primary, in August 2015, Hillary Clinton struck a deal with 33 state parties to launder millions of dollars to her campaign, a move that would be illegal under*

the election rules Democrats say they want to pass. This deal scared away most corporate politicians to the 2016 primary on the Democratic side and they had only five candidates. While Bernie followed the rules that Democrats say they want in terms of fundraising, Hillary did not. As we know from Wikileaks releases of DNC and Podesta emails, Hillary's campaign routinely violated federal law and her campaign coordinated with her super pacs. Hillary's campaign coordinated with media outlets to promote Trump's candidacy on the Republican side, as per the Pied Piper strategy. Podesta was able to change the primary schedule to fit both Hillary and Trump. Hillary's campaign told their friends in the media not to cover Bernie and her allies did not cover him. Hillary's campaign received advance copies of stories from the New York Times, CNN, MSNBC, the Washington Post and others and was able to pull unfriendly stories from these outlets. The debate schedule and set up were designed by the DNC and the media to favor Clinton. Google and Facebook executives were close to Podesta's people and worked to include superdelegate totals in delegate counts to make the race seem over when it was not. Polling places were closed in Arizona in a suspicious way. Hundreds of thousands of voters were kicked off the rolls in New York in a case that was called illegal by the Department of Justice. The Nevada caucus was a farce. In many states, such as New York, bizarre and arbitrary rules kept as many as 35% of eligible voters from voting. When the extent of the cheating was revealed in the DNC Wikileaks release right before the 2016 Democratic convention, Hillary Clinton did not make any major concessions to the progressive *faction of the party. Most Bernie delegates walked out of the convention in protest of their silencing to make the convention look better on TV. Hillary Clinton polled an average of 12 points worse than Donald Trump prior to the election. Polls after the nomination continued to show that Bernie was far superior to Clinton in a matchup against Trump. All available anecdotal and polling evidence, all empirical evidence, says Bernie was a better match up against Trump. When voters were not restricted from voting by closed primaries, the will of the people clearly favored Bernie, despite the media blackout conspiracy. Hillary Clinton's unfavorable ratings are the highest for any politician to run for president, except Donald Trump. The Clintons made 153 million dollars by giving speeches prior to the election. That these fees were in fact influence peddling is abundantly clear. Hillary was under FBI investigation for the entire period of the campaign. Hillary never campaigned in Wisconsin, paid little attention to Michigan and Pennsylvania, and consequently lost these states. Tim Kaine added no votes. Many counties that voted for Obama went for Trump. Trump got fewer voters than Republicans who lost in critical swing states like McCain, Romney and Bush. A higher percentage of Black men admitted they voted for Trump than other recent Republican candidates. More Hispanic men as well. More White women voted for Trump. About one out of five people who voted for Trump also said he was unqualified. Black households lost more than 50% of their wealth under Obama. Obamacare premiums are increasing far faster than inflation. Life expectancy for White people without college degrees declined under Obama. If Hillary had not had a private server in her home, Comey could not have been a factor in the election. Even if Russia was involved in the DNC/Podesta email releases, the emails are legitimate and not fake. The American people are better informed now than before the releases. The working class suffered significant setbacks under Democratic rule, Hillary's nomination was illegitimate, the Democratic party intentionally promoted a bad candidate over a good one, and Trump got a significant boost from the Pied Piper strategy. These factors explain most of the loss in 2016. Therefore, Hillary and the Democrats are responsible for the victory of Trump. If not for Citizen's United and McCutcheon v. FEC, Hillary Clinton would never have had a chance to run. Without the superdelegates purchased in August 2015, she would not have had an aura of inevitability. Without the media reporting the delegates in the totals, there would be no presumption of inevitability. These are known facts. Yet, the conclusion of these facts is that Hillary stole the election, before we even start talking about actual illegal fraud in the ballot box, which also seems to have occurred. She bought this election by taking advantage of right wing supreme court decisions that are anti-democratic.*

I don't see much difference between the global warming argument and the "Democrats gave us Trump" argument. You look at the available evidence and draw the most clear conclusion. I can't say how high the sea will rise but I can say that human activity is causing global climate change. If the Democrats had had a fair primary process, if the media were not colluding with the Hillary campaign, if federal law as to superpacs were enforced, if the primary calendar were different with open primaries, if Tim Kaine remained an unknown, then, clearly, Bernie Sanders would have been inaugurated president in January 2017. It's the best available evidence leading to the best conclusion in both cases.

It's true that Trump is a climate change denier. The Democrats are CIA-influenced crazed conspiracy theorists who generally think Russia actually hacked voting machines, a charge never actually levelled by the establishment. So, here we have an essay explaining the difference between an expert and an elite. An expert limits their conclusions to the most likely explanation. An elite uses power to push through a narrative, no matter how stupid and false the narrative may be. If the people rise up against the elite, they are not rising up against the experts. If people can't understand what the experts are saying, it's because the elites don't want them (us) to think systematically.

Another example: the US military has spent unbelievable amounts of money on violence over the last 50 years. Nothing good has come from all of this warfare. The narratives behind the wars in Iraq, Libya, Syria, Yemen, Central America and Vietnam were all false. Yet, if I were to propose that defense spending be cut 90%, and state that the American people would suffer exactly zero repercussions from this cut, that no one would attack the country, that chaos would not implode the world, I would be dismissed as unrealistic. No one can challenge the truth of what I just said about the US military's record of uselessness. The only arguments are the equivalent of threats, intimidation and some variation of "shut up."

Inequality is out of control. If the government were to redistribute the wealth by taxing stock transactions, inheritance, capital gains, and wealth, to fund education, healthcare, transportation infrastructure, open space, recreation, scientific research, space telescopes, medical research and art, nothing at all bad would happen to the economy at large. Growth would increase. Life expectancy would increase. Quality of life, the stock market: no major problems at all. No country should have a region called "the rust belt"—what a national disgrace. Racism is still alive and well after 400 years. Unbelievable. Breaking up the six largest banks and other antitrust actions would improve the functioning of the economy for the vast majority of the people.

## On Hillbots

Cut defense. No more war. Redistribute the wealth. Bring all the troops home. Reparations for Black America. Free Leonard Peltier. Snowden for head of the NSA. Harmony and respect among the different peoples of the nation. More transparency and democracy. Money out of politics.

Do I sound like a Republican to you? I'm also not poorly informed: you see what you have in your hands, right? It's a whole book. So, maybe there is a good reason to be on the left and hate Hillary? All of this agenda is possible, if not for shitty Democrats like CitiBank sellout warmonger Barack Obama and his Clinton/Podesta/Pelosi/Soros/Schumer allies.

My Hillbot friends have been brutal because I disagree with them. They don't see that their blind following of people like Obama and Clinton lead directly to Trump. They believe the MSM. They don't care about war in Yemen or Syria or Libya or deals to bailout CitiBank or declining wealth of Black families or declining life expectancy. Democrats gave us Trump, then blamed leftists who refused to participate in imperialism, buy propaganda or condone oligarchy rather than the 45% of eligible voters who stayed home, or, better yet, themselves. Obama played chicken with America and America got shot in the head. Maybe he shouldn't have played chicken with our future and sucked his ego up a bit, said no to DNC cheating, and endorsed Bernie. But guess what, his immortal soul is not yet condemned to hell. He still could redeem his soul from hell fire and admit he did wrong. It's not too late for him, or for America.

There are enough Blue Dog democrats for Donna Brazile to keep sending me fundraising emails and John Podesta's friends to get rich. There are not enough to win elections.

Now I get why Republicans dominate US politics. All they have, really, is disgust with self-righteous liberals. The right doesn't have an agenda to help working families. But liberals are so pompous, you don't need an agenda. You just have to not be Nancy Pelosi in her $10,000 necklace saying she is "fighting for working families" and, presto, the country is yours. No need to have a coherent governing agenda.

Somehow, this year, it became acceptable to ostracize, demonize and attack people because you have a different view. People, I mean, not leaders. I'm all for ostracizing, demonizing and attacking the leadership when the leadership fails. They stepped up and said, "I will lead!" When the party and world come crashing down around them, they should step aside. But Democrats don't ever seem to tire of their pathetic crop of losers.

All of a sudden, people began posting politics on social media this year. Most of these statements were not invitations to discuss the issue but groupthink, opportunities for like-minded people to confirm that they are the good people and the others bad.

If whatever point anyone happens to make was as obvious as that person thinks, and no discussion were necessary, there would be no reason to make the point. Yet, those were the majority of posts by all sides, including mine.

The purpose of this book is to backup my "obvious" points with evidence, at length. Online discussions don't work because we do not have consensus on the basic facts.

Let's consider an example of something I say all the time: Bernie would have won against Trump. Why do I say that? I cited the evidence at the beginning of this book, right up front, in the chapter on July 25, presented early in the book because this point is so important. Go check it out again. See, that's how you backup an argument. Can I prove a hypothetical completely? No, but this counterfactual is about as sure as a non-event prediction can be.

## On tin foil hats

**N**ow that the establishment went all nutty, conspiracy theory, wacko, blaming Hillary's just defeat on Russia and the FBI and Knights Templar and the Protocol of the Elders of Zion or the second shooter on the grassy knoll in Dallas in 1963 or the aliens in Area 51 or whatever it is that they blame her defeat on this week, can we stop excluding things like Pizzagate from national dialogue because they are "conspiracy theories"? We can exclude ideas because there is no evidence to support the claim, but with the outlandish "Russia did it" nonsense coming out of Obama's mouth and being repeated by the MSM, there is no longer an embargo on crazy theories just because they sound wacky.

**Reagan and Bush on chains, Iran yanking them**: It used to be if you said something like Iran had Reagan by the chain because he did a dirty deal in 1980 to keep the hostages locked up until after the election, and the Iranians had a video of Bush I or some other proof that it happened to keep Reagan to the deal after the election (insurance), then the Iranians DID keep the hostages locked up until after the 1980 election and Reagan was actually caught giving weapons to the Iranians, you were dismissed as a conspiracy theorist. I believe the Iranians did do a deal with Reagan based solely on the timeline of the release of the hostages and because Carter's offer of millions in military spare parts was rejected. The 2003 Bush Jr. invasion of Iraq benefitted the Iranian government tremendously. That same government may have been sitting on undeniable evidence of Bush Sr.'s treason at the time of the invasion.

**Nixon as traitor**: Or if you said Nixon undermined the peace talks in 1968 to win the election, treason, well, again, you're nuts. Guess what? "Yes, Nixon Scuttled the Vietnam Peace Talks: It's been rumored for years. Now we have real proof." Politico, June 9, 2014.

**Obama on a chain, CitiGroup yanking him**: The spreadsheet from Michael Froman to John Podesta in 2008—a document that shows that all of Obama's political appointees were vetted by a team of people at CitiGroup—proves that Obama was a CitiGroup plant and that the big banks had Obama on a chain. And guess what: his administration of the TARP program actually *DID* give billions to CitiGroup and the like. And there is documentary evidence of a plot.

You'd think Obama would have to answer some questions. But no. Instead he gives an emotional speech about how much he loves his wife to 20,000 of his fans.

Who worked on the spreadsheet? Was there anyone in your administration who ever proposed breaking up the big banks as a response to the 2008 crisis? Why did CitiGroup get to vet your political appointments? Did you bail out the banks or did you bail out the homeowners? Why the banks and not the homeowners? Didn't CitiGroup and its employees donate tons of money to Obama in 2008 and 2012? Doesn't it look like quid pro quo? He never has to answer those questions.

**Trump on a chain, yanked by Putin:** Now we know for sure Reagan, Bush I and II and Obama were all on chains, puppets to a certain degree. But that never got any real traction in the propaganda media. Instead, we're inundated with this Putin-Trump secret evidence story like we never heard about Michael Froman and what Obama did before he was elected, like it was just a coincidence that Iran kept the hostages locked up until Reagan took office and the Iran-Contra had nothing to do with October Surprise. No investigation of any of that.

I don't like Trump. The politics of Trump is a cancer. Maybe it's true that Trump's people met with Putin's people prior to the election. Maybe Trump has secrets and the Russians know what they are. Maybe even, although it seems highly unlikely given the statements by Julian Assange and Craig Murray, Russia had something to do with the DNC/Podesta Wikileaks publications. Maybe. Maybe not. And maybe it's kind of true but way overblown.

But you're not going to convince me with secret evidence. I don't care if John McCain agrees. I'm not impressed with the New York Times. You have to actually prove it with evidence in an open process in which the accused is allowed to present counter evidence. Otherwise, the Trump-Putin stuff is just a conspiracy theory. I don't respect authority, especially outlets with bad track records on truth, like the Washington Post, CNN and the New York Times, all of which are implicated in Wikileaks.

Wikileaks, Podesta and DNC releases, show that there is an elite club and the idea of a Deep State is as plausible as Chuck Schumer thinks it is. Never mind conspiracy theories: elections are fraudulent and insiders cheat and conspire with the rich to run the government for themselves. No doubt. CitiGroup has more sustained interest in America: sucking capital out of the real economy and creating a crony system of state supported larceny. Putin can't do any worse.

Mad nonsense running amok in America. I thought the silver lining of the Trump victory would be a reform of the Democratic party. That isn't looking too good. Now the Deep State may be overplaying their hand. Maybe not.

Anyway, real news is ignored: Wikileaks. I don't think we'll ever get a better look at how the Deep State functions then we got in 2016. A revolution would be the proper, logical response to the Podesta leaks, just to say the obvious that is not in the media. Propaganda is pushing a mad fog over a large nation.

## On not seeing

Many often assume a system of representative government with an element of democracy is the best possible form of government. We believe the efficacy, warts and all, of this system has been proven by the failures of monarchy, fascism and communism. We assume that we do in fact offer the hope of individual liberty, yet we quite explicitly do not tolerate any organized resistance to liberal democracy itself. Your individual rights do not include the right to overthrow the government and, say, set up a theocracy based on the bible or impose sharia law or military rule. You are allowed quite a bit of freedom as compared to people in the past but the system does not tolerate an effort to undo itself.

Of course, you might say. No system of human organization can allow for it's own destruction. That's anarchy! If you make this caveat, you might well be right. Just remember, as we will need the fact later, that among the liberties not protected under liberal democracy is the organized effort to resist or replace liberal democracy, whether that is a good thing or not. Tolerance is not unlimited.

Winston Churchill famously said, "Democracy is the worst form of government, except for all those other forms that have been tried from time to time." Monarchy, fascism, military dictatorship, communism: it's hard to find an example in the past few hundred years that would suggest this world of liberal democracy is not the best of all possible systems, flaws and all.

We are as blind as our ancestors to our own immorality. We cannot lord it over imperialist Victorian Britians, or Southern slave owners, or patriarchal classical Athenians unless we are willing to take a deep look at the structural cruelty and suicidal insanity of our world, as we wish the people of the past had opened their eyes to the injustice of their worlds. "Open our eyes" in a deep sense of not accepting our political-economic order, as slavery, imperialism, patriarchy were unacceptable in the past.

America in 2016 is a moral failure with a political structure that is not sustainable. We have something going on much like debt and social stratification in France in 1780 or slavery in America 1830 or the world economy in 1930: a fundamental failure not being addressed but festering. We do not have a functioning democracy that is capable of addressing environmental catastrophe, inequality, and militarism. The military of the United States of America is an enormous threat to world peace, given the wide engagement powers of the president. Global warming is real and not being addressed. The government at all levels, state, local and federal, is wholly undemocratic, self-interested and unresponsive to basic needs.

The members of dissenting religions who founded colonies in what is now the Commonwealth of Massachusetts in the 17th century escaped persecution only to immediately institute systems of persecution of those that dissented against the religious orthodoxy of these new communities. From a modern point of view, we might look back at the intolerance of those who were escaping intolerance as something strange, a bizarre and confusing fact, or some kind of logical breakdown in the early colonists' mental map of the world. "Hey, Puritans, you are doing to others what the Anglicans just did to you! Can't you see that?" You might want to scream back at your history book.

The confusion dissipates if we remember that for the pilgrims and other dissenters establishing new communities in Massachusetts the issue was not freedom of religion but whether or not a particular doctrine was a true representation of God's will. If you actually believe in God and you are sure that God's will is knowable on earth, then whether or not a community is right with God becomes critical and there is no room for tolerance of something God does not want to be tolerated. The problem was not that they were repressed in England prior to embarking for the new world. The problem for the dissenters was that they were repressed by people who were wrong about God.

I offer this example as an analogy for the way we think about liberal democracy. We are sure liberal democracy is, to quote Churchill, the best possible system, not a utopia certainly, but the the best of the possible. We can tolerate all kinds of religions, as our system does not depend on understanding the will of God. We cannot tolerate other political options outside of liberal democracy any more than the Puritans would have accepted Catholics into their communities.

The perception of ourselves as tolerant sometimes blinds us to the areas in which we are intolerant. Prohibition was, for many, part of the progressive movement. Obviously, more conservatives supported Prohibition than did progressives but there were some Prohibitionists in both ideological camps.

By freeing the workers from the evils of alcohol, family life would improve. People would lead longer and more productive lives. Some people put the abolition of alcohol in the same category of public good as ending child labor, compulsory education for children, limiting work hours, and providing for some kind of workmen's compensation when workers were injured or killed on the job. Many did in fact say, "Hey, you're not being tolerant. We just want to drink beer and wine without you interfering with our personal choice." But the progressives, those that favored Prohibition, were not swayed.

I offer Prohibition and early Massachusetts as examples of Americans not being tolerant without realizing how off base they were, at least as they appear to most of us now. The biggest example of this kind of blindness has to be slavery, of course.

The idea that no one should own another human being, that slavery is a moral wrong in all cases everywhere and always, was never clearly articulated until the 18th century. Socrates, Aristotle, the Apostle Paul, Jesus, the Buddha, Sir Isaac Newton, Mohammed, all the saints, popes, sages, prophets of Israel, Taoism, Confucius: it occurred to precisely no one that slavery was simply morally wrong, or if they did think about the morality of slavery, they didn't leave any evidence that they did. From enlightenment thinkers, broadly, plus

Quakers, the idea spread and now almost everyone in the world agrees that slavery is simply wrong. How is it that no one noticed a clear injustice for all those thousands of years before 1750?

We have been blind to injustice for almost all our time here on this planet. Consciousness and intelligence did not enable us to automatically see what we now consider obvious. For most of human history in the vast majority of societies the idea that a woman should be considered a political person, an equal to a man in the public realm, was impossible to imagine, including for women. We have no clear statement of a feminist ideology in writing by anyone until the modern era.

More examples: For long periods and many places, homosexuality was a serious crime. The first democratic election in Europe was after the French Revolution. The first election in the United States that allowed all white men to vote was 1828. The first election that allowed all Black people and women to vote was probably not until after the Civil Rights act in 1964. For most of history and in many places now, the assumption that people with more power and money deserve more power and money, thus excluding from politics those with less power and money, was not something whispered over a private meal (with the transcript from the Goldman Sachs leadership deep state summit later leaked to Wikileaks) but was the norm and the law.

So what aren't we seeing now? Maybe that the US is not a democracy, that we could end poverty, that we shouldn't tolerate the existence of urban ghettos or rust belts, that inequality isn't natural or healthy, that we don't need these wars, that we don't need spy agencies, that we don't need to put so many people in jail, that we could get rid of fossil fuels entirely in a few years, that there is nothing special about our so-called leaders, that we should ethnically integrate our schools and neighborhoods, that international law need not be a threat to America, that Bernie was cheated, that Podesta created Trump, and that voting is not the be all and end all of democracy. That there is a politics beyond and better than representative democracy that cannot be corrupted by money but in fact work as a counterweight to the market and technology in order to assume a human dimension to society.

# On closed primaries

Closed primaries are voter suppression. Unfortunately, the Supreme Court seems to be moving in the exact wrong direction on this issue, as argued in "Supreme Court To Consider Hearing Bipartisan Lawsuits Challenging Open Primaries" by Alex Gauthier in Electoral Reform Feb 7, 2017. As we move through history, we see all kinds of ways to restrict people from voting: literacy tests, property qualifications, ID cards, registration requirements. To varying degrees, these are all illegitimate and designed to distort the democratic process. Unfortunately, the Federal Courts have been on the wrong side of this story of increased access as often as on the right side.

We live in a winner-take-all system. If you have 49% of every congressional district vote for party X and 51% for party Y, party Y would have 100% of their people in congress. In European parliamentary democracies, each party gets a percentage of seats based on their percentage of the vote. So if party X gets 30%, party Y gets 30%, and party Z gets 40%, they all get about that many seats and have to work out a coalition.

In America, you have to work out your coalition before the election, which is why we need primaries. In a European-style parliament, in Israel or Spain, for example, Bernie and Hillary would have been in different parties, the people would have voted, then they would work out a deal after the election to govern together. In America, they have to work everything out before the election (or not and then lose).

This pertains to closed primaries because the idea behind closed primaries is false. The theory of the closed primary is that there are people called "Democrats" and "Republicans" and that these people have ideologies that are found in their respective parties. In fact, the parties are coalitions of many factions. They have to be. No one faction can in fact reach 50% of the voters.

The closed primary is like a loyalty oath to vote. In Eric Lipton, Democracy Can Stop Traffic, Washington Post, January 8, 1995, says, "In practice, many parties enforce loyalty oaths informally, as with controlling entry into the nomination setting in what are called 'firehouse primaries' (a 'firehouse primary' is a polling process conducted by a party without state supervision). In the mid-1990s, a news report indicated that Justice Antonin Scalia had 'questioned the legality of the oath' required from Republican voters who sought to participate in a firehouse primary in Fairfax, Virginia, but had then signed the form 'after getting an explanation from a party official.'

Were Justice Scalia's initial reservations well-founded? Less so in an unofficial primary. In the case of a state funded primary, not a "firehouse primary," there is even less justification for a loyalty oath. Insisting that a voter chose his or her party six months before the primary, as in New York in 2015-16, is like a loyalty oath to a party, as the voter does not know who the candidates will be or what issues they will advocate. The registration as a "Democrat" is tantamount to a loyalty oath.

Morse v. Republican Party of Virginia, 1996, held that

the Virginia GOP had no inherent right to conduct a primary. In Democratic Party v. Wisconsin, 1980, the Supreme Court did not allow the national DNC to refuse to seat the Wisconsin delegates chosen with an open primary, thus insisting that an open primary is constitutional. Now, we need to move the ball further along and get a ruling making closed primaries unconstitutional, as at least the 2016 New York rules are, requiring the equivalent of a loyalty oath to vote.

# On the Third World

The New York Times published a comparison of the average worker to the top 100 CEOs on June 8, 2014. The CEOs earn $30 million a year and the average worker $38,000, or 789 times more. Zimbabwe is ranked 167 of 194 in terms of per capita income at $890 per adult worker. The average American makes 43 times more than the average worker in Zimbabwe. The difference between a CEO and the American worker is 18 times more than the difference between an American worker and a very poor Third World worker.

We, as American workers, are 18 times closer to being among the Third World shanty town poor than we are to being among the oligarchs. Our interests line up more closely with the poorest Third World rural poor than with the billionaires who run America.

Of course, a difference of 43 times is a lot. If we consider a middle income country, the difference is more like three times between an American worker and a worker in Chile. There is more of a difference between Zimbabwe and Chile than between the US and Chile.

As workers in the First World, we should care if workers in the

Third World have things like social security. A minimum pension in Zimbabwe might be $50 a month while a retiree in the US should be assured of at least some $1500. Chile might be $400. But it is in our interest to insist that everyone be brought into the community of humanity in some way, and getting a pension when you retire is one way to do it.

I think of it like this: the boundary between the Roman Empire and the lands of Germanic tribes was more or less fixed for several hundred years. The Romans routinely sent ambassadors and other officers to divide and pit tribes against each other. Also, the superior Roman organization allowed a relatively smaller number of troops to be deployed efficiently to give an impression of superiority when no real military advantage existed. These strategies worked for a long time: confuse the opposition and divide them along ethnic lines.

Eventually, the German tribes unified behind charismatic leadership into larger military alliances (Visigoth was not an ethnic or religious designation). Increasing familiarity with Roman tactics dissolved the impression of superiority.

People on the Roman side had better lives in many ways. The people on the Germanic side knew that they were missing out. The point of the Germanic invasions was not to destroy Rome but to become Roman.

The Roman way of life stopped expanding into the Germanic areas following the final defeat of the legions on September 11, year 9 CE at the Battle of the Teutoburg Forest. The borders between the areas of Europe today with Latin-derived languages and Germanic languages depends on the outcome of this battle. From this point on, Rome gave up on making their way of life universal and settled for building a sort of "wall." The world was divided into us and them, the haves and have-nots, and it lasted for another 400 or so years, but not forever.

The progressive reforms of the late 19th century to early 20th century, such as child labor laws, social security, and universal education, followed by civil rights movements, made all the people in certain countries members of something like a community. We could stop there--Americans, Europeans, Japanese--or we could keep expanding the community. Trade deals could offer leverage to increase the reality of a world community. Or, we can build a wall. Walls do work, for awhile. Maybe a few hundred more years of this, we'll get away with it. Some day, though, they'll break through. Better to bring them in now, slowly, than lock them out forever. Immigration, trade policy, international law: in many areas we can start to rebuild the progressive compromise, this time on a global basis. Even the poorest of the poor should get their foot in the door of our social contract, starting with some minimal social security. If there are people in South Sudan and in a shantytown in India with no stake at all in the world system, then human beings have no rights, only citizens of particular nations have rights. The logical extension of the French revolution would be a social security card in Somalia. If we stop expanding our system and attempt to lock out the neighbors... well, 410AD sack of Rome is a possibility: deal them in now or wait until then break the door down later.

## On amendments and reform

First, Bernie Sanders or his successor wins the 2020 election with a landslide that puts progressives firmly in charge of the nation. Next, his agenda of Medicare for all, free college, higher minimum wage, increased taxes on the rich, reduced military spending, cements this majority for a generation, as life quality and opportunity dramatically and rapidly increase for the vast majority of voters. Then, we turn to making America more democratic and progressive permanently by writing the Bernie Sanders type of agenda into the infrastructure and constitution of the country.

Detroit was once one of America's wealthiest cities. Before that, the cities in upstate New York along the Erie canal was the richest part of the nation. Places that were once rich are now international symbols of ruin porn. This fact should be a national embarrassment.

Let's say we declare a national objective of reducing carbon emissions in transportation and produce 100% of our electricity from renewable energy by 2035. Next, the federal government and, say, the University of Michigan partner to build a massive research and development institution in downtown Detroit to figure out how we will rebuild our energy and transportation infrastructure. The mission of the new institution will be to invent, test and recommend new technologies: roads made with solar panels, ways to simultaneous bury roadside electrical lines while radically increasing free internet access for all, integrating new roads with driverless cars, high speed rail, integrating bike lanes into traffic plans, everything. If localities and metropolitan areas want to avail themselves of the trillions in infrastructure improvements, they will have to work with Detroit to develop a plan that increases the quality of life.

To attract and keep people in Detroit, the federal government will have to help build a network of parks, schools, increased security. In order to provide recreation and quality of life for the new prosperous and older residents now with more money to spend and time to go on vacation, we would want to preserve key ecosystems around the Midwest as recreational areas, with no destructive development.

As this project is too big for one city, there will be a high speed rail line connecting Detroit to Cleveland and from there across the midwest, from Toronto to Saint Louis. Other big projects will jump start other regions.

While moving to a carbon neutral economy, while rebuilding the rust belt, we will also abolish racism. Racism is written into the infrastructure and government structure and as we re-write these fundamental guiding systems, we will write racism out of the roads and highways, out of the financial system, education and out of the law, where is primarily lies.

Cities will be built to allow for quality of life and economic development and no areas of the country will be left behind. Rural areas will be integrated into regional, national, and international economies with high speed internet, transportation links, while preserving nature from development and protecting quality farmland for the present beauty and prosperity and future security of the nation.

When that's done, the majority will be yet more secure and we will reform the constitution. The US constitution has been good at providing stability over the centuries. Also, the idea of individual rights behind the constitution is critical to a democratic society. But it is a creaky old 18th century structure that includes many odd or antiquated provisions, when seen from a modern point of view.

How about an amendment to protect whistleblowers. We have 27 amendments to date and we could use some more. "Congress nor the states shall make no law punishing the revelation of information demostrating criminal activity by agents of the government"

**28th Amendment: judicial reform amendment:** *Federal judges will be limited to one 24 year term in office. After 24 years, all judges must retire from the bench. For ten years after leaving the bench, former judges cannot practice law and may not accept any employment or compensation from any other source than their federal pension. Congress will grant all retired judges a pension equal to the pay of a US senator for at least 24 years after leaving the bench.*

Why this amendment? Ray Kurzweil at Google research thinks we may conquer death. In the future, people may live to be 300 years old. Were this to become the case, we would still have the judges that voted against Dred Scott on the bench now. Also, every Supreme Court nomination is a huge battle because if you nominate a 40 year old judge, you may be looking at a shift in the country, either left or right, for 50 years. The stakes are too high. By reducing the term on the bench, the stakes are not as high and older candidates would be considered, adding diversity to the bench in terms of life expectancy.

**29th Amendment: electoral college reform amendment:** *Every state will allocate electors to the Electoral College on a proportional basis.*

Why? To reduce the possibility of a wide difference between the popular vote and the electoral college vote and to eliminate the concept of a "swing state" while not diluting the relatively larger power of small states vis a vis large states.

**30th Amendment: census reform amendment:** *Functions constitutionally assigned for determination based on the United States population census may be determined through statistical sampling if the results of sampling are more accurate than an actual head count.*

Why? In 1783, people assumed that counting every individual would be a better representation of population than statistical sampling a proportion of the population and extrapolating to the general figures. Turns out, sampling is more accurate than a head count. Why not bring the constitution up to date with current science?

**31st Amendment: election law amendment:** *Section 1: Corporations are not legal persons and do not have constitutional rights. Section 2: Laws and rules to increase access to voting, make elections more democratic, less subject to manipulation by those with more money are presumptively within legislative power.*

Why? To make this clear: you cannot grant "free speech" or other rights to corporations, only to actual human beings. Also, the courts can only overrule campaign finance laws if those laws restrict voting and make the problem of money in politics worse, not the other way around. Effectively, this amendment rescinds Citizens United and other anti-campaign finance decisions.

A broad amendment to allow for more democratic government is better than a narrow amendment reacting to a recent Supreme Court decision.

**32nd Amendment: independent information and technology agency:** *This amendment establishes an Independent National Office of Information Services (INOIS). The purpose of INOIS is to publish information, provide systems for the exchange of information and opinion between the public and government officials, assure that legislation is clearly written, and track and publish information on the performance of government agencies and programs.*

Section 1, governance: All United States citizens over the age of 18 interested in serving for four years on the board of INOIS may submit their names to a database of potential candidates. From this database of citizens, twenty individuals will be chosen randomly to be finalists to serve on the board every other year. A term of office will last for four years. From the pool of twenty (20), six (6) officers will be selected by the House of Representatives. In two years, from a different random list of twenty (20) candidates from the database of interested citizens, the House will select another six (6) board members. Thus, the full board will be twelve (12) officers, changing half of the board every two years. If a member resigns or dies or otherwise does not finish his or her term, that seat can be filled by congress by selecting an individual from the same list of twenty (20) from which the resigning officer was selected. All decisions of INOIS are made by majority vote. A tie vote means no action is taken. The board has the authority to delegate and oversee its authority to others as needed.

Section 2, funding: Congress shall allocate and the President approve funding for INOIS equal to or more than the funding for the offices and entities of congress itself.

Section 3, government documents: as guided by case law and FOIA, state FOIL provisions, INOIS will provide a public searchable database of all government documents for national, state and local government.

Section 4, public input on legislation: INIOS will ensure a forum for the public to read, comment on and conduct nonbinding votes on all legislation prior to passage by congress.

Section 5, re-writing legislation: If public comment or voting suggests to the INOIS board that a specific piece of legislation is confusing, poorly written or too complicated, the board may return the proposed legislation back to the elected representatives to be re-written. The proposed law will have a "hold" on it until the INOIS board is satisfied that the public can understand the legislation. Likewise, if a representative has not responded adequately to comments pertaining to a proposed law, as determined by the INOIS board, the board can place a hold on the proposed legislation. No legislation can be voted on by congress, state legislatures or local bodies if INOIS has an outstanding hold on the wording of the proposed legislation. Legislatures can seek judicial review of a hold if they are unable to work out an agreement with INOIS after 90 days.

Section 6, using data for good government: INOIS shall gather data on government services and activities and create systems to compare and guide the conduct of these aspects of government. Data on local, state and federal agencies including budgets and variable outcomes, will be published to help guide judges in determining sentences, legislators in considering legislation, the public prior to voting on candidates, or for any other purpose deemed appropriate by the INOIS board.

Why this amendment? Data is powerful and there should be an agency outside the control of congress and the president to track what the other agencies are doing. It's an additional check on government power. Congress should not be allowed to cover up unpleasant facts by not allocating money to research matters they do not want to be provided with good information.

I would like to be able to, say, type in the name of a particular police department and see 1) how much all the employees get in salary, 2) how many arrests they made, 3) conviction rate, 4) overall budget, 5) number of disciplinary actions, etc. That way

I'd get a better sense of what I'm getting as a citizen, whether my city is wasting money or not. Judges should have data available to them when they sentence people for crimes and not make arbitrary decisions. I would like to know exactly how much the US is spending on a particular weapon system.

### 33rd Amendment: national anti-corruption agency

*No employee, officer, official, elected representative or contractor of the government of the United States or the states of the union or jurisdictions within those states may profit from his or her position so as to enrich themselves or their families or associates by using the collective general power of the state for personal benefit. They may not take property or money from the general fund, nor may they sell access to the power inherent in their public positions, nor may they take money in any form after they leave government positions such that they or their associates appear to benefit from previous public positions. This amendment establishes an agency, Public Integrity Authority (PIA) with the mission of ensuring that individuals as listed above use their governmental powers only to serve the public interest.*

Section 1, PIA board: All Unites States citizens over the age of 18 interested in serving for four years on the board of PIA may submit their names to a database of potential candidates. From this database of citizens, twenty individuals will be chosen randomly to be finalists to serve on the board every other year. A term of office will last for four years. From the pool of twenty (20), six (6) officers will be selected by the House of Representatives. In two years, from a different random list of twenty (20) candidates from the database of interested citizens, the House will select another six (6) board members. Thus, the full board with be twelve (12) officers, changing half of the board every two years. If a member resigns or dies or otherwise does not finish his or her term, that seat can be filled by congress by selecting an individual from the same list of twenty (20) from which the resigning officer was selected. All decisions of PIA are made by majority vote. A tie vote means no action is taken. The board has the authority to delegate and oversee its authority to others as needed.

Section 2, funding: Congress shall allocate and the President approve funding for the anti-corruption agency equal to or more than the funding for the offices and entities of congress itself. All fines paid to the agency can be used by PIA to continue to enforce good government actions.

Section 3, process: PIA may bring charges of self-dealing or other actions not in the public interest against any current or former government employee, contractor, official, or representative, from the President of the United States to local government personnel. Any covered individuals may be charged with self-dealing or non-public interest behavior even if they have not violated a specific statute or law. The charges, as prepared by PIA, will be presented in a hearing before a duly convened jury of randomly selected American citizens. Procedures for the hearings will be set by the PIA board.

Section 4, powers: PIA has the power to remove officials from office, to ban individuals from running for office in the future, to revoke government pensions and post-employment benefits, and fine covered individuals, with no fine so onerous as to ruin or impoverish a covered individual.

Section 5, grants: PIA may also accept solicitations from impoverished or poor covered individuals for grants. If found worthy of a grant by a jury, covered individuals may receive grants to compensate them if they are poor and they have not used their public positions to benefit themselves.

Why this provision? Sun Yat-sen was right: where is the branch of government to control corruption? Trump has personal business interests but cannot be impeached, as congress is a partisan body. Let a semi-random board track the elected officials and oversee an agency designed to root out corruption.

In these last two ideas, I throw in the idea that there might be other ways to get representation other than elections. Randomly selecting (with some provision to get the most reasonable people within a random group) some people in power seems like a good check on the parties and lobbyists. They can't know who they have to corrupt beforehand, as any random person could suddenly find themselves in a position of power, as with a jury.

By selecting the governing board by lottery we might avoid partisanship. These two proposed independent agencies have limited power, one mostly to expose and reveal information, the other to remove elected officials from office, mostly. We should be able to trust this power to average citizens. If juries can decide who lives and dies, they ought to be able to figure out what to do with information and which politicians have crossed the line and need to find a new job.

I propose new provisions for complete transparency. All documents go right online—no need to FOIL/FOIA any invoice, any proposed legislation, anything—it all goes online immediately and is searchable. This is now possible, not so in 1783 when the constitution was written. It's easier to put documents online than to print them out and file them in a cabinet so let's open this sucker up.

No more Mr. and Ms. Bigwig. You are in the Senate. Therefore, you think you're a hot shot. You get staff. You get travel allowances. You get member items, taxpayer money you get to claim with your name on it, to put your name on a playground. Aren't you special?

How about we restructure what being in "public service" is about and take a page out of Vermont's playbook? In Vermont, being in state government is really service. There are way more reps per capita and there are too many to corrupt. They don't get perks. They are regular people. My mother's neighbor was in the state senate and her husband plowed my mother's driveway. No bigwig at all.

Stuff like that. Re-think this a bit.

## On writing this book

John Brown met with Frederick Douglas before his raid on Harper's Ferry and laid out the plan: get the weapons, then spark a slave uprising. Douglas looked at Brown's plan and said, "This is not going to work." Brown looked back at Douglas and said, "What's your plan? To write more books? Give more speeches? If you're against slavery, we have a gun for you. Join us."

The Brown-Douglas meeting epitomizes just about every political movement. Writing is only worth so much. Douglas wasn't against some kind of direct action. He wasn't writing because he thought writing was better than action. He just didn't like Brown's plan. If Brown had presented him a better plan, he would have grabbed a gun. Instead, Douglas went to England, as he had prior knowledge of the raid and could have been arrested as a co-conspirator.

Violent action, as in Brown's case, was only called for because slavery itself was such an abomination. There is no comparable issue before us today and the action anyone might propose now should certainly not be violent.

And while America is not a democracy, it is also not a totalitarian state. Non-violent direct action has worked in American history before and can work now. I take the results of the Princeton Study on democracy seriously and believe we don't live in a democracy. I take the DNC/Podesta Wikileaks releases seriously and I know exactly why Princeton got the results they got in their study: the process that produces oligarchic rule.

The 2016 Bernie Sanders campaign woke a lot of people up. The Trump election scared more people. Some kind of action is called for. But some kind of narrative is also called for. Until I see some place to invest the action, something compelling, taking a few weeks out to write a book is not a waste of time. John Brown is not knocking on my door.

UNITED STATES NEWS

## STUDY BY MIT ECONOMIST: U.S. HAS REGRESSED TO A THIRD-WORLD NATION FOR MOST OF ITS CITIZENS

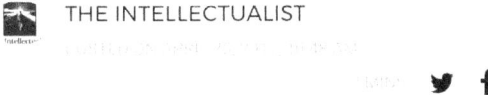

THE INTELLECTUALIST

# On the argument

**N**ow, let's consider some of the Blue Dog truisms, or statements that Democrats believe to be so obvious that they do not need to offer evidence, postulates of corporatists.

"The democrats didn't cheat Bernie. That's just normal hardboiled politics." No, the fraud clearly included routine criminal violation of election law, unprosecuted to date, likely outright ballot cheating, unfair elections that should be voided and an extreme level of media manipulation.

"Bernie wasn't a real Democrat and should be grateful he was allowed to run." Wrong. In a winner-take-all electoral system to pretend that primaries are private functions of private organizations undermines the possibility of democracy.

"Wikileaks didn't reveal anything that interesting in the DNC/Podesta releases. Just political people being political as usual." Wrong. The leaks in 2016 were the most profound demonstration in detail ever of how our oligarchic system works. What we learned was a thousand times worse than Watergate in terms of the scale of the criminal corruption and the fact that this degree of larceny was covered up by the legacy media only compounds the profundity and depth of the horror.

"Russia intervened in the American election in 2016." This claim doesn't even pass the minimal examination of logical consistency, let alone evidence. What did Russia do? What's your proof? Julian Assange and Craig Murray said that an insider leaked the emails.

"Obama was one of our greatest presidents." No, Obama failed as party leader in a catastrophic way, routinely violated the war powers provisions of the constitution, was a proponent of American imperialism, belonged to the banks, not the people, and left an imperial presidency intact for Trump. Trump is Obama's legacy.

"We need to join together on the left, not divide by bringing up the past." Wrong. The horrible leadership that gave us Trump is still leading the Democratic party.

"The Clinton Foundation was/is a charity." Obviously not true. If it was a charity, why did the money dry up minutes after Hillary lost?

"Michelle Obama and Bill Clinton really feel our pain and are great speakers." Yes, they are impressive as people, but their emotional, soaring language has debased rhetoric, both of them. You can walk away from an Obama speech inspired… and that is terrible, because Obama now means CitiBank sellout, American imperialist, failure. I don't want my emotions played with through electronic media.

"It's you Bernie or Bust people who gave us Trump!" I thought you said we should unify the party? By bashing the base? We told you Hillary was going to lose on July 25 and the leadership steered the party into the Hill-iceberg.

"Trump is Hitler!" He's bad, but the Hitler shouting is counter productive too, and also a terrible analogy that is doomed to come back and bite you in the ass. All he has to do is not be Hilter to make you look silly.

I expect to be ignored by people who disagree with me. I expect Blue Dogs to get infuriated and Trumpers to laugh. I have zero chance of presenting this narrative in any mainstream, corporate media outlet. And those who agree with me don't necessarily have to read much of the book: many already know it. Nevertheless, in the ongoing battle of narratives, this book might well be a useful tool.

The relentless hysterical alarmism about everything Trump does or says in the mainstream media and its social media echo chamber is intended to put predictable and controllable neocons back in charge. It's not okay to ban Yemenis from the US, as the nightly MSM tells us (the Muslim ban is an abomination), but to participate in a Saudi led action that leads to more than 10,000 starving to death never makes the news. Both are wrong. People should protest any president outside of the law.

Everything was not okay before Trump was elected and would not be well if the corporate Democrats took power back. Yes, down with Trump. But also down with Pelosi, Schumer, Clinton and Obama, or whatever corporate imperialist banker steps up to take us back to the bad old days of the Brock doctrine of crookery.

Team establishment is lowering the bar for Trump. Democrats: if you think 2016 was bad, 2020 might be worse if you keep lowering the bar and Trump turns out not to be moronic. All he has to do is not be Hitler, not bring on an economic disaster, not implode, and he may well succeed with only half a brain. It's the scarecrow scenario. If Trump were to push through a part of Bernie's program with Democratic votes, Medicare for all… the corporate Democrats new brilliant "alarmist" strategy will collapse, as did the Pied Piper strategy that gave us Trump in the first place.

## On Big Brother

No convincing evidence of Russian interference in the 2016 election through the Wikileaks releases will ever exist. Nice try FBI, DHS, Obama and "17 intelligence agencies" are lying.

Trump may have troubling or illegal ties to the Russian mafia or government. The Putin government may have met with the Trump campaign to plan to undermine the integrity of the 2016 election. We can't yet know all of these questions.

We can know with almost complete certainty, however, that Craig Murray and Julian Assange's statements that Russia had no role in the DNC and Podesta leaks will almost certainly remain the best and final word on the subject of how the emails got to Wikileaks.

Any one of dozens of individuals no longer or never associated with the CIA could have left evidence to suggest Russia was hacking the DNC. The files created by the CIA are now out there, floating around, and have been for months or years. The Russians, the CIA, a friend of a guy who worked for the CIA in 2014… too many suspects, all have the same fingerprints.

The individual who passed the Vault 7 information to Wikileaks to publish did so, perhaps, in the hope that software companies and individuals would put fixes in place to protect privacy. Wikileaks and the leaker behind Vault 7 are providing a public service in revealing the extent to which our information is still being hacked by the government, even after Obama promised to stop it following the NSA Snowden releases.

We cannot know who hacked the DNC: no authentic "Russian" trail is possible. If the government wants to make the contrary claim, that we can know Russia did hack the DNC and Podesta, they'll have

20   L.+                     THE NEW YORK TIMES, MONDAY, APRIL 25, 1966.

## The C.I.A.: Maker of Policy, or Tool? Agency Raises Questions Around W

**SURVEY DISCLOSES STRICT CONTROLS**

But Reputation of Agency Is Found to Make It a Burden on U.S. Action

The 1966 *New York Times* article from which the now famous quote by John Kennedy ("I will splinter the CIA into a thousand pieces and scatter it into the wind.") This serious and thoughtful article would not appear in a MSM publication today.

### Kennedy's Bitterness

And President Kennedy, as the enormity of the Bay of Pigs disaster came home to him, said to one of the highest officials of his Administration that he wanted "to splinter the C.I.A. in a thousand pieces and scatter it to the winds."

Even some who defend the C.I.A. as the indispensable eyes and ears of the Government—for example Allen Dulles, the agency's most famous director—now fear that the cumulative criticism and suspicion, at home and abroad, have impaired the C.I.A.'s effectiveness and therefore the nation's safety.

They are anxious to see the criticisms answered and the suspicions allayed, even if—in some cases—the agency should thus become more exposed to domestic politics and to compromises of security.

## iOS Exploits Data

| Name | Type | Access Created | Born Date & iOS Version | Modification Date | Death Date | Found by | Description |
|---|---|---|---|---|---|---|---|
| Archon | technique | Remote Architecture Detection | | | | (came with purchase) | Critical vulnerability in U.S. devices given to foreign government known to spy on journalists and human rights groups |
| Dyonede | macho-parsing | Codesign Defeat | | | | JDW  GCHQ | |
| Earth/Eve | | Remote Exploit | | | | Purchased by NSA / Shared with CIA / Ported by GCHQ | |
| Peppermint | | | | | | Peppermint NSA / VR Contract | |
| Elderpiggy | | Sandbox Escape | | | | Implemented by GCHQ at JDW | |

**Edward Snowden** @Snowden · 8h
If you're writing about the CIA/@Wikileaks story, here's the big deal: first public evidence USG secretly paying to keep US software unsafe.
pic.twitter.com/kYi0NC2mOp

a hard time proving it. Anything that looks Russian isn't.

CIA Hacker is a fun job. Vault 7 Wikileaks release includes CIA hackers having what seems like a great time. They keep in shape, do push ups (cms/page_16385149.html). They love their work, even if they complain a bit from time to time (ciav7p1/cms/page_15728740.html).  Who are they fighting and why? Never seems to come up. They get to travel to Germany and play spook (ciav7p1/cms/page_26607630.html).

CIA is all in, for themselves. The CIA itself has a clear mission: to avoid any scrutiny of their budget and to have as much latitude to act as independently as possible. Do the president and congress have any control over these guys?

The idea that there is a real foreign enemy out there, the idea that the CIA represents the good guys fighting this foreign enemy seems utterly absurd at this point. The CIA has to prop up the enemies in order to justify their budget. Thus, the CIA is making Russia malware stronger and more scary. Imagine what would happen in the Russians were not that bad or not that effective: the CIA would have a hard time justifying their secret budget of some unknown billions of dollars.

Scary stuff from the CIA. Vault 7 is filled with strange and disturbing comments. In one correspondence we read (/ciav7p1/cms/page_14588670.html), "Mendicant Engineer—reserved for the next tool delivered during a gov't shutdown." Nice to know they are ready for the shutdown. The rest of us? Not so much.

Fake off mode is scary. "Suppress LEDs to improve look of Fake-Off mode. Turn on or leave WiFi turned on in Fake-Off mode… Parse unencrypted audio collection… During initial development, a rough approximation of bit rates for different audio quality settings were made. Quality 1 settings required 100 kB/minutes. Quality 5 settings required 250 kB/minutes. Quality 7 settings required 350 kB/min. Quality 5 seemed to provide very nice results and is usually used." Hello, Big Brother. Can you hear me?

The CIA intentionally uses Russian malware and disguises their tracks to look like Russians. ID /ciav7p1/cms/page_14587109.html#efmA-OBCQ discusses how to hide your tracks and look like the Russians. In these instructions for hiding your origins, we read "DO NOT leave dates/times such as compile timestamps, linker timestamps, build times, access times, etc. that correlate to general US core working hours (i.e. 8am-6pm Eastern time)." More of those in that same link.

Meanwhile, the Department of Homeland Security (DHS) in their joint statement on Russian hacking of October 7, 2016, said, ". . . are consistent with the methods and motivations of Russian-directed efforts. These thefts and disclosures are intended to interfere with the US election process. Such activity is not new to Moscow—the Russians have used similar tactics and techniques across Europe and Eurasia, for example, to influence public opinion there. We believe, based on the scope and sensitivity of these efforts, that only Russia's senior-most officials could have authorized these activities."

So, who are you going to believe, the DHS or your own eyes? There is no such thing as evidence "consistent with the methods" of the Russians because those same methods are consistent with the CIA.

In the FireEye report called "APT28: A WINDOW INTO RUSSIA'S CYBER ESPIONAGE OPERATIONS?" commissioned to prove Russian hacking, we read, "The second was that malware compile times from 2007 to 2014 corresponded to normal business hours in the UTC (+) 4 time zone, which includes major Russian cities such as Moscow and St. Petersburg." Right, just as the CIA instructed their hackers to do.

The FBI in their December 29, 2016 report "GRIZZLY STEPPE—Russian Malicious Cyber Activity" said, "The U.S. Government confirms that two different RIS actors participated in the intrusion into a U.S. political party. The first actor group, known as Advanced Persistent Threat (APT) 29, entered into the party's systems in summer 2015, while the second, known as APT28, entered in spring 2016." The systems were old Russia malware, as reported in 'Seven years of malware linked to Russian state-backed cyber espionage. F-Secure report details "The Dukes" malware family and its Russian connections.'

Old, well-known Russian malware is just what the CIA would use. Here is the Wikileaks summary on UMBRAGE:

"The CIA's hand crafted hacking techniques pose a problem for the agency. Each technique it has created forms a "fingerprint" that can be used by forensic investigators to attribute multiple different attacks to the same entity.

This is analogous to finding the same distinctive knife wound on multiple separate murder victims. The unique wounding style creates suspicion that a single murderer is responsible. As soon one murder in the set is solved then the other murders also find likely attribution.

The CIA's Remote Devices Branch's UMBRAGE group collects and maintains a substantial library of attack techniques 'stolen' from malware produced in other states including the Russian Federation.

With UMBRAGE and related projects the CIA cannot only increase its total number of attack types but also misdirect attribution by leaving behind the "fingerprints" of the groups that the attack techniques were stolen from.

UMBRAGE components cover keyloggers, password collection, webcam capture, data destruction, persistence, privilege escalation, stealth, anti-virus (PSP) avoidance and survey techniques."

We can now say that the "Russia did it" story is over in anything other than an "alternative fact" universe. There is not now nor will there ever be any evidence that Russia gave the Podesta and DNC leaks to Wikileaks. If Russia influenced the 2016 US election, they did it some other way, without Wikileaks, without revealing Podesta's emails.

Driverless cars, smart TVs: big brother has infected tech: Can the CIA murder anyone at any time by turning their own car against them? Michael Hastings was investigating the CIA, then died in a car crash, as reported in The Blaze, "Journalist Michael Hastings Was Investigating CIA Director John Brennan Before He Was Killed in Fiery Car Crash" August 13, 2013. According to ciav7p1/cms/page_13763790.html, the CIA was interested in hacking into a car to potentially conduct just such an assasination.

If they are listening to you through your TV can you dismiss the idea they killed Kennedy?

Have you seen this Kennedy quote? "I will splinter the CIA into a thousand pieces and scatter it into the wind." John F. Kennedy's quote has been pretty prominent since Wikileaks used it as the password to decrypt their torrent file for Vault 7. It is a real quote and it is interesting to see it in the context of the 1966 New York

Times article, coming around discussion of the Bay of Pigs invasion of Cuba.

The writers of the April 25, 1963 New York Times article got the quote from someone in the Kennedy administration. He was really murdered and the idea that the CIA did it is tin-foil hat stuff... like the CIA listening to you through your television, which they can do right now.

This release confirms the seemingly obvious statement by John McAfee back in December: "if it looks like the Russians did it, then I can guarantee you it was not the Russians."

70 billion dollars buys you a lot of code and newsprint. With 70 billion dollars in the budget, the CIA can give money to Amazon to buy the Washington Post and pay software developers to let them in. Edward Snowden offered his assessment that the CIA was in fact buying access to operating systems on Twitter on March 7, 2017

70 billion a year... for what? The Federation of Scientists publishes a nice index to spending at fas.org.

MOM, A RUSSIAN BEAR CAME IN AND MADE A BIG MESS

# On Obama

Obama sang "Amazing Grace" at the funeral for the Emanuel African Methodist Episcopal Church victims in Charleston, South Carolina. He sang beautifully and his performance seemed to go over well in the service. But it bothered me. I know he can sing well. But he's president and nine people died. Is he trying to prove something?

In Argentina, he danced a tango. In Kuwait, he sank a three point shot. On the Tonight Show, he slow jammed the news. I get it Barack: you can do it all. Then why did you fail at being president?

Make no mistake: he ran on "hope and change" and then passed the keys to Donald Trump. If he had come through with real change and a real reason to hope, he would not have left the Democratic party in a shambles, life expectancy falling for many populations, Black household wealth miniscule compared to where it was in 2008 or compared to White households, Obamacare imploding, war in the Middle East, and Africa unstable. Even with all those errors, he could have salvaged his legacy by passing the baton to Bernie but he was too arrogant to consider the possibility.

Obama let CitiBank and the insurance companies exclude all opinion beyond a very narrow range of acceptable, elite, inside the beltway, opinion. Everyone around him was a servant of the oligarchs to such an extent that he did not know there could be another way.

Why did he want Hillary to be secretary of state in 2008? Maybe there was a secret deal in 2008, when Tim Kaine stepped down as DNC head and Debbie Wasserman Schultz took over the post. Maybe the plan for 2016 was set up in 2008. The evidence against this scenario is that Bill Clinton bad-mouthed Obama in

private until 2012, including oblique criticism at times in his 2011
book *Back to Work: Why We Need Smart Government for a Strong
Economy.* In any event, by the time of the 60 Minute interview with
Hillary in 2013, Obama was set on passing his baton to Hillary, the
voters be damned.

He missed chance after chance to be an independent, creative
leader. Obama plodded and stumbled into war crimes. He spent
political capital on a program, Obamacare, without figuring out if
it would actually help the healthcare delivery system in the US.
Sloppy, careless, Obamacare was bad politics and bad policy. He
was afraid of the health insurance lobby. That's not leadership.
Obama was a great candidate and a great symbol. But as president
and party leader, he failed. You're either down or you're not. Obama
is not down with the people.

## A tale of two countries

The share of U.S. pre-tax income accruing to the bottom 50 percent and top one percent of income
earners, 1962-2014

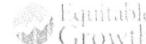

# On Bernie

**B**ernie Sanders lives in a strange alternate universe called congress. On May 16, 2016 Gallup found that a substantial majority of Americans want single payer government health insurance. Polls in 2017 found a substantial minority of Republicans, about one-third, also favor this policy. Politifact concluded that this majority has existed for 70 years. Yet in congress, as part of the alternative universe of Democrats and Republicans inside the beltway, where Bernie lives, the idea of copying Germany, Canada, the UK and every other rich country is considered absurd or ridiculous. Hillary Clinton famously said on January 28, 2016 that Medicare for all, a system similar to what exists in Canada, will "never, ever" be passed by the US congress.

Do you see the problem Bernie has? His policy proposals are generally popular with Americans but considered absurd and ridiculous by his colleagues. If Bernie were operating in a democratic political system where the will of the public had a substantial impact on policy, he would have a much easier life. He could boldly present mainstream, popular, effective, moderate proposals like a tax on stock and bond transactions or beefed up financial regulation on the six biggest banks, including breaking them up or nationalizing parts of their operations. He could propose shifting money from the military to programs designed to turn the entire electricity grid of the United States green by 2030. All of these proposals would be generally popular with the voters and would make the economy function better. No one but a small number of rich special interests would suffer.

Unfortunately, the media, congress and judicial system all have as their prime mission to protect and enhance the interest of a small number of oligarchs. Bernie somehow manages to survive in this environment without becoming disconnected from the worldview of the vast majority of Americans. When he talks to regular Americans, he is rational, moderate and consistent. When he has to go back to congress, he begins to say things that seem strange or irrelevant and some of his supporters think he might be a sell out.

He isn't a sell out. It's just if you live in congress, you have to say things like the lunatic obsession about Russia is based on evidence that is "troubling." Maybe he knows that what is troubling is his collegues going off the tin-foil hat deep end, but he can't say that.

Bernie didn't have a steady job or any possible "career" in politics until he was 40. He ran for office on third party lines, getting few votes, for years. Nothing he did as a young man at the University of Chicago or in his 30s in Vermont suggested he had tremendous personal ambition for himself.

That he was a full adult, 40, without ever having the accoutrements of power and authority is part of what makes him the solid person he is. If we are going to live to be 300 in a generation or two, we will need different arcs to our biographies as well.

Vermont is a special place politically. Elected officials cannot really front as bigwigs in Montpelier. The political culture of Vermont also produced this idiosyncratic politician. His sense of himself, the fact that he was not particularly needy about status, were part of his appeal.

Officially, Bernie doesn't believe in personality cults. If anyone is going to be the subject of a personality cult, it should be someone who is suspicious of the phenomenon itself. Even if you are intellectually suspicious of adoration of a person, when they adore you, you might start to like it and it can still go to your head.

Before the DNC convention opened, around July 25, Bernie spoke to his delegates, streamed live on Facebook by the delegates themselves. His own delegates boo-ed him when he said they had to support Hillary Clinton. You see? Compliance is fading. His people will support him if he throws up his fist and says "revolution" but not when he says "go back to sleep." He can lead his people, but only in one direction.

In the senate he has a difficult job. The corporate Democrats are unsympathetic to Bernie's base and do not tolerate him saying the things he needs to say to represent us. We want him to say the DNC has to reform. If he stops saying these things, we will desert him. But if he alienates the DNC types completely, he cannot execute a takeover of the party. Bernie seems to think that the Democratic party is salvageable and that progressives have a chance to take it over. If he didn't think that it was possible to force the party to reform, he could give them a lot more hell.

He wants to come in as a committee chair, not go out as a hero. If he can thread this needle and keep his base with him and put pressure on the party until it bends, it'll be a miracle. Maybe a catastrophic Democratic defeat in the midterms, which is quite possible given the complete incompetence and incompetent characters of Nancy Pelosi and Chuck Schumer, will help finally drive home the truth to the establishment that we hate them, that the primary in 2016 never ended, even if Bernie conceded, and they can't win without us.

Caitlin Johnstone's February 19, 2017 article, "Let's Talk About Bernie's Capitulation To The Democratic Establishment" is pretty much perfect, so go read that and I don't need to write much more.

# On the Berniecrats

On February 28, 2016 Tulsi Gabbard, congresswoman from Hawaii, resigned her post as Democratic National Committee Vice Chair to endorse Bernie. "I think it's most important for us, as we look at our choices as to who our next commander in chief will be, is to recognize the necessity to have a commander in chief who has foresight, who exercises good judgment," she said. In January 2017 she visited Syria and met with president Assad, declared an enemy of the United States by Obama and Clinton. Both of these bold moves prove that Gabbard is not bullied by elite consensus, sees right through propaganda and is not afraid to take the kind of bold action Obama never took in his time in office. She is a courageous leader with foresight and judgement. The establishment Democrats have tried to smear her as an Islamophobe.

Keith Ellison, congressman from Minnesota, did well in debate at the DNC rule committee meetings. He held his own, expressing interesting ideas on trade and immigration. In the past, he has explored radical ideas, as would anyone who is both genuinely concerned about the state of American race relations and highly intelligent. The establishment Democrats have tried to smear him as an anti-semite.

Nina Turner, former state legislator from Ohio, is, like Bernie Sanders, clearly herself when she speaks to television reporters. You can't listen to her over months and not feel sure that she does not have a "private and public position." She's genuine, her real beliefs right there for you to see. With experiences of deep poverty in her background, police officers in her family, and firm convictions, her fans completely trust her. The establishment Democrats denied her the right to address the DNC convention in Philadelphia. Nina Turner is some ex-state senator of no particular importance to the

DNC insiders, apparently, but millions of us out here think she's great.

The Democrats love minorities and women, and here we have two women, a Hindu, and Black American Christian, two Black politicians, all backing a Jewish candidate. They are from Ohio, Minnesota, Hawaii and Vermont, nice regional diversity, nice religious and ethnic diversity, and diversity between rural, urban, suburban, West, Midwest, East...  but somehow that isn't the diversity the Democrats want. Why? They think for themselves and tell the truth. They haven't bowed down to George Soros and Goldman Sachs or genuflected before the almighty dollar.

If Ellison were head of the DNC, Gabbard minority leader of the house, Bernie, senate minority leader and Nina leading Our Revolution or winning as Governor of Ohio, there would be zero chance of Trump winning in 2020. The Democrats would re-gain the house and senate. We'd be on our way to a more progressive America.

The Republicans and Trump are not in the way. With this team in place, the left would roll over them like a runaway train. The impediment to progress-- the only problem in American politics-- is the Democratic party establishment. They like their positions. They have nothing to say and a record of utter failure but they hold on, right to the bitter end of the human race if necessary. Schumer, Pelosi, Obama, Clinton, Biden, Booker: they are the most significant threat to American democracy, creaky and dysfunctional as it is.

*Military Industiral Complex anyone?*

# On the constitution

**U**nder Trump, key portions of the constitution will definitely be suspended... because the US has been operating outside of the norms of the Anglo-American tradition of the rule of law since at least 2001.

Here is a tale of farewell wisdom: George Washington and Dwight Eisenhower gave the two best presidential farewell addresses. Eisenhower warned us about the military-industrial complex. Washington warned us about political parties and foreign entanglements.

Washington wanted to:

> *"warn you in the most solemn manner against the baneful effects of the spirit of party generally... The alternate domination of one faction over another, sharpened by the spirit of revenge, natural to party dissension, which in different ages and countries has perpetrated the most horrid enormities, is itself a frightful despotism. But this leads at length to a more formal and permanent despotism. The disorders and miseries which result gradually incline the minds of men to seek security and repose in the absolute power of an individual; and sooner or later the chief of some prevailing faction, more able or more fortunate than his competitors, turns this disposition to the purposes of his own elevation, on the ruins of public liberty."*

The conventional wisdom is that the Founding Fathers' hostility to the notion of political parties was somewhat elitist, that the "best" people of society should sort things out without whipping up groups of masses against each other. Washington and his generation probably did fail to see that in a winner-take-all election a system of two parties (or in a system of proportional representative government, more parties) is somewhat natural and not necessarily inherently evil.

On a deeper level, Washington was right that if party is ALL that matters in politics, if society swings back and forth between two factions, if we have nothing but factions squabbling over spoils with no substance for the people at large beyond the coalitions of insiders behind the factions, the people will become hostile to the process. Then, a single individual can step forward and become a dictator. The dynamic of meaningless party vendettas and the appeal of a strong man to end the squabbling, as Washington described the situation, was on display in 2016. Washington was right about the danger of hyper-partisanship leading to undemocratic government.

**HYPER-PARTISANSHIP AND THE ILLUSION OF CHOICE**: Oddly, America is plagued both by hyper-partisanship and the illusion of choice between parties. For 60 to 70 percent of the public, including real independents and non-voters, the two parties are equally terrible. For the 30 to 40 percent of kool-aid drinking partisans, Democrat versus Republican is tantamount to good versus evil, traitors and racists. The difference between the partisans and the disillusioned majority is that the partisans pay attention to and believe the mainstream media.

Many people, maybe most, can see that the Democrats and Republicans basically agree on all the important issues facing the country and offer no real choice. Both parties are for endless war and empire. Both parties are funded by insurance companies and financial service companies to make sure banking regulation and healthcare, among other issues, work out to favor the elites.

Both parties think international trade deals exist only to make multinational corporations more rich and powerful. TARP, NAFTA, TPP, NSA, CIA: both parties obey the same masters, multinational corporation, banks, oligarchs and the Deep State.

The one-party wall fell in 1989. When will the two-party wall fall? Both parties literally take money from the same people. The seamless transition from Bush to Obama in terms of TARP funding (taking care of banker friends) and military operations (empire and war) should have tipped us all off on the fact that his election stuff is for suckers.

I often say, "If Lenin had set up the Soviet Union as a two-party state instead of a one-party state, the USSR would still be up and running." They could have had a "FOX Pravda" and a "CNN Pravda" and two people, each from a different party of state communism ideologues, argue vehemently on TV and the Soviet people never would have noticed they didn't live in a democracy.

Even though there is no real difference between Democrats and Republicans, the two factions contest each other in presidential elections, in congress and the Supreme Court. Although we talk about "conservatives" and "liberals" on the court, they are really no different than congress people and are partisan operatives, in general. We really have Democrats and Republicans on the court. And, like their counterparts in congress, the judges disagree on abortion and gun control but agree on corporate domination of politics and do not question the imperial, endless war presidency.

**FACTIONS, FACTIONS EVERYWHERE BUT NOT A DROP OF TRUTH:** We're supposed to have a separation of powers, but all three parts of the government are dominated by the same two parties. If one party gets control of all three branches, then that party or faction can ignore the other faction.

Washington was worried about that possibility. Also, as the factions worry about fighting each other in the three branches, the interest of the people are completely ignored. Frustrated with the log jam, the people will back a dictator.

If we are counting on the parties and the courts to step in, the constitution is done: stick a fork in it: Trump is in flagrant violation of the emoluments clause. In 2011, Jay D. Wexler, a law professor at Boston University, published "The Odd Clauses," a book about the Constitution's more obscure provisions. He said such obscurity could be impermanent, as the recent attention to to Emoluments Clause demonstrates.

> *"I've seen over and over how parts of the Constitution that were considered vestigial or irrelevant for decades or more can suddenly resurface and take on enormous importance with a quick change of events… The framers were prescient men who created a government that could withstand the worst of human foibles—corruption, vindictiveness, the thirst for tyranny—and wrote a Constitution to combat those foibles in many of their forms, not all of which will always be present, but which emerge in different guises in different eras."*

Trump's ventures include multimillion-dollar real estate arrangements—with Trump's companies either as a full owner or a "branding" partner—in Ireland and Uruguay. The Bank of China is a tenant in Trump Tower and a lender for another building in Midtown Manhattan where Mr. Trump has a significant partnership interest. Here is the clause:

No Title of Nobility shall be granted by the United States:

And no Person holding any Office of Profit or Trust under them, shall, without the Consent of the Congress, accept of any present, Emolument, Office, or Title, of any kind whatever, from any King, Prince, or foreign State. Article I, Section 9, Clause 8

No doubt, Trump is violating his clause of the constitution. But that's not the only clause in the document. What about Article I, Section 8, Clause 11 of the U.S. Constitution?

> *The Congress shall have power to declare war, grant letters of marque and reprisal, and make rules concerning captures on land and water.*

When did congress authorize Obama to overthrow Gaddafi? Obama authorized the death of Abdulrahman al-Awlaki, a 16-year old American citizen, born in Denver. Abdulrahman was killed in a U.S. drone strike in Yemen on October 14, 2011. The killing violated the right to due process under the Fifth Amendment to the Constitution, the prohibition on unreasonable seizures under the Fourth Amendment, and, with respect to his father, Anwar Al-Aulaqi, the ban on extrajudicial death warrants imposed by the Constitution's Bill of Attainder Clause. The killings also violated international law, which is incorporated through the Constitution, as you can read in the complaint linked above from the ACLU.

War or murder? Here's the kicker, either the killing was an act or war or murder. If it was an act of war, when did congress authorize the war?

If you are worried about Trump getting out of control as president, indict Obama for the murder of Abdulrahman al-Awlaki and extradite George W. Bush to Italy for the kidnapping and torture of Hassan Mustafa Osama Nasr (aka Abu Omar) on 17 February 2003. That'll set Trump on the straight and narrow and restore

American rule of law along the way. You can be president without breaking the law if you want to.

Obama trashed the war powers provision of the constitution by engaging in illegal acts in Libya, Syria, Pakistan, Yemen, Somalia, Sudan, Iraq and Afghanistan without congressional approval, including actions that seem to be premeditated murder with no oversight, with no public presentation of evidence of wrongdoing, when the individual in question, a minor and American citizen in one case, posed no imminent danger to anyone, as he was in a restaurant 4000 miles away from the United States.

If the constitution is worth anything, the government is not supposed to be in your business without a warrant and probable cause. Now, let's consider the Fourth Amendment.

> *The right of the people to be secure in their persons, houses, papers, and effects, against unreasonable searches and seizures, shall not be violated, and no Warrants shall issue, but upon probable cause, supported by Oath or affirmation, and particularly describing the place to be searched, and the persons or things to be seized.*

Note the word "papers." Email is digital paper. Yet, thanks to Edward Snowden, we know the NSA was routinely storing all of our email without a warrant. NSA employees were abusing their power to read the emails of their spouses and exes. Reuters says, "At least a dozen U.S. National Security Agency employees have been caught using secret government surveillance tools to spy on the emails or phone calls of their current or former spouses and lovers in the past decade, according to the intelligence agency's internal watchdog." If they can read their boyfriend or girlfriend's email without permission, they could read your email with permission.

Obama promised to stop this trashing of the Fourth Amendment. But he didn't. The CIA, as we now know through the Wikileaks Vault 7 release, was deliberating leaving Apple and Samsung devices unsecure, or paying for insecurities and back doors to be left open in software, or installing malware on devices themselves.

Here is a summary or some of what we know from the Vault 7 release: With UMBRAGE, the CIA can hijack malware from other countries for false flag cyber attacks. In order to invade Smart devices from tablets to TVs and listen to conversations, the CIA created malware. It then lost control of that malware, allegedly giving "the entire hacking capacity of the CIA" to anyone who manages to dig up the code; the CIA's covert hacking program, including exploits against products like iPhone, Android, Windows, and Samsung TVs. The CIA has an extensive hacking division, WikiLeaks said, which is composed over over 5,000 registered users and more than a thousand hacking systems and malware. Using the "monitor mode" featured in many Smartphones and embedding a tool in the code of music player app, the CIA can use Android devices to harvest data from all neighboring WiFi traffic. That spiffy new "Smart" Samsung TV in your living room? The CIA can use its microphone to listen to everything you say.

The MSM would tell us this is no big deal. Isn't it clear that that Fourth Amendment is suspended.

The abrogation of the constitution continues into other critical areas. The constitution says our word is bond; but no, Uncle Sam's signature does not mean much, as the US government lies in the world's face like a petty swindler.

Article II, Section 2, Clause 2 of the United States Constitution, includes the Treaty Clause, which empowers the president of the United States to propose and chiefly negotiate agreements, which must be confirmed by the Senate, between the United States and other countries, which become treaties between the United States and other countries after the advice and consent of a supermajority of the United States Senate.

A treaty passed by the Senate has the force of US law. In 1988, the US senate ratified the United Nations Convention Against Torture. Here are some provisions of this treaty with the force of US law:

> *Each State Party shall ensure in its legal system that the victim of an act of torture obtains redress and has an enforceable right to fair and adequate compensation including the means for as full rehabilitation as possible. In the event of the death of the victim as a result of an act of torture, his dependents shall be entitled to compensation…. No exceptional circumstances whatsoever, whether a state of war or a threat or war, internal political instability or any other public emergency, may be invoked as a justification of torture… Each State Party shall ensure that all acts of torture are offences under its criminal law. The same shall apply to an attempt to commit torture and to an act by any person which constitutes complicity or participation in torture.*

Yet, under Bush, torture was routine and unpunished.

What kind of "conservative" ignores 500 years of tradition? Further, the US is a signatory to the Geneva Convention which does not allow the abuse of prisoners of war. Sometime in Medieval England, or maybe later, jurisprudence settled on the idea that to lock someone up the detainee must either be charged with a crime and appear before a judge, or the individual can be classified as a prisoner of war. A prisoner of war does not have a right to habeas corpus. He will be released when the conflict ends. The George W Bush administration invented a category called "enemy combatant," thus upending hundreds of years of jurisprudence.

The war powers provision, the provisions as to treaties and the rule of law, and the Fourth Amendment have been so completely ignored and undermined that it's impossible to square the reality of how the US government actually operates with the constitution. Three important parts of the constitution have been clearly suspended or overturned in fact if not on paper under Bush and Obama. Now, with Trump, a fourth provision of the constitution is invalidated, emoluments.

If it's wrong, it's wrong; if it's illegal, it's illegal... is that so hard to get, party people? When Washington warned about the dangers of faction, he might have been thinking of just the scenario we now see in America. Democrats were (or claimed to be) upset by Bush unilaterally abrogating the convention on torture. Democrats claimed to be upset by the abusive and arbitrary nature of the enemy combatant status, allowing for detention forever without charge. Under Bush, a declaration of war against Al Qaeda in 2001 was used to justify kidnapping, or extraordinary rendition, and torture, including individuals with no connection to Al Qaeda. Yet, with Obama in the White House, Democrats suddenly didn't mind the administration using this same declaration of war against one Jihadi group, Al Qaeda, as the justification for war against another non-state group, Isis, that did not exist in 2001.

Meanwhile, Republicans made all kinds of charges against Obama, accusing him of working outside the constitution but generally failing to note his violation of the war powers act, as they intended to violate the same provision if they ever re-gained the White House. Nevertheless, Republican calls for constitutional government now all ring hollow as they allow Trump to enrich himself and continue Obama's illegal war in Syria.

You see what Washington was talking about right? He kind of had a point. If we are going to be members of parties, we cannot allow these factional differences blind us to the abrogation of the constitution itself.

The situation is so bad that it is difficult to argue that the United States is currently a constitutional state with a true system of the rule of law. Without the Fourth Amendment protection of individual rights, without a system to debate the monumental decisions involved in war making, without honoring treaties, including on such a fundamental issue as torture, what is there really left of the constitution?

If we had listened to Washington, maybe we wouldn't have had to get a refresher from Eisenhower. But nevermind all this "constitution" nonsense, let's get back to the important agenda for America: hyping Russian influence. You know, serious journalism.

**WikiLeaks**

John F Kennedy and Bernie Sanders both called for breaking up the CIA #vault7

**John F. Kennedy And Bernie Sanders Both Called For Abolishing The CIA**
On Tuesday, WikiLeaks published a batch of internal CIA documents to its site that exposed the breadth and scope of the Central Intelligence Agency's spying and

# On history

**F**undamental, indisputable facts should not be ignored. This statement would seem to be entirely too obvious to dispute. You probably don't want to have a thorough discussion of the geology of mountains without mentioning Mount Everest. You might want to point out that on Mars, with lower gravity, there is a mountain that is taller than Everest. The inter-planetary comparison would not be relevant for all discussions of the formation of mountains but if you have a hypothesis about gravity, the fact that Olympus Mons stands about two and a half times as tall as Mount Everest's height above sea level cannot simply be ignored as inconvenient.

On August 6, the U.S. dropped a uranium bomb on Hiroshima, and American President Harry S. Truman called for Japan's surrender. Three days later, on August 9, a plutonium bomb was dropped on Nagasaki. Also on August 9, 1945, the Soviet Union invaded Manchuria, Inner Mongolia, northern Korea, Karafuto, and the Chishima Islands. Japan announced its surrender to the Allies on August 15.

Why did Japan surrender? Because of the atomic bomb or the specter of a Soviet occupation of some part of Japan itself? Apologists for the American decision to drop nuclear bombs on Hiroshima and Nagasaki are welcome to make a case that an invasion of Japan would have been worse than the destruction caused by the bombs and therefore justified. However, anyone advocating such a position should not be allowed to simply ignore a massive Soviet invasion across a wide swath of northern Asia. Maybe the bombing of Japan did not lead to the surrender. Maybe concerns about the possibility of a replay of Europe, with the Red Army occupying a large part of Asia, was critical in the decision to drop the bomb. You can't simply ignore something that massive and clearly substantiated in the historical record.

Likewise, about 50% of the inhabitants of the Soviet Union were non-Russians. The Soviets themselves tried to cloud this fact by referring to both Ukrainians and Russians as "East Slavs," estimated at about 70% of the Soviet population in 1989. But the powers behind cold war America were also never candid with the general population about demographics in the USSR from about 1945 to 1990 either. Most Americans in the 1970s and 1980s did not know that evil empire was built on a foundation of sand, of inter-ethnic tension, that could undermine this apparently daunting enemy at any time. If you want to argue that the Reagan military build up somehow triggered the fall of the Soviet Union, you cannot ignore the fact that ethnic nationalism, not lack of resources due to excessive military spending, was clearly front and center in the minds of many of the people who actually took the USSR apart region by region.

You can see why people would want to say that Reagan brought down the Soviet Union. Otherwise, all that defense spending was wasted, as is likely all the current defense spending. You can see why Americans might like to think that the atomic bomb was the only or even the critical factor in Japan's quick surrender. Otherwise, maybe the bombing cannot be justified morally. These convenient arguments might also have some truth to them. If they are somewhat true, they are undermining their own credibility by ignoring massive, irrefutable and relevant facts: ethnic nationalism, in one case, and the Soviet invasion, in the other.

Elite points of view backed by money and power, assuming ideologies of American nationalism, have in the past regularly determined how most Americans see history. In order to present a vision of American righteousness, some rather huge facts are generally simply left out of mainstream narratives. The Vietnamese communists fighting France, the United States and China in the 1950s, 1960s and 1970s were never puppets of the Soviet Union or China or any other world communist movement. The Vietnamese were supposed to be maybe world communist puppets, or maybe Chinese puppets at one point, then Soviet puppets. But the truth is now clear: there was never a good reason for the United States to be involved in Vietnam. Even now, discussions of American history rarely make this point clearly enough.

Trump was elected president in 2016. If the Democrats had not cheated in the primary, if not for the Pied Piper strategy, if not for the liberal echo chamber created with the help of John Podesta in 2007, if not for media collusion and black out of Bernie Sanders, if the Democrats had not nominated Hillary Clinton against the will of the majority of Americans, Trump would not have been elected president in 2016. If you want to make a counter argument, you have to respond to the evidence presented in this book. I expect this straight-forward, evidence-based argument to be ignored for twenty years or so, then accepted as gospel truth.

Maybe the election of Trump was a minor failure: the Democrats fumbled. If it was a local failure, then Trump being president should not be a big deal, assuming the system of checks and balances works. If Trump's election is a big deal and a crisis, then the American system must be flawed. If the system were as good as most claim, Trump wouldn't have been elected, or his election would not be a crisis.

If his election is a crisis, then we are not talking about a minor or one-time mess up by the Democratic Party. If Trump's election is critical or dramatic, a shock to the system, and a real danger to the people, then a radical view of US history should go mainstream. Our system is fake Democracy. Checks and balances and institutions don't protect us. We need systematic reform: constitutional amendments, new parties, something dramatic.

Either the Democrats screwed up and we need new Democratic leadership or we need something more revolutionary. Returning to the days of CNN, focus groups, Time magazine fluff pieces on plutocrats, and stage managed made-for-TV political conventions doesn't make logical sense. That world of image management, media lies and fake politics with both parties taking money from the same oligarchs obviously failed in some way, unless you like Trump. If you think everything is fine the way it is, then you don't like Trump because he says the America that elected him was not great and needed to be made great. We've got some logic problems involved in any argument other than the call for systematic change, unless Trump is the systematic change, which appears not to be the case.

Since Trump was elected, among the terrible policies, we might see a few glimmers of hope politically. More voters on the right seem to have developed a genuine antipathy to the CIA. The sooner we can get rid of the CIA, the better. Trump has shown disdain for the MSM without much damage, suggesting that the MSM reign of error may be ending. The the New York Times and the Washington Post have clear agendas and standing up for the 99% of workers is not one of them. We can live without the propaganda machine and the unelected spooks. We also don't need the Democratic or Republican parties. The response to Trump cannot be to go back to the good old days of 1992 or 2008.

# On the Supreme Court

**N**eil Gorsuch is on the supreme court due to Republican partisan tricks. The Republicans in the senate held up Obama's nominee for a year (trick one), then used the "nuclear option" to override a Democratic filibuster (trick two). The nuclear option has only been used twice in all of American history, once in 2013 and now here in 2017. Two aggressive parliamentary maneuvers worked for them. Presumably, the use of the so-called nuclear option means all court nominations are to be approved by 51 senators from now on, not the tacit consent of at least 60.

In 2000, the "conservatives" on the court acted in as partisan a way as senators or congressmen and installed a president, George W. Bush. The "conservative" justices turned out to be "Republican" justices. In these two cases, we see extreme partisanship dominating the Supreme Court.

Justices like Gorsuch get on the bench by working with Republican politicians, then justices like Scalia act like Republican politicians when ruling as judges. Naturally, Gorsuch, had to praise Scalia as a "legal lion" when he accepted the nomination. But this whole "lion" paradigm is a distortion. A sharp intellect, a person who communes with deep ideas about justice, fairness, process, and all the philosophical implications of these ideas and actually attempts to put these principles into action: such a "lion" has no chance of getting on the Supreme Court.

Justices are cogs, not fierce defenders. Gears in the machine: pretending to be "intellectual" is a role. Verbal gymnastics to rationalize the imposition of power in the context of a decision is not an intellectual activity, it's a form of high propaganda. The liberals in recent history include a couple of good examples that might qualify as "lions" but the current crop is not quite up to snuff. Unless you clearly say that the American system of justice is broken and take bold steps to stop the routine grinding up of a large segment of the population, unless you note that endless war is not compatible with democracy, you are no fierce defender of the people.

Gorsuch was groomed to be in a position to get a nomination by something of a conservative judge production machine. Law school, court appointment, he was pushed along by rich backers at every step, from the day he was born. He is from a rich, Republican family and his career was initiated and backed by a Republican billionaire. It's a regular "cat pretending to be lion" creation factory.

It would be nice if it were possible for someone who, say, drove a truck got into a position of power. Maybe if Gorsuch had driven a truck he might have had a little more sympathy with Alphonse Maddin, forced to chose between freezing to death and losing his job. Gorsuch only had sympathy for the trucking company, seeing an employee not as a human being but as a production unit, you know, sort of like a slave.

Gorsuch is not a Supreme Court judge because he has good judgement or because he is smart or charming or worked hard. No lion: he rose to power by being the man's pussy cat. Even if any of those attributes apply to him, lots of other people fit all of those criteria and they will never get on the Supreme Court. The only reason for his rise is that he worked with a partisan organization, the Republican Party, and that party in turn worked with oil and gas billionaires like Philip F. Anschutz. That's how he got on the bench in 2006.

If a party that is directly funded by billionaires to promote an ideology that allows for more billionaires to get more billions puts up a judge, he will rule in favor of their interests. And, of course, Gorsuch has reliably served big business and oligarchs like Anschutz and he will continue to do so for the rest of his life.

He is not in fact a man of reason, a judge, a person deeply concerned with the implications and philosophical implications of government policy. He is, like other politicians, a product of a system that just keeps rolling on: rich billionaires keep drilling for gas, buying politicians, getting rich, and on and on.

Meantime, I would point out, there are more than 25 people walking around free and alive today in the United States who were convicted of murder, sentenced to death, but later exonerated by DNA evidence. I present this one little fact—many fine people have obviously been executed by the state who could not avail themselves of DNA evidence of their innocence—as just one little hiccup to get us started on the idea that everything is not okay with the system rolling on and on, keep on rolling. If you suck up to billionaires you get on the Supreme Court. If you happen to be in the wrong place at the wrong time, you might by dumb luck be executed for a crime you didn't commit.

And since I mentioned the Republican party, I would point out that while Bush v. Gore (2000) was an abomination in a long history of horrible Supreme Court decisions, if Gore had been president, the world might not be all that different. Gore supported the invasion of Iraq. And if Obama's nominee had gotten on the court, Merrick Garland, had gotten on the court, there would have been absolutely no danger to the interests of oligarchs like Anschutz and the others to whom both Gorsuch and Garland kowtow. The Republican partisan machine is simply better and more coherent than the equivalent Democratic machine but neither party in any way wants to check or turn let alone stop the system from rolling, rolling, rolling. Rolling over innocent people who were executed, rolling over the war powers provisions of the constitution to allow for endless war, rolling over the environment, rolling over treaty obligations to native people and to the world through the UN Convention on Torture, etc.

We have an undemocratic system in which the people's voices don't matter here in America. Proof: "I guess it takes a study to point out the obvious." If there is a study, and the results are obvious to John Podesta and his kind, the state "the United States is a not a democracy" should be a simple, uncontroversial fact.

Is the current partisanship leading to bad Supreme Court rulings something that just happened? The naked partisanship isn't new. FDR found a Republican court in control when he got into office in 1932 and had to deal with it in a partisan way.

How about bad decisions? Is the Supreme Court a venerable and august institution in decline? Should we respect the Supreme Court?

No, as I will now argue, hell no. For almost the entire some 230 year history of the United States constitutional structure, the Supreme Court has stood for racism, big business, sexism, and the power of the state over the individual. For about 90% of the history of the court, the big and strong have used the judicial branch to bash the weak and powerless. In the rhetoric of the Federalists in 1788, the court was supposed to protect individual liberty and minorities from factional rule, from a faction that is a majority, and be there to stand by the dissident or the outsider when the majority controls the other branches of government. In general, the court has actually done the exact opposite.

We know the Supreme Court was a good friend of the

slave owner. We know that the court did nothing in the face of exonerations of death row inmates. We know that the president can apparently bomb any target anywhere in the world without congressional approval. We know that presidents have arbitrarily and on their own abrogated and defied treaties ratified by the US Senate with the force of US law. We know the Supreme Court tried to stop the New Deal. We know about Citizens United. We know about "separate but equal." The court undermined the Civil Rights amendments to the constitution and allowed for White supremacy to take over the all aspects of government in the late nineteenth century. The FBI spied on Americans because of their politics in the 1970s, framed them, and sometimes killed them in staged raids. Eugene Debs and many others went to jail because they were against World War I and the court didn't protect them. Jehovah's witnesses were lynched for not taking the Pledge of Allegiance and the court was on the side of the lynch mob. We saw the court install a president in 2000.

You can see it. It's not a great institution that went off the rails here and there. The Dred Scott decision was not a blemish in an otherwise perfect history of justice. The proper conclusion of a fair consideration of history is that the Supreme Court sucks and always has and is entitled to no respect and deference.

Generation after generation, the court has issued horrible decisions (or fails to rule at all) such that they knock the chair out from under vulnerable people and leave ordinary Americans and people around the world at the mercy of tyrants. If the proof of the pudding is in the eating, the Supreme Court of the United States is a shit stew.

The framers of the constitution decided for a strong federal judiciary to control factional government, especially when a faction become a majority. In Federalist Paper 10, for example, Madison said, ""the most common and durable source of factions has been the various and unequal distribution of property." Wikipedia says, "Madison feared that a majority faction of the unpropertied classes might emerge to redistribute wealth and property in a way that benefited the majority of the population at the expense of the country's richest and wealthiest people."

When the proponents of the new US constitution came out with their new document, they did not advertise the idea that the courts could rule a law unconstitutional. It seems Madison and Hamilton and their allies hoped to sneak the notion of a court throwing out a law into our system of government without explicitly debating the issue in public.

In some of their earlier writing, you can read that they believed in judicial review. The issue was discussed at the constitutional convention and the majority seemed to agree that courts should have the final say on what is and is not allowed under the constitution. They weren't sure, however, how the general public would react to the idea, so they tried to slip it passed the rest of the country.

The opponents of the constitution first brought up the fact that under the new system, it seemed like courts could overrule legislatures, including the Supreme Court over Congress. Brutus and Federal Farmer, two pen names for the opponents of the constitution, pointed out that the Supremacy Clause and Article III, Section 2 would give the courts vast powers. Like in Britain, they wrote, the constitution will allow the courts to "mold the government into almost any shape they please." Judges should not be allowed to sit for life unless they commit a crime, as that would leave "no way is left to control them but with a high hand and an outstretched arm." They concluded that through "our inattention to limiting properly the judicial powers, we may fairly conclude, we are more in danger of sowing the seeds of arbitrary government in this department than in any other."

Only after Brutus and the Federal Farmer outed judicial review as part of the constitution did the Federalists like Madison and Hamilton fess up to what they had in mind and present an argument in favor of judicial review. They tried to slip this judicial power into the structure of government without an open discussion and, failing with that strategy, they went with plan B, and presented a case for a strong federal judiciary openly in the Federalist Papers.

Madison got his way. The court has been powerful and largely in the service of the wealthy since the inception of the Republic.

Here are some bad decisions: Dred Scott 1857 (ruling black people aren't citizens), Plessy v. Ferguson (allowing separate-but-equal) 1896, Buck v. Bell 1927 (permitting compulsory sterilization), and Korematsu v. United States 1944 (upholding Japanese internment camps), Slaughter-House Cases / United States v. Cruikshank 1873 / 1875 (undoing Reconstruction), Chae Chan Ping v. United States 1889 (upholding Chinese exclusion act), Bowers v. Hardwick 1986 (allowing laws against homosexual), Lochner v. New York 1905 (against workers rights), Hammer v. Dagenhart 1918 (voiding child labor law), Lucas v. South Carolina Coastal Commission 1992 (preventing the protection of the environment), Exxon Shipping Co. v. Baker 2008 (increased Exxon stock by 23 billion in one day), Citizens United v. FEC 2010 (big money politics).

These are not aborations, exceptions. The anti-labor decisions in the period of Lochner were widespread. Plessy, Cruikshank are part of a pattern.

In every period of US history, the court has stood by the powerful against the weak, except for the period when FDR and others who followed him appointed the judges, from about 1954 and Brown v. Board of Education through the early 1970s. There are no really terrible decisions in this period. The rest of it? Crap. 1850s siding with slave owners, in the 1870s with racists, in the 1900s with the bosses, in the 1920s with the eugenicists, in the 1930s against the New Deal, in the 1940s against the Japanese, and in the 1980s, 1990s and 2000s with big business.

Does a legal lion stand by and let Japanese families get imprisoned? Exclude people from the country because they're Chinese? Be lynched because they're Jehovah Witnesses? Be a slave? Execute an innocent man? Deny education to Black people? Give money to Exxon to pollute the environment? The US system was never designed to be a democracy. And it isn't.

# Conclusion

I started writing this book around the time Trump took office, January 20, 2017. Here's the urgency: I could feel in the first week of Trump in office that an important truth was slipping away. I know a self published, late night book is unlikely to change the flood of power narratives working to pump bullshit into every corner of the American mind, doing psy ops for the oligarchy during this period of cracks and holes with millionaire talking heads pretending to be serious. My book is unlikely to make any difference. I flail away at my poor keyboard.

We the people face a future of technology beyond our control, market forces beyond our control and a government ungrounded by constitutional principles. This problem is not a left problem or a right problem.

Your kids are excited that today they will see images of a newly discovered planet with liquid water only five light years away at school. Nothing is more important than visions for the future and education, as robots and AI take over more and more of the economy and as people tend to live to be 150 to 200 years old. In school, the kids learn that there once was a phrase called "The Rust Belt" before the people took control back of the government. In those days, race determined where many people lived. The president could start a war without consulting anyone and the military budget was determined by the defense contractors who benefitted from the high level of senseless spending. The robber barons of that era had billions of dollars and could simply leave all that money to their children, guaranteeing inequality for generations. A semi-literate White supremacist president was elected as a "businessman" as a sign of desperation, frustration and due to the corruption of the Democratic Party.

You say goodbye and head downtown. You leave your home a few minutes from the center on a road made of solar panels, bike path on the side of the road safe enough for kids. Your electric self driving car lets you out at the research center for transportation technology in downtown Detroit: an office complex combined with a aircraft hanger type of testing grounds. You walk out for lunch on a sidewalk cafe, then take the fast train to Chicago to be there before dinner.

All energy energy generated in America comes from renewable sources. Everyone on earth has access to decent water, air, food, health care and at least a small pension. The World Trade Organization guarantees that all member nations provide basic needs to citizens as a condition of membership. Some systematic way of sharing wealth directly to citizens guarantees that all people have some stake in the world.

That kind of future is entirely possible, and in only a few years. We can set ourselves on the path to a sustainable, fair society. But how many more two trillion dollar Iraq war mistakes can we afford? The money spent on the Iraq war should have been spent on Michigan and Ohio, on rural West Virginia, Mississippi and upstate New York.

How many more chances will be get to turn this ship of state in the right direction? If America heads in the wrong direction, how much of the world will it drag down with it?

Bernie represented a turn toward making the government at least accountable to the mass of people. The market and technology do not have even the seeds of a notion of "citizen." There is no other institution or force or god other than the state that can attend to the basic needs of humanity. As of 2016, that institution is entirely in the hands of special interests who no more care about the general welfare than do the agents driving the market and improvements in technology.

The people of the world are doomed unless we can get control of the government and turn it into an instrument that recognizes the category of citizen, or individual, that allows for the expression of ration human values. Barack Obama did nothing—not one thing—as president to move the possibility of a collective expression of humanity forward in any way. He is a celebrity. With mass media and electronic imagery, the celebrity president played off images and words to which he was not connected politically or emotionally, impressions and rhetoric out of Black American history while not taking steps to reverse mass incarceration or wealth and income disparities, the ambiance of progressive change while siding with CitiGroup over homeowners. He didn't even really write Dreams of My Father. Podesta, Wasserman Schultz and the Clintons played him like a fool. He couldn't bring himself to let Bernie win and handed the imperial presidency to Trump. The soundtrack to this paragraph is Wu Tang clan, Old Dirty Bastard. Read it again with that playing in the background. You know which track, right?

If Bernie had won, I would not be writing this book in this form right now, but a book similar to this one would still be needed at some point. The ideas here for how to deepen or reform liberal democracy would still be valid. If Bernie had won, his agenda would not have magically materialized. The military industrial financial tech complex would not simply have given up the ghost and disappeared.

If the DNC had not fumbled and put Trump in the White House, this book would have the same ideas for making our society more democratic. We would need to think again about how important a communal space is, government, when we live in a world of powerful technology and a powerful market. If we are to have a powerful government to check the other gods, tech and market, that god had better be constrained and uncorrupted.

You know what the Soviet Union did wrong? It was a one party state. If the communists had come up with the idea of a two party state, they'd still be around. If they had "debates" between one party led by a charismatic minority cosmopolitan arguing for foreign intervention with oligarchic control of government, against a man of the people, straight shooting local nationalist arguing for foreign intervention with oligarchic control of government, they could have continued a policy of foreign intervention with oligarchic control of government forever.

If instead of a single, obviously state-owned newspaper, Pravda, they had had six apparently independent media outlets that were in fact owned by a small gang of party insiders, the propaganda environment would not have been as obvious. In this apparently diverse but actually controlled and narrow media environment, the two apparently different but actually the same parties could have pretended to have a debate, and communism never would have fallen.

We have a two-party system in which both parties agree on militarism, big banks, media consolidation, money in politics, deference to insurance and pharmaceutical companies on healthcare, and tax policy that favors the acquisition of enormous fortunes of inherited wealth for a small group of oligarchs over building infrastructure and education for the mass of working people. We have a media controlled by a small group of owners with overlapping interests with these billionaires. And guess what?

This media gives us a narrow debate, never mentioning options that would in fact make a real difference in people's lives, like redistribution of wealth.

And under all that, we have the Deep State that Chuck Schumer warned Donald Trump not to tangle with right before that same Deep State sank one of Trump's appointees by tapping his phone then leaking the call to the establishment media.

Three things remain as true as the mount on high but as obscured as if behind an autumn fog: one, the Bernie Sanders agenda of decreasing militarism, environmental protection, racial justice and redistribution of wealth is the only coherent strategy to improve the conditions for working people in the United States, fight climate change and reduce war around the world, the only program built on the world as it is and true to the reality of economics and government, not spin, not pre-approved elitist narratives designed to sound good but do nothing; two, the rise of Trump is due to years of phony politics, with a limited debate between oligarchic corporate pro-war Democrats and oligarchic corporate pro-war Republicans topped off with the cherry of the Democrats robbing Bernie Sanders; and three, the Democrats have learned nothing and if there is no change in the party Trump will win in 2020 and have loyalists throughout the government, judiciary, law enforcement and military.

Certainly, the constitution and the interests of the American people will not be protected unless there is a change to who runs the "left" and why. Or forget "left" and just give us a party for the 99% and an end to war. We need a positive vision of a better America. Socialists have that. The Blue Dogs only have an MSM powered lie. Everything they say is a lie because Obamacare is lousy.

When in history has there been a moratorium on history? Histories will be written on what happened, the path to 2016 and the victory of Trump. This book is meant to jump into that fray. I won't (and can't) power my way through with media clout and fame, so I'll have to use, well, evidence, logic and truth.

We will see narratives based on power. The authors of the power histories of 2016 will claim authority based on some past experience. Selective evidence will avoid the elephants in the room. The discussion of the 2016 Wikileaks releases will be fundamentally dishonest and superficial. These authors certainly will not point out how often we read in these leaked emails that the people closest to Hillary Clinton did not like, respect or trust her or that team Podesta says point blank that the United States in not a democracy (Wikileak ID 23756, 15762, 3723), as they go on to master corruption, even if they know, and admit, it's wrong. The conclusion of the power narrative will blame the regular people for failing: Trump supporters are racist and sexist. Minorities are lazy or disengaged or something. Leftists are stubborn and hardheaded. After blaming the people, the power narrative will blame random actors Blue Dogs don't like. Wikileaks sucks for some reason. The FBI is biased. And, of course, RUSSIA!

This "punch it through" power story will be a crock of crap but the mainstream media will eat it up. Interviews. The lie machine will kick into gear. Those people who still think with the nostalgic brains cultivated in the middling, fake debate, corporatist, limited soup of the PBS/CBS/ABC/NYT/WAPO/CNN/Fox/Limbaugh bullshitistic paradigm will share the "proof" and the "debunking" on social media with an assist from the algorithms of Google and Facebook.

This complex of corporate brainwashing may be sufficient to prevent a sustained awaking of the people to the fakeness of the entire so-called "democracy." Propaganda will not be sufficient to return American politics to PBS Newshour when you had a "Republican" and a "Democrat" pretend to have a debate about something that matters to the people. The good old days: when the elites could have beauty contest elections, then write how much they admired each other in their memoirs when they retire.

FOR REPUBLICANS: "Enemy combatant" is outside of the framework of English (and later American) jurisprudence going back to the middle ages. You are either a prisoner of war or accused of a crime. Torture is cruel and inhumane punishment. Treaties are to be honored. When the United States president signs and the senate ratifies a treaty, that treaty has the force of law in America. We don't sign, ratify then ignore a treaty. Yet, Bush-Cheney tortured people after our country signed on to the United Nations Convention on Torture. Those values are what make Anglo-American conservatism unique and important. The current crop of Trump-loving European style Volk racists are outside the tradition of Anglo-American conservative insistence on law. Trump's effort to ban people from entry in the country explicitly based on religion is an affront to the establishment clause. No official religion is a bedrock principle of American government. Having a military general as secretary of defense upends civilian control of the military. The president's generalized rhetoric about the press is disturbing. Trump launched various radical attacks on our ancient constitutional liberties in his first weeks (when I am writing this book). Trump and Bush were both radicals from an Anglo-American traditional, Edmund Burke Conservative point of view: aggressive war, disdain for tradition, looking at people as groups, not individual actors, like we were in the Habsburg Empire and not a Republican nation in the tradition of Locke, Hume, and even Reagan and Thatcher. Trump holds on to his businesses and plans to make money off being president, apparently, like his friend Putin, who in fact may be the richest man in the world. Trump may be engaging in shady deals with Russia and we would not know. Republicans have been using dog whistle racism for years to win White voters and they shouldn't be surprised when their party turns into the party of White nationalism.

So, are no Republicans also conservatives? Is the Republican party and the "conservative" movement 100% racist, self-interested, cowardly bullshit? Where are my conservatives? Not in congress, I can guarantee you that. They seem afraid of their base. Do Republicans think a sitting president should make money off his office?

FOR DEMOCRATS: Only congress can declare war is another central principle of our constitutional framework. Barack Obama did not think he should even pretend to talk to congress before removing a head of state, Muammar Gaddafi, and creating a new, more chaotic order in a huge swath of the globe, northern and western Africa, as was reported in the New York Times on February 28, 2016. Obama bombed Yemen with drones and from ships. As many as 10,000 Yemenis may have already died in the conflict as of the beginning of 2017 with starvation a real possibility in a country that shares a border with the obesity capital of the world, Saudi Arabia and the Gulf States. The Fourth Amendment guarantees the individual personal liberty from the state. Obama essentially tossed the Fourth Amendment in the trash with the NSA spying program revealed by Edward Snowden. Chelsea Manning revealed that Egyptian torturers were trained by FBI—although allegedly to teach the human rights issues. We learn that the State Department under Hillary Clinton knew the US-backed 2009 coup in Honduras was "illegal and unconstitutional." Hillary Clinton knew Saudi Arabia and Qatar were arming Isis Daesh but continued to sell arms and take bribes from Saudi Arabia and Qatar. Hillary got almost $200 million in wealth through bribery, unprecedented greed and corruption that would make Richard Nixon blush. Google tried to influence this election (see Eric Schmidt on Wikileaks). Possibly the two most powerful entities in the history of the world, the United States government and Google, should not be intermixing and if the idea of an algorithm driven politics doesn't send shivers down your spine… you haven't got a spine. Obamacare isn't working and was weak tea. Black household wealth dropped 50% during Obama's time in office. Life expectancy dropped under Obama for many communities in America. All of Obama's cabinet positions were vetted by CitiGroup, as a team of bank employees sent him a list of acceptable applicants, following which CitiGroup got more TARP funding than any other bank (Wikileak ID 8190). Free elections are an essential ingredient of democracy and the Democratic party now stands firmly against free and fair primaries. The superdelegate system is an undemocratic abomination.

So, do no Democrats care about constitutional protections? Are no Democrats against war? Do no Democrats care about democracy in Central America? Starvation in Yemen? Free and fair election in the US? Do they care about working people? Do Democrats think CitiGroup should have a veto on political appointments and come out of the crash better than before, unlike Black households? Do Democrats think a secretary of state should take money from foreign powers?

Religion, civilian control, search and seizure, war powers, treaties, torture, cruel and inhuman punishment, no self-dealing: what rights and principles have not been trampled since 9/11? Democrat, Republican: it makes absolutely no difference in terms of respect for the constitution. What aspect of life important to working people has been enhanced and protected by the elite one party cabal? Both parties suck so completely from a historical point of view, or by comparing our rules and politicians to other countries in terms of self-dealing and legalized bribery, that you cannot seriously call the United States a democracy.

Abraham Lincoln suspended habeas corpus (Habeas Corpus Suspension Act 1863) but even in the middle of the worst crisis in American history he 1) respected the Supreme Court's decision that only congress can suspend the writ, even though many of the judges were Southerners; 2) limited the geographic and temporal dimensions of the suspension; 3) was quite clear that the act was allowed under the constitution, Article I, Section 9. But if anyone were to ask Obama on what authority he moved troops into Iraq, bombed Yemen, Somalia, Pakistan, contributed to the death of the head of state in Libya, armed Daesh/Isis in Syria to oppose secular Assad, he might just act as if the question were merely impolite and move his hands slowly and his voice would get very deep and he would say nothing of substance. Trump would roll his eyes and wave his hands, such a nuisance, constitution, bullshit. If you asked Bush Jr. why he was able to void the United Nations Convention on Torture as approved by the Senate, he would babble incoherently.

You know, there is a reason Abraham Lincoln is considered a great president and a great man. Bush, Obama and Trump are midgets who seemed to have been rolling around in the playpen rather than standing on the shoulders of giants.

If there is something valuable about Anglo-American conservatism is it the respect for these traditions of individual liberty and limited government, of process and prudence. Since our elites are giving us none of the benefits of conservatism and all of the pain of inequality and war, the right response of the people is resistance to oligarchs.

Obama Titanic iceberg crasher. We have a date and a time: July 25, 2016. Crash. Who was the captain of the ship? Go back and read the quotes above again. See the dates. See what happened. Now, you Blue Dogs, will you listen? No? Then when will you listen? Iceberg 2.0 ahead, 2020.

The Republican party was founded in 1854 and by 1861 it controlled every part of the government. Who would have guessed that the Soviet Union would disappear in 1985? Not too many. Yet, by 1991, it was gone. It doesn't happen often, but sometimes a solid looking impediment is not as strong as it looks and things give way. We need that kind of change now in America: kick over the oligarchy and let the people breath, end racism, end imperialism, and stop polluting. We might be closer than you think.

The Democrats cannot be allowed to whitewash their crimes with anti-Trump sentiment. Madeleine Albright can tweet that she wants to register as a Muslim in solidarity, yet when asked if the deaths of Iraqi children under sanctions was a price worth paying for ending Saddam's rule. Her reply? 'I think this is a very hard choice, but the price — we think the price is worth it.' Then there's Hillary Clinton, who was retweeted tens of thousands of times for saying of Trump's order: 'This is not who we are.' Given the drone strikes and interventions in seven muslim countries when she was secretary of state, I would have to disagree. It appears to be exactly who we are.

Trump is dangerous. So why did Obama hand him the White House with an intact imperial presidency when he could have stopped it with three little words in May, June or July 2016? It would have been easy for Iceberg Obama to stop him. He chose not to. Three little words would have done the trick. Obama, in his pride, could not say them. He's a great orator. But the three words he didn't say are more important than the thousands he did speak. He sat for an interview with 60 minutes in 2013 with Hillary and stuck with his sitting position, never changing his position, never standing up. Thus, Obama, by failing to lead, fucked the world up. What three little words he never got up from his 2013 sit down with Hillary and CBS would have saved the world?

One word: I. Next word: endorse. Last word: Bernie. If he had done that, his legacy would be up and running, America would be leading the world in green energy, democracy would have been renewed. Pride indeed is a deadly sin, President Iceberg, Mr. Obama. You had a tremendous responsibility. And you let down the human race and the planet. Your own pride made you blind, Dr. Smooth.

Team oligarchy, Hillary/Obama, gave us Trump. If Obama or Hillary or Schumer or Pelosi or Podesta want to meet me in debate or for an interview any time any place, I will politely ask them questions, with follow up, and send them the questions in advance. Yet, if they don't leave the room in a panic at having to give real answers to real questions, in 45 minutes the truth of every word in this book will be so clear that the Democratic party will be on the floor crying like a baby. They have nothing to say. I want a chance to prove it. I would love to have 30 minutes with Obama. Has he no time for the people? Including people who don't unquestionably accept everything he says anyway? This hypothetical interview would be the defining moment of his political career, as it will reveal that he failed America and the world. He has style and he is a great symbol. But he failed and he knows it. So, he won't take me on. My email is easy to find. I'm ready.

See, you Blue Dogs have to read this book. If Obama would call me, you could watch the interview and the effect would be the same: the destruction of the web of lies that keeps the Democratic party from having to face their primary, indeed key, critical, essential, role in the rise of Trump. Since Obama won't talk to the people, preferring to chit chat with friendly but mediocre South African comedians, you, Blue Dog, have an obligation to see in print what would be obvious in the give and take of a real interview. Obama has never done a real interview in his life, never had to answer real questions, so he has deprived you of the obvious truth, forcing you to live in ignorance or read this book.

During one of his many journeys the Roman Emperor Hadrian was pestered by a woman, but the emperor brusquely said that he did not have the time to deal with her. Her yelled response, "Then stop being emperor!" immediately made him stop and listen to her petition. Marcus Aurelius was renowned for the time he devoted to hearing any case brought before him. A conscientious emperor spent long hours in often dull work.

A citizen of Rome could appeal to the emperor. Trevor Noah is not a citizen of the United States. I am. I appeal to Obama as a leader of my former party and former emperor to hear my appeal and to engage in 30 minutes of questioning with follow up in the venue and time of his choosing with questions provided in advance.

Were Obama merely an emperor! The emperor and his party have no clothes. The only thing propping up these Democrats is that they never have to answer hard questions. The mainstream media is propping them up.

2008 was the year of the New Deal 2.0. The crisis was there to use, to leverage the power of the state to reform the economy for working people. Obama has admitted in interviews that he does not think presidents can transform society. He never took his "hope and change" rhetoric as anything more substantial than Bush's "compassionate conservatism" or Hillary's "stronger together." He might be an ass, and the slogan incoherent, but Trump actually believes he can "make America great again." He's spinning, but not just spinning. Obama was just spinning, full stop.

So, we were sold a bill of goods in 2008 and Obama was not the president he advertised himself to be in the 2008 campaign. He ran as a populist progressive then governed as a hawkish Republican elitist, entitled, White banker. He stabbed Black America in the back as the average wealth and life savings of the majority evaporated in the housing crisis. Oh well, it's just blood money made by sweat and work. That's not as important as keeping CitiGroup "liquid."

In 2016, the United States is not a democracy. We were robbed. It was the party's chance to redeem itself but Obama's genius for blase inaction struck again. Blue Dog, Blue Dog, 2016 was the year of Sanders, of rebirth, of a new bloom, if not for your evil crimes. The little bird descended but you did not heed the warning of the mother earth goddess.

The devil was at the door. The bird told you what to do. The voice from on high was as clear as it has ever been in the history of mankind. But the Democrats were having fun, feeling important is fun, and they wanted more money and power. So… dark descended on America. Woe to you, Barack Obama: the stain of complacent evil is upon your soul.

Bernie Sanders was the man of the year in 2016. He got a knife in the back. He fell. Trump stepped over his body into the White House. Who wielded the knife? Barack Obama and the Blue Dogs. Then, with Trump in the White House, they voted to approve his Nazi cabinet into power.

We're not in a democracy, but we also don't live in a totalitarian state. Not yet. Meanwhile the rank and file Blue Dog (Blue Sheep in this case) democrats are off to the slaughter house, mad at me because I think they should learn from their mistakes, stop losing elections, and clean house before it's too late.

We can still wake up. We can still organize. We can still write. We can still force team D for dummy into retirement. If we don't, woe. We told you on July 25, 2016 and you did not heed the warning. The mother goddess sent a messenger and you ignored her wisdom. You must reform now. Clean house.

Now, you see that mother goddess quote? Now, just one paragraph later, I'm telling you that the quote was hyperbole intended for us, the Bernie true believers, and not to be taken literally. Watch what happens to the quote anyway.

Rebuilding your democratic infrastructure means making the constitution mean something again: war powers, treaty obligations, no established religion, all of it. Congress and the courts should be bodies on constitutional matters (as opposed to policy) and not just forums for partisan conflict. The Democrats screwed up by not protesting Obama's wars in Libya, Yemen, Syria, Somalia, Iraq and elsewhere. The Democrats should not have let Obama rule by executive order.

This recent past matters. When a Trump supporter says, "Where were you protesters when Obama was in charge?" the right answer is not some long winded illogical defense of Obama's stupid and illegal imperialism but, "Yeah, you're right: we should have protested Obama too."

If you love Obama, you also love lawless American imperialism. There is nothing more central to his "legacy" than

American intervention without authorization from congress or any kind of strategic success. He kept the reasons for bombing Yemen, Pakistan, Somalia, etc. secret even from congress. He routinely violated domestic and international law to kill whoever he wanted whenever he wanted, including a head of state. He went back into Iraq after declaring that intervention over in 2011. It's not an asterisk on the Obama presidency and this kind of endless war is not a footnote on the American government in the 21st century. It's a disgrace and blemish on America for all time: a barbaric, arrogant, destructive murder machine. And then he passed it all to Trump intact.

Here is my unrealistic dream:the base of the Democratic party will realize that their leadership fucked up, sold out the working class since well before 2008, robbed Bernie, is in the pocket of the banks and the military industrial complex and they are the ones who gave us Trump. Then, the rank and file will abandon the Democratic party as it currently exists. Without the current leadership in place, a new generation of progressives will take over, and Trump will cease to be a danger to America. Reforms will follow.

The only thing that is preventing the Democratic base from rising up and overthrowing their bad leadership is confusion sown by the media as part of the conspiracy that is this fake democracy. This Pied Piper media is part of the cabal that gave us Trump by coordinating with Podesta and company. Turn them off. Obama, Clinton, Pelosi, Schumer, Podesta, and the rest of them sold us out to CitiGroup, the Deep State and the war machine, then handed America to Trump. Death to the Democratic party, that's what I hope this book accomplishes. They richly deserve to go out of business. Probably won't happen, not by writing a book anyway, but that's my dream. They'll have to lose some more elections I guess.

The Democratic party is mostly responsible for 16 years of war, rising and extreme inequality, the Deep State, Big Brother, and President Trump. If you are still in the thrall of Obama and disagree, ignoring my arguments or trying to silence me might work among a set of Blue Dogs such as yourself but will not work in the long run. Why? Because their is such a thing as truth.

The 2017 Russia hysteria has a huge flaw in terms of "resistance" to Trump as a strategy: aside from being irrelevant to the lives of the American people, it's also not true.

Barack Obama is a con man. "Hope" and "change" were advertising slogans. On October 11, 2011 Obama murdered Abdulrahman Anwar al-Awlaki. He should be arrested and charged with murder. Obamacare was a flop. Libya. CitiGroup. Isis.

The Domino Theory used to justify the Vietnam war was wrong. The communist party of Vietnam was never a puppet of the Soviet Union or China. A million people died in an unnecessary war.

The Iraq War was launched by the son of the man who likely made a deal to keep the American hostages in Iran until after the 1980 election. The Iraq War benefited Iran, who is still sitting on the evidence of the 1980 October surprise, but cost the American taxpayer US two trillion dollars and killed a half million people for no good reason. Weapons of mass destruction was a lie.

The fall of the Soviet Union: the CIA fails to predict this most important event of the Cold War. Democratic presidents were overthrown and/or murdered by the CIA in Iran, Chile, Congo, Guatemala, Laos, Haiti, Dominican Republic, Indonesia, Bolivia, Cambodia, and more.

There is nothing natural or healthy about inequality. Inherited wealth generation after generation: there is no excuse morally and no benefit to society practically.

Four hundred years of racism should probably be enough. We have ghettos, a Rust Belt, and rural poverty because some people don't count and the government doesn't care if some citizens of the nation live or die. Some people count as legal persons and others are disposable.

The US never developed a labor party because the workers were divided, black and white, and because of state violence against the people. If not for state murder of striking workers, we would all have government health care, better working conditions and live about two years on average longer, for a total of some 600 million more years of human life.

We have forgotten what money means. America is not a democracy. The way we pick leaders and make decisions is irrational.

We have wasted vast sums on the military. We let a few billionaire hoard so much wealth. If we just stood up to the oligarchs and stopped US imperialism, our lives would be much better and longer, and the environment could be better. There is no upside to war and aristocracy.

Here are the conclusions of what we now know to be reality:

The Princeton Study of American democracy is not a statistical straw man. By confirming that the conclusion of the study is true, professional anti-democratic operators Podesta and Mook have turned a finding based on empirical evidence into an irrefutable fact. Remove the phrase "American democracy" from your vocabulary.

Both parties serve their donors and only their donors: financial services, insurance companies, military contractors, technology companies and other oligarchs.

The 2016 Wikileak publications reveal massive, complete and systemic corruption in foreign and domestic policy in the United States. Crimes are routinely committed by the powerful, including Clinton and Obama, include FEC violations and murder, without consequence for elites.

The Democratic Party raised more money than any political organization in the history of the world under Obama and yet lost more seats and ended up weaker than at any time since 1920. In response, the party instituted no reforms. Anyone who donates to the Democratic Party or to Democratic candidates is likely an insider looking for favors or a fool. If this Russia hysteria doesn't pan out (which it won't) and Trump isn't Hitler (which he isn't), the Democrats will keep losing.

Bernie Sanders would have been the party nominee if the US had a free press and open and fair elections, including at the primary stage. If Bernie had been the nominee, he would have been elected president.

The Pied Piper strategy worked. The free media Trump by Podesta and company and the changes the Democrats put into the primary calendar allowed Trump to win the Republican nomination. Then, in the general election, many Republicans did in fact abandon Trump for Johnson, or stayed home, or in some cases voted for Clinton. The reason that the Pied Piper strategy did not work well enough to win the White House was that more people were alienated from Clinton than Trump, although vast numbers were alienated from both.

Under Obama, White households earned, on balance, twice

as much per year in income as Black households and held about twelve times as much net worth wealth. The gap between Black and White income and wealth as great or greater under Obama than at any time in modern history since records were kept. The first Black president was a great symbol of progress and he can now bask in his celebrity.

In health care, the United States is off the charts in terms of spending but heading the wrong way in terms of life expectancy. In education, the US is among the top five spenders but down about 30th in results. In military spending, the US spends more than the next eight countries combined and yet our actions, such as invading Iraq, have more strategic benefits for our enemies (jihadis and Iran) than our own nation.

When people act out: a media total blackout. Static is the soundtrack of the fade out of the social contract. How you made out, when all you're laid out? The Democratic party is played out. Fade out.

Establishment Democrats Only Care About Making Money, Not Rebuilding A Movement - T...

Before serving as chairman of the Democratic National Committee while employed as Obama's labor secretary, Tom Perez encouraged the Clinton campaign early on in the primary election cycle to demean her opponent by labeling him as a favorite of white men and unpopular with the African American, female, and the Latinx demographics. According to emails leaked by WikiLeaks, **Perez encouraged Clinton campaign chairman John Podesta** to use the Bernie Bro myth in order to win the Nevada caucus:

**The survey**, conducted by Harvard University and The Harris Poll, disproves the "Bernie Bro" trope with hard numbers. According to the survey results, which were conducted among 2,027 registered voters between April 14 and April 17, 2017, Sanders is actually more popular among women, African Americans, Hispanics, and Asian Americans than white people and men.

The poll shows 55 percent of men and 52 percent of whites approve of Bernie Sanders. However, Sanders is approved by 73 percent of African Americans, 68 percent of Hispanics, 62 percent of Asian Americans, and 58 percent of women. And even though Sanders identifies as independent, 80 percent of Democrats approve of him.

## JOHN PODESTA: ENJOY YOUR TWISTED, PEDOPHILIA, CANABALISTIC ART COLLECTION. YOU EARNED IT.

Russia wasn't a factor in the outcome of the 2016 election.

## AMERICAN INTERVENTION IN SYRIA HAS NOTHING TO DO WITH HUMAN RIGHTS.

I'm not mad my candidate lost in 2016. I'm mad I don't live in a democracy, where urban ghettos and rust belts are taken for granted.

**THE NEW YORK TIMES IS FAKE NEWS.**

I'm not mad my candidate lost in 2016. I'm mad
I don't live in a democracy.

**THE CIA DOMINATES CONGRESS.**

No military action in the last 60 years has
benefited the American people in any way.

**WALL STREET RULES WASHINGTON.**

Sometimes we have banking crises that need
immediate attention. Racism is allowed to fester
unattended for 400 years.

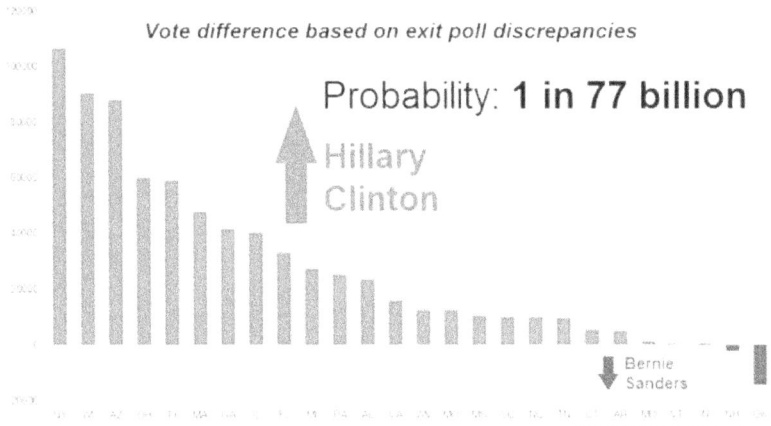

Vote difference based on exit poll discrepancies

Probability: **1 in 77 billion**

Hillary
Clinton

Bernie
Sanders

www.ingramcontent.com/pod-product-compliance
Lightning Source LLC
Chambersburg PA
CBHW062121280526
45788CB00001B/15